AF870607

VOLUME 4

BUSINESS & LEADERSHIP

Covering

Financial Management

Financial Planning

Financial Compliance

Financial Reporting

HR Management

Performance Management

Workforce Planning

Training & Development

Risk Management, and much more

DR. SATHYAPRIYA GOVINDARAJULU
ZAHEER SIDDIQUI

VRA TEXTBOOKS SERIES

Business & Leadership

Volume 4

Covering:

- Financial Management
- Human Resources Management

RELEASE 1.0

© Vocational Resources Australia

© 2023 Vocational Resources Australia

ALL RIGHTS RESERVED. No part of this work covered by the copyright herein may be reproduced, transmitted, stored, or used in any form or by any means graphic, electronic, or mechanical, including but not limited to photocopying, recording, scanning, digitizing, taping, web distribution, information networks, or information storage and retrieval systems, except as permitted under The Commonwealth Copyright Act (1968), without our prior written permission.

Vocational Resources Australia specialises in development, publishing, and distribution of learning resources for Australian Vocational Education sector.

Visit our website www.vocationalresources.com.au for further information or to shop online.

For product information or for permission to use material from this publication, send us a message/ request through our website.

"Where possible, we have arranged the topics, within each chapter in alphabetical order. We hope this will help you easily locate the information you need, making the search process smoother and giving you more time to enjoy your reading."

.... Dr. Sathya and Zaheer

Copyrights 2023 Vocational Resources Australia. All Rights Reserved.

ABOUT DR. SATHYAPRIYA

Dr. Sathyapriya Govindarajulu is a highly accomplished academic and researcher, possessing an impressive educational background that includes a PhD in Finance, an MBA, and a Post-Doctoral Researcher position at Charles Darwin University.

In addition to her academic achievements, she is a lecturer at Central Queensland University and has gained significant experience working in the VET sector. Her post-doctoral research work has received grant funding from the ACSDRI, highlighting the importance of her research in advancing the field of finance. Moreover, Dr. Sathya is actively involved in academia and currently supervises students in organisational leadership as a co-supervisor.

Dr. Sathya's contributions to the field of finance include two published papers in international journals, three papers in national journals, and a book.

She has presented her research at more than ten conferences, including the Latrobe University in Melbourne. Her research article on financial inclusion won the Best Paper Award at Finance Track in India.

Copyrights 2023 Vocational Resources Australia. All Rights Reserved.

ABOUT ZAHEER

Zaheer Siddiqui is an accomplished professional with over 35 years of experience that spans various roles and levels of responsibility, from grassroots to CEO positions. With a master's degree in economics, an MBA, and an MS in computer science, Zaheer has a strong foundation in both business and technology. He has also attained Diploma of Vocational Education and Diploma of Training Design & Development.

In addition to his formal qualifications, Zaheer has also accumulated an impressive lifelong learning portfolio that includes hundreds of vocational and applied courses from various institutions. This breadth of knowledge and experience allows Zaheer to bring a unique perspective to any project or endeavour he undertakes, making him a valuable asset. He assisted several organisations in improving their market presence and sustainability.

Drawing upon a wealth of experience in business and leadership, Zaheer has expertly contextualized this volume to the Australian Vocational Education sector. His strong grasp of the BSB training package has enabled him to create a resource that is equally valuable to trainers, students, team leaders, and managers. Through careful consideration of the needs and expectations of each group, Zaheer has crafted a comprehensive guide that is both informative and accessible.

Copyrights 2023 Vocational Resources Australia. All Rights Reserved.

FIVE INCREDIBLE VOLUMES

Volume 1:
Workplace Communication, Critical and Creative Thinking, Emotional Intelligence, Personal Development, Leadership, Workplace Technology

Volume 2:
Continuous Improvement, Innovation, and Quality Management, Sustainability, Change Management, Health, Safety, and Risk management, Business Development and Marketing

Volume 3:
Business Operations, Business Continuity, Business Performance, Business Systems, Corporate Social Responsibility, Customer Service, Meetings, Resource Management, Operational & Strategic Planning, Supply Chains

Volume 4:
Financial Management, Financial Planning, Financial Compliance, Financial Reporting, Human Resources Management, Workforce Planning, Training & Development

Volume 5:
Project Management

Copyrights 2023 Vocational Resources Australia. All Rights Reserved.

UNIT MAPPING

For Australian Vocational Education Readers: All the five volumes have been mapped to over 160 units in BSB Training Package. Chapter-wise mapping has been populated for your convenience.

#	Unit of Competency	CHAPTERS														
		1	2	3	4	5	6	7	8	9	10	11	12	13	14	15
1	BSBCMM211	x														
2	BSBCMM411	x					x									
3	BSBCMM412	x			x											
4	BSBCMM511	x					x						x			
5	BSBCRT201	x	x													
6	BSBCRT311	x	x													
7	BSBCRT411		x	x	x											
8	BSBCRT413	x	x													
9	BSBCRT511		x										x		x	
10	BSBCRT611		x										x			
11	BSBESB301											x				
12	BSBESB401												x			
13	BSBESB406												x			
14	BSBFIN301													x		
15	BSBFIN302													x		
16	BSBFIN401													x		
17	BSBFIN501													x		
18	BSBFIN502													x		
19	BSBFIN601													x		
20	BSBFIN801												x	x		
21	BSBHRM411														x	
22	BSBHRM412														x	
23	BSBHRM413														x	
24	BSBHRM415														x	
25	BSBHRM521														x	
26	BSBHRM523														x	
27	BSBHRM524														x	
28	BSBHRM525														x	
29	BSBHRM527														x	
30	BSBHRM613														x	
31	BSBHRM614														x	
32	BSBHRM615												x		x	
33	BSBINS302												x			
34	BSBINS303												x			
35	BSBINS501												x			
36	BSBINS601												x			
37	BSBLDR301	x				x									x	
38	BSBLDR411	x			x	x							x			
39	BSBLDR412	x														
40	BSBLDR413	x				x										
41	BSBLDR414					x										

Copyrights 2023 Vocational Resources Australia. All Rights Reserved.

UNIT MAPPING

For Australian Vocational Education Readers: All the five volumes have been mapped to over 160 units in BSB Training Package. Chapter-wise mapping has been populated for your convenience.

#	Unit of Competency	CHAPTERS														
		1	2	3	4	5	6	7	8	9	10	11	12	13	14	15
42	BSBLDR521														x	
43	BSBLDR522					x					x				x	
44	BSBLDR523	x			x	x							x			
45	BSBLDR601									x						
46	BSBLDR602				x			x		x			x			
47	BSBLDR811				x	x				x						
48	BSBLDR812			x						x	x	x	x			
49	BSBMKG431											x				
50	BSBMKG433											x				
51	BSBMKG434											x				
52	BSBMKG435											x				
53	BSBMKG436											x				
54	BSBMKG438											x				
55	BSBMKG440											x				
56	BSBMKG541											x				
57	BSBMKG623											x	x			
58	BSBOPS101												x			
59	BSBOPS201	x											x			
60	BSBOPS202												x			
61	BSBOPS203												x			
62	BSBOPS301												x			
63	BSBOPS304												x			
64	BSBOPS305	x											x			
65	BSBOPS401												x			
66	BSBOPS402												x			
67	BSBOPS403										x					
68	BSBOPS404												x			
69	BSBOPS405												x			
70	BSBOPS501												x			
71	BSBOPS502												x	x	x	
72	BSBOPS504										x					
73	BSBOPS505											x	x			
74	BSBOPS506X												x			
75	BSBOPS507X												x			
76	BSBOPS601												x			
77	BSBPEF101				x											
78	BSBPEF201				x											
79	BSBPEF301				x											
80	BSBPEF302			x	x											
81	BSBPEF401				x						x					
82	BSBPEF402	x			x	x										

Copyrights 2023 Vocational Resources Australia. All Rights Reserved.

UNIT MAPPING

For Australian Vocational Education Readers: All the five volumes have been mapped to over 160 units in BSB Training Package. Chapter-wise mapping has been populated for your convenience.

#	Unit of Competency	CHAPTERS														
		1	2	3	4	5	6	7	8	9	10	11	12	13	14	15
83	BSBPEF403			x	x											
84	BSBPEF501	x									x				x	
85	BSBPEF502			x												
86	BSBPMG420					x										x
87	BSBPMG421															x
88	BSBPMG422							x								x
89	BSBPMG423													x		x
90	BSBPMG424	x				x									x	x
91	BSBPMG426										x					x
92	BSBPMG427															x
93	BSBPMG428															x
94	BSBPMG429															x
95	BSBPMG430										x					x
96	BSBPMG530															x
97	BSBPMG531															x
98	BSBPMG532							x								x
99	BSBPMG533													x		x
100	BSBPMG535															x
101	BSBPMG536										x					x
102	BSBPMG537															x
103	BSBPMG538												x			x
104	BSBPMG539												x			x
105	BSBPMG540															x
106	BSBPMG633					x					x				x	x
107	BSBPMG814					x							x		x	x
108	BSBSTR301							x								
109	BSBSTR401							x								
110	BSBSTR402							x								
111	BSBSTR501							x								
112	BSBSTR502							x					x			
113	BSBSTR801		x			x		x					x		x	
114	BSBSTR802										x		x			
115	BSBSTR803							x					x			
116	BSBSTR601					x		x	x		x		x		x	
117	BSBSTR602												x			
118	BSBSTR603												x			
119	BSBSUS211								x							
120	BSBSUS411								x							
121	BSBSUS511								x							
122	BSBSUS601	x								x			x			
123	BSBTEC202						x									

Copyrights 2023 Vocational Resources Australia. All Rights Reserved.

UNIT MAPPING

For Australian Vocational Education Readers: All the five volumes have been mapped to over 160 units in BSB Training Package. Chapter-wise mapping has been populated for your convenience.

#	Unit of Competency	CHAPTERS														
		1	2	3	4	5	6	7	8	9	10	11	12	13	14	15
124	BSBTEC301	x					x									
125	BSBTEC302	x					x									
126	BSBTEC303						x									
127	BSBTEC401	x					x				x					
128	BSBTEC402	x					x				x					
129	BSBTEC403						x						x			
130	BSBTEC404						x						x			
131	BSBTEC601	x					x	x								
132	BSBTWK201	x				x							x			
133	BSBTWK301														x	
134	BSBTWK401											x				
135	BSBTWK502	x				x							x			
136	BSBTWK503												x			
137	BSBWHS211										x					
138	BSBWHS307										x					
139	BSBWHS308										x					
140	BSBWHS309										x					
141	BSBWHS311										x					
142	BSBWHS411										x					
143	BSBWHS412										x					
144	BSBWHS413										x					
145	BSBWHS414										x					
146	BSBWHS415										x					
147	BSBWHS504										x					
148	BSBWHS516										x					
149	BSBWHS517										x					
150	BSBWHS521										x					
151	BSBWHS522										x					
152	BSBWHS603										x					
153	BSBWHS605										x					
154	BSBWRT311	x					x									
155	BSBWRT411	x														
156	BSBXCM301	x														
157	BSBXCM401	x					x						x			
158	BSBXCM501	x														
159	BSBXTW301	x				x										
160	BSBXTW401	x				x									x	
161	TAELED803							x							x	

Copyrights 2023 Vocational Resources Australia. All Rights Reserved.

Table of Contents

Copyrights 2023 Vocational Resources Australia. All Rights Reserved.

Copyrights 2023 Vocational Resources Australia. All Rights Reserved.

Copyrights 2023 Vocational Resources Australia. All Rights Reserved.

Copyrights 2023 Vocational Resources Australia. All Rights Reserved.

Copyrights 2023 Vocational Resources Australia. All Rights Reserved.

Copyrights 2023 Vocational Resources Australia. All Rights Reserved.

Copyrights 2023 Vocational Resources Australia. All Rights Reserved.

Copyrights 2023 Vocational Resources Australia. All Rights Reserved.

Copyrights 2023 Vocational Resources Australia. All Rights Reserved.

Copyrights 2023 Vocational Resources Australia. All Rights Reserved.

Copyrights 2023 Vocational Resources Australia. All Rights Reserved.

Copyrights 2023 Vocational Resources Australia. All Rights Reserved.

Copyrights 2023 Vocational Resources Australia. All Rights Reserved.

Copyrights 2023 Vocational Resources Australia. All Rights Reserved.

Copyrights 2023 Vocational Resources Australia. All Rights Reserved.

13 Financial Management

For Australian Vocational Education readers:
Some of the topics in this chapter have been mapped to the following Units of Competency:

BSBFIN301, BSBFIN302, BSBFIN401, BSBFIN501, BSBFIN502, BSBFIN601, BSBFIN801, BSBPMG423, BSBPMG533, and BSBOPS502.

Copyrights 2023 Vocational Resources Australia. All Rights Reserved.

Chapter 13: Financial Management

Accounting

At its fundamental level, accounting entails the systematic monitoring of an individual's or an organisation's financial transactions. Accountants document and scrutinize these transactions to produce a comprehensive overview of their employer's financial well-being.

Principles of Accounting

Basic accounting principles form the foundation for accurate and reliable financial reporting. These principles guide the recording, analysis, interpretation and presentation of financial data effectively. Some of them are discussed below:

- Accrual Principle
  The accrual principle requires that revenues be recorded when they are earned, not necessarily when cash is received, and expenses should be recorded when incurred, rather than when they are paid.

  This principle is important in ensuring that financial statements reflect a company's financial performance accurately.

- Consistency Principle
  The consistency principle refers to the practice of using the same accounting methods and procedures consistently throughout a company's accounting records. This helps enhance the comparability of financial statements between periods.

Copyrights 2023 Vocational Resources Australia. All Rights Reserved.

- Historical Cost Principle
  According to this principle, assets are recorded at their original cost when acquired, and not their current market value. This provides an objective measure of the company's investment and aids with decision-making by enabling comparability within the database.

- Materiality Principle
  The materiality principle suggests that only materially significant items, those that would alter the judgment of someone relying on those statements, ought to be recorded in financial statements. Immaterial or insignificant information may negatively impact actual events making them difficult to analyse.

- Objectivity Principle
  The objectivity principle stresses the need for impartial, verifiable evidence to support a company's transactions. All entries must be supported by verifiable documentation.

- Prudence Principle
  Also referred to as conservatism, the prudence principle suggests that estimates and assumptions should be made in favour of being prudent and cautious when valuing assets or estimating losses in order to mitigate risks and uncertainties.

- Going Concern Principle
  Businesses are assumed to continue operating into the foreseeable future or the period covered by financial statements unless there is substantial evidence proving otherwise.

Copyrights 2023 Vocational Resources Australia. All Rights Reserved.

- Matching Concept Principle
  The matching concept principle involves recording expenses in the same accounting period as the corresponding revenues which they helped in earning. This principle ensures that the expenses and revenues associated with a particular product or service are reported in the same accounting period.

- Generally Accepted Accounting Principles (GAAP)
  GAAP are a set of guidelines and standards used in accounting to ensure that financial statements are accurate, consistent, and understandable.

  GAAP covers a range of accounting concepts, including revenue recognition, expense recognition, asset valuation, and financial statement presentation. It is important for companies to adhere to GAAP guidelines in order to provide transparency and accountability to investors, creditors, and other stakeholders.

These principles provide a framework to ensure that financial statements are prepared in a uniform and standardised manner, making them comparable across different organisations and industries.

Copyrights 2023 Vocational Resources Australia. All Rights Reserved.

Principles of Double Entry Bookkeeping and Accrual Accounting

- Dual Aspect Principle
  Every financial transaction affects at least two accounts - a debit account and a credit account - in equal amounts, ensuring that the total debits always equal the total credits.

- Entity Principle
  The accounting records of a business should be kept separate from those of its owners or other enterprises to ensure clarity and transparency.

- Going Concern Principle
  Financial statements are prepared on the assumption that the business will continue to operate indefinitely, providing a reliable basis for forecasting and decision making.

- Historical Cost Principle
  Assets and liabilities are recorded at their original cost (or value), ensuring consistency and accuracy in financial reporting.

- Accruals Principle
  Revenues and expenses are recognised when they are incurred and not when cash is received or paid, providing a more accurate view of a business's financial performance.

Copyrights 2023 Vocational Resources Australia. All Rights Reserved.

- Consistency Principle
  Businesses should use consistent accounting methods from one period to another to ensure comparability and consistency in financial reporting.

- Materiality Principle
  Only significant items should be disclosed in financial statements, avoiding unnecessary clutter and ensuring that key information is clearly presented.

- Prudence Principle
  Businesses should be cautious in their accounting practices, recognising any potential losses or liabilities even if they have not yet occurred, to ensure accuracy and transparency in financial statements.

Audit Trial

An audit trail is a series of documents, records, or electronic files that provide a complete record of all the activities and transactions that have taken place in a business's accounting system. The audit trail is created as a result of the process of auditing, which involves reviewing a company's financial records and documentation to determine the accuracy and completeness of its financial statements.

The audit trail typically begins with the original source documents, such as invoices and receipts, which provide evidence of transactions. These source documents are then entered into the accounting system through a series of journal entries, which reflect the debits and credits associated with each transaction.

Copyrights 2023 Vocational Resources Australia. All Rights Reserved.

Each journal entry is then posted to the general ledger, a comprehensive record of all the business's financial transactions. The general ledger is organised into various accounts, such as accounts payable, accounts receivable, and cash accounts. Each account includes a balance that reflects the total amount of transactions associated with that account.

As transactions are recorded and posted to the general ledger, they are also linked together through reference numbers, dates, and other identifying information. This linkage creates a complete audit trail that allows auditors to trace transactions from their original source documents to the final financial statements.

The audit trail is essential for ensuring the accuracy and integrity of a company's financial records. It provides evidence of all the transactions that have taken place and allows auditors to identify errors, discrepancies, or instances of fraud.

In addition to providing a record of financial transactions, the audit trail also includes various control measures designed to prevent errors and fraud. For example, the use of purchase orders, receipts, and invoices can help ensure that goods and services are accurately accounted for and that payments are properly authorised.

Copyrights 2023 Vocational Resources Australia. All Rights Reserved.

Budgeting

Budgeting is the process of creating a financial plan that outlines the projected revenues, expenses, and profits for a given period, typically a fiscal year. It is a detailed financial plan that serves as a roadmap for the organisation's finances over the upcoming period. Budgets help organisations to allocate resources effectively, prioritise expenses, and make informed decisions to achieve their strategic goals.

Some of the key benefits of budgeting include:

- Helps in planning and allocating resources effectively
  A well-defined budget helps an organisation to plan and allocate resources based on their strategic priorities.

- Facilitates performance monitoring and evaluation
  Budgeting allows businesses to set benchmarks against which they can measure actual performance.

- Helps in decision-making
  By providing a detailed view of resources available and expenses, budgeting offers insights to inform strategic decisions.

- Supports accountability
  By tracking the actual performance of the business, budgets hold stakeholders accountable for their financial performance.

Copyrights 2023 Vocational Resources Australia. All Rights Reserved.

Budget Components

Key components of a budget are discussed below:

Estimated Revenue

Projected revenue refers to the amount of money a business anticipates generating from the sale of its goods or services.

This estimation is typically based on two key factors: sales forecasts and estimated costs of goods sold, or services rendered.

For established businesses, past experience can be used to estimate revenue. However, for new businesses, it may be necessary to research revenue figures of similar local businesses and use those as a conservative estimate. It is important to remain realistic and avoid overestimating, regardless of the business's age.

Fixed Cost

In a business budget, expenses that remain constant, regardless of sales volume or other business activities, are known as fixed costs.

Examples of fixed costs include rent, mortgage or utility payments, employee salaries, internet and accounting services, and insurance premiums.

It is crucial to include these costs in the budget to ensure that sufficient funds are available to cover them. Fixed costs can also be used as benchmarks to identify any financial issues if the business is not meeting its financial objectives.

Copyrights 2023 Vocational Resources Australia. All Rights Reserved.

Variable Costs

Variable costs are expenses that fluctuate based on the level of business activity. As your business grows or shrinks, so do your variable costs.

Examples of variable costs include the cost of raw materials, direct labour costs, shipping and handling costs, and sales commissions.

When creating a budget, it's important to accurately estimate these expenses based on the level of business activity you anticipate. This can help you identify areas where you may be overspending or where you could potentially cut costs to increase profitability.

One-Time Expenses

Unforeseen expenses that arise irregularly are categorised as incidental expenses in a business budget. These costs are usually one-time expenses and can be difficult to predict.

Examples of incidental expenses include replacing broken equipment, unexpected repairs, or buying new technology. While it may be challenging to estimate the exact amount needed for these expenses, it is a good idea to set aside a contingency fund to cover them.

Cash Flow

Cash flow refers to the movement of money in and out of a business. By reviewing previous financial records, you can estimate the cash flow for the upcoming year.

Analysing the amounts, timing, and uncertainty of cash flows is crucial for financial reporting. It helps determine a

Copyrights 2023 Vocational Resources Australia. All Rights Reserved.

company's liquidity, flexibility, and overall financial performance.

Positive cash flow is an indication that a company's liquid assets are growing, which enables it to fulfil obligations, invest in its business, pay expenses, return money to shareholders, and build up reserves to prepare for future financial challenges.

Companies with strong financial flexibility are better positioned to take advantage of profitable investment opportunities and are more resilient during economic downturns, as they can avoid the costs associated with financial distress.

The cash flow statement is a standard financial statement that provides information on a company's cash sources and uses over a specific time period. It is a critical tool for corporate management, analysts, and investors, as it helps determine a company's ability to generate cash to pay its debts and cover operating expenses.

The cash flow statement is among the most important financial statements issued by a company, along with the income statement and balance sheet.

A negative cash flow occurs when a company's outflows exceed its inflows.

Copyrights 2023 Vocational Resources Australia. All Rights Reserved.

Types of Cash Flow

Cash flow types are discussed below:

- Cash Flows from Operations (CFO)
  CFO, also known as operating cash flow, pertains to the movement of cash directly related to a company's regular business operations involving the production and sale of goods. This type of cash flow is a key indicator of a company's ability to settle its bills and cover operating expenses.

  A company must have more cash inflows from operating activities than cash outflows to ensure long-term financial sustainability.

  To calculate operating cash flow, cash received from sales is subtracted from operating expenses that were paid in cash for the period.

  The cash flow statement, which is issued quarterly and annually, reports operating cash flow. This figure helps determine whether a company can generate enough cash to maintain and grow its business, but it can also indicate when a company may require external financing to expand capital.

  It's important to note that CFO is useful for separating sales from cash received. For instance, a large sale to a client would increase revenue and earnings, but this additional revenue wouldn't necessarily improve cash flow if there are issues with collecting payment from the customer.

Copyrights 2023 Vocational Resources Australia. All Rights Reserved.

- Cash Flows from Investing (CFI)
  CFI pertains to the movement of cash as a result of various investment-related activities within a specific time frame.

  These activities may involve the purchase or sale of assets or securities and other similar transactions. Negative CFI, which indicates that more cash was spent on investments than generated from them, may not necessarily be a red flag since it could be due to substantial long-term investments for the betterment of the company, such as research and development (R&D)

- Cash Flows from Financing (CFF)
  Financing cash flow, also known as CFF, represents the movement of cash resulting from financial activities such as issuing debt or equity, and distributing dividends. By analysing CFF, investors can evaluate a company's financial stability and how efficiently it manages its capital structure.

- Cash Flow vs. Profit
  Although they appear similar, cash flow and profit are not equivalent. It's easy to mistake the two terms, but cash flow pertains to the cash that enters and exits a company, while profit refers to the amount of money earned after deducting all expenses.

  Profit is a metric that quantifies a company's financial performance and reflects the amount of money it earns after paying off all its expenses. It is the difference between a company's revenue and its expenses.

Copyrights 2023 Vocational Resources Australia. All Rights Reserved.

- Analysing Cash Flows
  The cash flow statement, when used in conjunction with other financial statements, can assist analysts and investors in determining several metrics and ratios, which can be used to make well-informed decisions and recommendations.

Profit

The last piece of the budget puzzle is profit, which you can calculate by deducting your estimated expenses from your projected revenue.

A higher profit indicates that your business is expanding, which is a positive indicator.

Once you have determined how much profit you anticipate for the year, you can allocate the funds to various functional areas of your business.

For instance, you might consider using your profit to boost advertising or marketing efforts to increase sales.

Copyrights 2023 Vocational Resources Australia. All Rights Reserved.

Budget Development

Steps involved in developing the budget are listed below:

1. Review past performance
   The first step is to review past financial performance, including revenues, expenses, and cash flow. This information can help provide a baseline for developing the new budget.

2. Establish goals and objectives
   Once you have reviewed past performance, you need to establish goals and objectives for the upcoming period. These goals should be specific, measurable, achievable, relevant, and time bound.

3. Estimate revenues
   The next step is to estimate the amount of revenue you expect to generate during the period. This can be based on historical data, market trends, and other factors that impact your revenue.

4. Estimate expenses
   After you have estimated your revenue, you need to estimate your expenses. This includes fixed expenses (like rent and salaries) and variable expenses (like supplies and utilities).

5. Analyse the budget
   Once you have estimated your revenues and expenses, you need to analyse the budget to ensure that it is realistic, balanced, and aligned with your goals and objectives.

Copyrights 2023 Vocational Resources Australia. All Rights Reserved.

6. Finalise the budget
   After you have analysed the budget, you need to finalise it by making any necessary adjustments and ensuring that it is aligned with the organisation's overall strategy.

7. Monitor and review
   Finally, you need to monitor and review the budget regularly to ensure that you are on track and making progress towards your goals.

Budget Governance

Budgetary governance involves developing the annual budget, monitoring its implementation, and ensuring that it aligns with public objectives.

The recommendation on budgetary governance comprises ten principles that present a brief overview of effective practices related to budgetary activities. These principles aim to offer practical guidance for designing, implementing, and enhancing the budget systems.

Additionally, the Recommendation emphasises the significance of budgetary principles in other aspects of good governance, such as integrity, open data, strategic goal attainment, and building trust between the government and citizens.

Copyrights 2023 Vocational Resources Australia. All Rights Reserved.

Principles of Budgetary Governance

Principles of budgetary governance help to ensure that budgetary governance is effective, efficient, and accountable, and that public funds are used in ways that benefit citizens and support the achievement of public policy objectives.

They are discussed below:

- Transparency
  This principle emphasises the importance of openness and accountability in the budgetary process. Organisations should provide clear and accessible information about their budget plans, including the revenues they expect to collect, the expenditures they plan to make, and the reasons behind their decisions.

- Participation
  This principle emphasises the need for citizens and stakeholders to have a meaningful role in the budgetary process.

  Organisations should create opportunities for workers' input and feedback and use this input to inform their budget decisions.

- Predictability and Stability
  This principle emphasises the importance of stability and predictability in the budgetary process.

  Organisations should set clear and consistent policies and procedures for budget planning, execution and avoid

Copyrights 2023 Vocational Resources Australia. All Rights Reserved.

sudden changes that could disrupt the economy or public services.

- Flexibility
  This principle emphasises the need for governments to be able to adapt their budget plans to changing circumstances.

  Organisations should have the ability to adjust their budgets in response to unforeseen events or changing priorities, while still maintaining overall fiscal discipline.

- Accountability
  This principle emphasises the need for governments to be accountable for the use of public funds.

  Organisations should establish clear lines of responsibility for budget management, monitor the effectiveness of their budget plans, and take corrective action when necessary.

Budget Types

There are many different types of organisational budgets, each designed to help managers plan and allocate resources effectively. The type of budget that an organisation chooses will depend on its goals, objectives, and the nature of its operations.

By implementing a budgeting process that aligns with its strategic plan, an organisation can ensure that it is using its resources effectively and achieving its performance goals.

Copyrights 2023 Vocational Resources Australia. All Rights Reserved.

Some of the budget types are discussed below:

Operating Budget

An operating budget is a plan for an organisation's income and expenses over a specific period of time, usually a year. This type of budget is designed to help managers allocate resources effectively to meet the organisation's objectives. The operating budget includes all of an organisation's operating expenses, such as salaries, utilities, rent, and other costs that are necessary to run the organisation's day-to-day operations.

Capital Budget

A capital budget is a plan for an organisation's long-term investments, such as purchasing new equipment, buildings, or other fixed assets. This type of budget is designed to help managers plan for major expenditures and allocate resources accordingly.

Cash Budget

A cash budget is a plan that outlines the organisation's expected cash inflows and outflows over a specific period of time, usually a month or a quarter. This type of budget is designed to help managers ensure that the organisation has enough cash on hand to meet its obligations and pay its bills.

Sales Budget

A sales budget is a plan for an organisation's sales revenue over a specific period of time. This type of budget is designed to help managers forecast sales and allocate resources accordingly. The sales budget is usually based on historical sales data, market research, and other factors that could affect sales.

Copyrights 2023 Vocational Resources Australia. All Rights Reserved.

Production Budget

A production budget is a plan for an organisation's production output over a specific period of time. This type of budget is designed to help managers allocate resources effectively to meet the organisation's production goals. The production budget is usually based on sales forecasts, historical production data, and other factors that could affect production output.

Master Budget

A master budget is a comprehensive financial plan that includes an organisation's operating budget, capital budget, cash budget, sales budget, and production budget. This type of budget is designed to help managers forecast revenues and expenses over a specific period of time and allocate resources accordingly.

Zero-Based Budget

A zero-based budget is a budgeting process where all expenses must be justified for each new period. This type of budget is designed to help managers identify areas where costs can be reduced and allocate resources more efficiently. In a zero-based budget, each line item must be justified, regardless of whether it was included in the previous budget cycle.

Flexible Budget

A flexible budget is a budget that adjusts for changes in the volume of activity. This type of budget is designed to help managers forecast revenues and expenses over a specific period of time and adjust for changes in the level of activity. A flexible budget allows managers to adjust their budgets

Copyrights 2023 Vocational Resources Australia. All Rights Reserved.

based on changes in the organisation's operations, such as changes in production volume or sales levels.

Program Budget

A program budget is a budget that is organised by program or activity area. This type of budget is designed to help managers allocate resources effectively to meet the organisation's program goals. The program budget is usually based on the organisation's strategic plan and includes the costs associated with each program or activity area.

Performance Budget

A performance budget is a budget that is organised around the outcomes or results that an organisation hopes to achieve. This type of budget is designed to help managers allocate resources effectively to meet the organisation's performance goals. The performance budget is usually based on the organisation's strategic plan and includes the costs associated with achieving each performance goal.

Budget Variance

Budget variance refers to the difference between the actual performance of a business or organisation and the projected performance stated in its budget.

It is a measurement used in budgetary control which aims to analyse the financial and operational performance against the budgeted or expected values.

Budget variance can be expressed both in absolute terms or in percentage terms. Positive variance means that the actual results surpassed the budgeted results, while negative

Copyrights 2023 Vocational Resources Australia. All Rights Reserved.

variance implies that actual results fell short of the budgeted ones.

There are several reasons why budget variance may occur, such as changes in market conditions or unexpected events that affect the business's operations, among others.

Budget variances can be classified into two types: favourable variance and unfavourable variance.

- Favourable Variance
  This indicates that the actual revenue or the cost-reducing activities are better than expected, resulting in higher profitability. For instance, if the business budgeted for a cost of $1,000 on a project, but the actual cost was just $800, then the company has a favourable variance of $200.

- Unfavourable Variance
  This indicates that costs are higher than the budgeted amount, or the revenue generated is less than the budgeted amount, leading to a lower profitability. For example, if the business budgeted for $10,000 in revenue but only generated $9,500, then it has an unfavourable variance of $500.

Interpreting budget variances accurately is significant in decision-making process, as it helps in identifying the underlying causes of the variance and taking appropriate corrective actions to address them.

The business should analyse each variance in detail to ascertain the reason for deviation and assess if the reasons

Copyrights 2023 Vocational Resources Australia. All Rights Reserved.

are controllable or uncontrollable. Controllable variances arise due to actions taken by the company and can be corrected by the organisation such as reducing costs or improving sales processes.

On the other hand, uncontrollable variances are those where external factors have contributed to the variance in the budget and are not in control of the business.

Developing Action Plan to Remedy Budget Variation

Developing action plans to remedy significant deviations from an organisational budget typically involves a series of steps. First, it's important to identify the causes of the deviation. This could involve reviewing financial records, analysing expenses, and looking for patterns or trends.

Once the causes have been identified, the next step is to develop a plan of action to address the issue. This might involve reducing expenses, increasing revenue, or a combination of both. The plan should be specific, measurable, and achievable, with clear timelines and action items.

It's also important to engage key stakeholders in the process, including managers, department heads, and employees. This helps to ensure buy-in and accountability and can also generate new ideas and perspectives.

Finally, it's critical to monitor progress and adjust the plan as needed. Regular reporting and review can help to identify any issues or challenges early on, so that corrective action can be taken before the situation becomes more serious.

Copyrights 2023 Vocational Resources Australia. All Rights Reserved.

Revising Budget Priorities

In order to revise the organisational budget priorities to meet operational contingencies and risk management, it's important to first assess the current budget and identify areas where adjustments can be made. Then, you can consider the potential risks that the organisation may face and allocate resources accordingly.

One approach could be to create a contingency fund that can be used to mitigate unexpected costs and risks. Another approach could be to prioritise investments in technology and training to help the organisation adapt to changing circumstances and reduce future risks.

Revising organisational budget priorities is a critical process that allows organisations to adapt to changing circumstances and respond to risks and unexpected events.

To revise the budget effectively, it's important to consider factors such as the organisation's mission and strategic goals, the competitive landscape, and the potential risks and opportunities that may arise.

Operational contingencies refer to unexpected events or circumstances that can impact the organisation's operations, such as natural disasters, supply chain disruptions, or changes in market conditions. By creating a contingency fund, the organisation can be better prepared to address these unexpected costs and mitigate risks.

Risk management involves identifying, assessing, and mitigating potential risks that could impact the organisation's operations or financial performance. By investing in

Copyrights 2023 Vocational Resources Australia. All Rights Reserved.

technology and training, the organisation can better adapt to changing circumstances and reduce future risks.

It's also important to regularly review and adjust the budget based on the organisation's performance and changing circumstances, and to involve all stakeholders in the process to ensure buy-in and support for the revised budget priorities.

Copyrights 2023 Vocational Resources Australia. All Rights Reserved.

Business Activity Statement (BAS)

To comply with tax obligations, businesses in Australia are required to submit a BAS to the Australian Taxation Office (ATO). GST reporting makes up a significant portion of the BAS. Other tax liabilities such as PAYG withholding and instalments, wine equalisation tax, fuel tax credit, and fringe benefit tax may also be included in the BAS, depending on the business.

BAS Form

The BAS form is used to report and pay tax liabilities to the ATO, with a significant portion of the form dedicated to GST.

The form includes other taxes such as PAYG withholding, instalments, wine equalisation tax, fuel tax credit, and fringe benefit tax where applicable to the business.

When you complete a BAS form, you're reporting the amount of goods and services tax collected on your sales, subtracted by the GST paid on your purchases. The difference between the two amounts determines whether you owe money to the ATO or are eligible for a refund.

For instance, if you charge a customer $50 for a product or service, the extra $5 added to the bill is the GST that you need to remit to the ATO. When your business buys supplies, you may be charged 10% in GST, which you can claim back as a credit from the ATO.

Copyrights 2023 Vocational Resources Australia. All Rights Reserved.

Preparing the BAS

There are three main steps to completing your BAS:

1. Prepare your information
   To ensure the accuracy and completeness of your financial information, it's important to reconcile your accounts regularly.

   This involves comparing and verifying your business transactions, such as receipts and invoices, to your accounting records to identify any discrepancies and ensure that all information is up to date.

2. Calculate your totals and enter figures
   After verifying the accuracy of your information, the next step is to determine your totals.

   This can be done by generating a report through your accounting software or by manually adding up your figures (using a GST calculation worksheet, for instance).

   Once you have your totals, you can then input them into your BAS form.

3. Lodge and update
   To lodge your BAS, you have three primary options: sending a hard copy of your BAS form to the ATO via mail, using the ATO's Business Portal to lodge your BAS statement online, or hiring a BAS or Tax agent to do it for you.

Copyrights 2023 Vocational Resources Australia. All Rights Reserved.

Regardless of the method you select, it's crucial to keep a copy of your BAS statement and update your accounting information with the figures you've submitted.

Lodging the BAS

Businesses that are registered for GST are required to submit a BAS on monthly, quarterly or yearly basis. ATO determines and communicated the submission frequency, based on the business' turnover.

Copyrights 2023 Vocational Resources Australia. All Rights Reserved.

Common Types of Financial Entries

The two main types of financial entries are credit and debit. They are used to record transactions in accounting, bookkeeping, and financial reporting systems.

Here's a brief explanation of each type of financial entry:

Debit

A debit entry in accounting refers to an increase in assets or a decrease in liabilities or equity. When a debit entry is made, it means that money or assets are flowing into the company.

Debits are recorded on the left-hand side of financial statements or accounting ledgers. For example, if a company purchases goods on credit, the entry on the accounting ledger would be a debit to the inventory account, representing an increase in inventory.

Credit

A credit entry in accounting refers to a decrease in assets or an increase in liabilities or equity. When a credit entry is made, it means that money or assets are flowing out of the company.

Credits are recorded on the right-hand side of financial statements or accounting ledgers. For example, if a company sells goods on credit, the entry on the accounting ledger would be a credit to the accounts receivable account, representing an increase in sales revenue.

Copyrights 2023 Vocational Resources Australia. All Rights Reserved.

Other types of financial entries that are frequently used include:

Journal Entries

Journal entries are used to record specific transactions manually in accounting ledgers.

Adjusting Entries

Adjusting entries are made at the end of the accounting period to reconcile accounts and ensure that the financial statements accurately reflect the exact financial status of the company.

Closing Entries

Closing entries are made at the end of an accounting period to transfer temporary accounts such as revenue and expenses into permanent accounts like retained earnings.

By keeping accurate records of financial entries, companies can use the data to create financial reports, make informed business decisions, and comply with regulatory requirements.

Copyrights 2023 Vocational Resources Australia. All Rights Reserved.

Compliance Requirements

The key financial compliance requirements for Australian organisations include:

- Australian Taxation Office (ATO) compliance
  Businesses must comply with various tax obligations, including income tax, Goods and Services Tax (GST), and Pay As You Go (PAYG) withholding.

  The ATO requires businesses to file annual tax returns and to report their financial transactions on Business Activity Statements (BAS).

- Australian Securities and Investments Commission (ASIC) compliance
  ASIC monitors corporate activity in Australia and regulates the conduct of companies, businesses, and financial services providers.

  ASIC requires companies to file annual financial statements and keep accurate records.

- Australian Accounting Standards Board (AASB) compliance
  The AASB sets the accounting standards for Australian organisations to ensure they comply with legislative and regulatory requirements.

  AASB standards cover areas such as financial reporting, auditing, and disclosure.

Copyrights 2023 Vocational Resources Australia. All Rights Reserved.

- Australian Prudential Regulation Authority (APRA) compliance
  APRA regulates banks, insurance companies, and other financial services providers to ensure they operate in a financially sound and stable manner.

  APRA requires these organisations to maintain adequate reserves and to have risk management systems in place.

- Anti-Money Laundering (AML) and Counter-Terrorism Financing (CTF) compliance
  Businesses are required to comply with AML/CTF laws, which are aimed at preventing the use of financial systems for illegal activities such as money laundering and financing of terrorism. This includes customer identification and verification, record-keeping, and reporting obligations.

- Superannuation compliance
  Businesses must comply with superannuation requirements, which include contributing to employees' superannuation funds and complying with SuperStream data and payment standards.

- Trade Practices compliance
  The Australian Competition and Consumer Commission (ACCC) regulates trade practices and enforces competition and consumer protection laws in Australia.

Compliance with these laws is essential for organisations to avoid hefty fines and penalties.

Copyrights 2023 Vocational Resources Australia. All Rights Reserved.

Critical Dates

Following is a list of possible critical dates to assist with some of the compliance requirements:

- End of Financial Year (EOFY) - June 30
- Annual Tax Return Due Date - October 31
- Quarterly Business Activity Statement (BAS) Due Dates - February 28, April 30, July 31, October 31
- Superannuation Guarantee Contributions - Due on the 28th day of each quarter
- Company Annual General Meeting (AGM) - within 5 months after end of financial year
- Fringe Benefits Tax (FBT) Due Date - March 31
- Payroll Tax Filing and Payment Due Date - Monthly or Quarterly depending on state/territory
- Goods and Services Tax (GST) Filing and Payment Due Dates - Monthly or Quarterly depending on turnover
- Annual Financial Statements and Reports - Within 4 months after end of financial year
- Dividend Payment Dates - Determined by the company and declared at AGM

Please note that these dates may vary depending on the specific organisational structure, industry, and location. It's always a good idea to consult with a financial expert to ensure compliance with legal and regulatory requirements.

Compliance - Methods & Tools

With effective methods and tools, organisations can develop and implement financial compliance strategies to ensure adherence to regulatory and legal requirements.

Copyrights 2023 Vocational Resources Australia. All Rights Reserved.

Some of the methods and tools used in organisational financial compliance include:

Financial Risk Assessment

Organisations need to assess their financial risk levels to identify potential financial compliance gaps. This process can be achieved through conducting regular audits or assessments of financial operations, policies, and procedures.

Policies and Procedures

Developing comprehensive financial policies and procedures is crucial in achieving financial compliance. Policies and procedures help set the standards for expected behaviours and actions, enhance transparency and accountability, reduce errors, and mitigate risks.

Compliance Management Software

Compliance management software is a powerful tool to aid in managing financial compliance. The software can track and monitor regulatory changes, automate policy dissemination, and alert employees of compliance obligations.

Internal and External Audit

Audits are essential in ensuring compliance with legal and regulatory requirements. Internal audits help identify gaps in financial processes and controls, while external audits provide an unbiased assessment of an organisation's financial compliance.

Copyrights 2023 Vocational Resources Australia. All Rights Reserved.

Employee Training and Education

Employees need to be aware of compliance obligations and understand their role in achieving financial compliance. Employee training and education programs enable employees to have a clear understanding of compliance policies and procedures.

Whistleblowing Policy

A whistleblowing policy is essential in creating an environment where employees can report any potential financial irregularities without fear of retaliation.

Organisations should communicate their whistleblowing policy to employees and ensure they understand the reporting process.

Security and Data Protection

Ensuring the security of financial data is essential to achieve financial compliance. Organisations should implement data protection measures, such as access controls, encryption, and data backups, to prevent unauthorised access or data theft.

Relevant Legislations

Some of the legislations relevant to financial industry are:

- Corporations Act 2001
- Australian Securities and Investments Commission Act 2001
- Anti-Money Laundering and Counter-Terrorism Financing Act 2006
- Banking Act 1959
- Financial Sector (Collection of Data) Act 2001

Copyrights 2023 Vocational Resources Australia. All Rights Reserved.

- Insurance Act 1973
- Life Insurance Act 1995
- National Consumer Credit Protection Act 2009
- Superannuation Industry (Supervision) Act 1993
- Payment Systems (Regulation) Act 1998 etc.

Copyrights 2023 Vocational Resources Australia. All Rights Reserved.

Cost Control

Cost control is a critical aspect of organisational management. It involves the management of an organisation's expenses to ensure that they remain within the budgetary constraints, while still meeting the organisation's objectives.

Cost control is an essential aspect of organisational management as it helps to minimise expenses and maximise profits.

Organisations that do not have efficient cost control mechanisms in place are likely to experience financial problems, such as cash flow problems, operational inefficiencies, and other financial constraints that can impede growth.

Moreover, cost control plays a significant role in the sustainability of an organisation. When cost control measures are in place, the organisation can increase efficiency and improve overall performance. Reduced expenses also mean that the organisation can invest more in innovation and development, thus leading to increased competitiveness.

Strategies for Cost Control in Organisations

Effective cost control requires the implementation of strategies that address different areas of the organisation. Here are some strategies that can be employed to ensure successful cost control in organisations:

Copyrights 2023 Vocational Resources Australia. All Rights Reserved.

Budgetary Control

The first step towards cost control is to set a budget. The budget should be realistic and based on the organisation's objectives. The budget should also be monitored regularly to ensure that expenses remain within the set limits. Any deviations from the budget should be addressed promptly.

Zero-Based Budgeting

Already discussed in previous pages.

Outsourcing

Outsourcing is an effective way to reduce expenses in an organisation. Outsourcing allows the organisation to focus on its core functions while leaving other non-core tasks to external vendors who can provide these services more efficiently and cost-effectively.

Automation

Automation of processes can help reduce operational costs in an organisation. Automating repetitive tasks can free up employees' time and reduce the need for manual labour, thus leading to significant cost savings.

Asset Management

Effective asset management is critical for cost control in an organisation. The organisation should ensure that assets are utilised efficiently and that they are not underutilised or not utilised at all. Proper asset management also involves ensuring that assets are maintained well to extend their useful life and reduce repair and replacement costs.

Copyrights 2023 Vocational Resources Australia. All Rights Reserved.

Negotiation

Negotiation is a fundamental skill in cost control. Organisations can negotiate with suppliers for better prices or payment terms, reduce interest rates on loans, and also negotiate better deals with clients to maximise revenue.

Credit Terms

Credit terms refer to the specific conditions and requirements that regulate the extension of credit from one party to another. These terms outline the details of the arrangement, including the duration of the credit period, the interest or fees charged, and any penalties or consequences for non-payment.

For example, a supplier may offer a customer credit terms of net 30, which means that the customer has 30 days from the date of the invoice to pay the supplier in full. The credit terms may also include a certain interest rate or late payment fee if the customer fails to pay within the given timeframe.

Credit terms are often negotiated between two parties prior to the extension of credit and are typically outlined in a contract or agreement. Clear and mutually agreed-upon credit terms are important for managing financial risk, maintaining cash flow, and building trust between parties.

Debt Collection Procedures

1. Establish a clear and consistent communication protocol for debt collection activities. This protocol should outline the appropriate channels of

Copyrights 2023 Vocational Resources Australia. All Rights Reserved.

communication, such as phone, email, or mail, and specify the frequency and timing of communication.

2. Train all staff members who will be involved in debt collection activities on the communication protocol, including what to say and how to say it. This will help ensure that all communication is professional, respectful, and consistent.

3. Develop templates for communication, such as collection letters or scripts for phone calls, to ensure that all communication is consistent and meets legal requirements.

4. Set clear expectations for debtors, such as payment deadlines and consequences for non-payment, and communicate these expectations clearly and consistently.

5. Monitor communication with debtors to ensure that it is effective and respectful. Regularly review and update your communication protocol as needed to ensure that it is meeting the needs of both your organisation and your debtors.

Copyrights 2023 Vocational Resources Australia. All Rights Reserved.

Ethical Requirements in Financial Management

Organisations have ethical obligations and responsibilities that extend beyond mere financial performance.

Ethical requirements in organisational financial management pertain to the moral and ethical responsibilities that a company has towards its stakeholders, including its shareholders, employees, customers, suppliers, and the general public.

The following are some of the ethical requirements that organisations must adhere to in financial management:

- Honesty and transparency
  Organisations must be honest and transparent in all their financial dealings with stakeholders. This includes providing accurate and reliable financial information, disclosing all material information in a timely manner, and being truthful in all communication.

- Fairness
  Organisations must be fair in their treatment of stakeholders. This includes ensuring that all stakeholders have equal access to information, resources, and opportunities, and that financial transactions and decisions are made fairly and responsibly.

- Confidentiality
  Organisations must maintain the confidentiality of sensitive financial information and ensure that it is not disclosed to unauthorised individuals or parties. This includes protecting the privacy of employees, customers, and suppliers.

Copyrights 2023 Vocational Resources Australia. All Rights Reserved.

- Compliance
  Organisations must comply with applicable laws and regulations governing financial management. This includes maintaining accurate and complete financial records, conducting regular audits, and complying with accounting standards and principles.

- Accountability
  Organisations must be accountable for their financial performance and management. This includes establishing clear lines of authority and responsibility, ensuring that financial decision-making is transparent and accountable, and taking responsibility for any financial mismanagement or misconduct.

- Social responsibility
  Organisations should recognise the broader social, environmental, and ethical impacts of their financial decisions and management practices. This includes promoting sustainability, ethical behaviour, and social responsibility in all financial operations.

Copyrights 2023 Vocational Resources Australia. All Rights Reserved.

Financial Bids and Estimates

Financial bids and estimates are an integral part of any organisational context. Bids and estimates are critical tools in helping organisations to plan, budget, and execute their projects. Bids are essentially proposals that organisations submit to potential clients, outlining the scope of work, the costs involved, and the timeline for completion. Estimates, on the other hand, are the projected costs associated with a particular project. In this discussion, we will delve into the significance of financial bids and estimates in an organisational context.

First, let's look at the importance of financial bids in an organisational context. Bidding is a crucial aspect of any organisation that seeks to win a project or contract. A winning bid is one that not only meets the client's needs but also provides value for money. Bids that are too high can result in clients rejecting the proposal outright. On the other hand, bids that are too low could result in the organisation incurring losses or not making enough profit to make the project worthwhile. Therefore, accurate financial bids are essential for the success of any organisation.

The organisation's financial team plays a significant role in the bidding process. The team's responsibility is to evaluate the costs involved in executing the project, such as labour, materials, and equipment. The team must also consider factors such as market pricing, profit margins, and overhead costs. By considering these factors, the financial team can develop a competitive bid that is both profitable and attractive to potential clients.

Copyrights 2023 Vocational Resources Australia. All Rights Reserved.

Once the financial bid has been submitted and accepted, the organisation must then prepare an estimate outlining the projected costs associated with the project. An accurate estimate is essential in ensuring that the project stays within budget. The estimate should include all the costs associated with the project, including labour, materials, equipment, and overhead costs. By developing a detailed estimate, the organisation can ensure that it has adequate resources to complete the project and that it can deliver the project within the agreed timelines.

In an organisational context, financial bids and estimates also play a vital role in decision-making. Organisations must be able to evaluate whether a particular project is profitable or not. By developing accurate financial bids and estimates, organisations can make informed decisions about whether to pursue a particular project or not. The organisation must also consider the risks involved in executing the project, such as market trends, changes in regulations, and other external factors.

Working with financial bids and estimates requires careful consideration of the following key factors:

- Accuracy
  The accuracy and reliability of the bid or estimate are crucial. Any inaccuracies could potentially result in higher costs, project delays, or legal issues.

- Detail
  A detailed bid or estimate should include all aspects of the project, including the scope of work, timelines,

Copyrights 2023 Vocational Resources Australia. All Rights Reserved.

resources needed, and any assumptions made during the estimation process.

- Competitive pricing
  In some cases, multiple bidders may be submitting financial bids for the same project. It is important to review each proposal and ensure that the pricing is competitive without compromising quality.

- Realism
  Bids and estimates should be realistic and based on actual market conditions, labour rates, material costs, and other relevant factors. Unrealistic bids or estimates may lead to under-budgeting or over-promising.

- Contingency planning
  Every bid or estimate should include contingency plans for unexpected challenges or changes in scope that could affect costs or timing.

- Contract constraints
  The terms and conditions of a contract can significantly impact the final cost of a project. It is important to review all contract requirements before submitting a bid or estimate.

- Communication
  Communication is essential throughout the bidding and estimating process between all parties involved in order to keep everyone informed throughout and avoid potential misunderstandings or surprises.

Copyrights 2023 Vocational Resources Australia. All Rights Reserved.

Financial Goals

Financial goals for a business are tangible economic objectives that a company can aim for, whether in the short term or the long term, they help the business achieve broader organisational goals.
In order to survive, your business needs to be financially self-sustaining. In order to truly succeed, it needs to achieve a continually growing profit margin.

Financial goals help to ensure the former and make possible the latter.

Business financial goals take many forms. They can be decidedly short-term and tangible, for example, saving money to buy a piece of equipment. They can also be longer-term and more numerical, such as achieving a certain profit margin over the course of a financial year. But one thing that all great business financial goals have in common is that they're clear, measurable and achievable.

Importance of Financial Goals

One of the most important reasons for setting organisational financial goals is to ensure that a company has a clear sense of direction. Without goals, it can be difficult to know where to focus your efforts, and this can lead to a lack of direction and purpose. By setting goals, a company can have a clear sense of what it wants to achieve and can create a roadmap to get there.

Another important reason for setting organisational financial goals is to help ensure that a company is financially stable. Financial stability is crucial for any business, as it allows the company to weather economic storms and maintain its

Copyrights 2023 Vocational Resources Australia. All Rights Reserved.

operations even in difficult times. By setting financial goals, a company can ensure that it has enough money to cover its expenses, meet its financial obligations, and invest in growth opportunities.

Organisational financial goals can also help a company to improve its financial performance. By setting specific, measurable goals, a company can identify areas of weakness in its financial operations and take steps to improve them. For example, if a company is struggling with cash flow, it can set a goal to improve its cash flow position by a certain percentage over the next year. This will provide a clear target for the company to work toward and help it to focus its efforts on improving its cash flow management.

In addition to improving financial performance, organisational financial goals can also help a company to manage risk. By setting financial goals, a company can identify potential risks and take steps to mitigate them. For example, if a company is heavily dependent on a single customer for revenue, it may set a goal to diversify its customer base in order to reduce the risk of losing that revenue stream.

Organisational financial goals can also help to improve communication within a company. By setting goals, a company can ensure that everyone is working toward the same objectives and has a clear understanding of what needs to be done to achieve them. This can improve collaboration and teamwork, as well as provide a sense of shared purpose among employees.

Copyrights 2023 Vocational Resources Australia. All Rights Reserved.

Types of Organisational Financial Goals

There are many different types of organisational financial goals that a company can set. Some examples include:

Revenue Goals

These goals focus on increasing the amount of revenue that a company generates over a certain period of time. This can include goals related to sales growth, market share, and customer acquisition.

Profitability Goals

These goals focus on improving the profitability of a company. This can include goals related to reducing costs, improving margins, and increasing efficiency.

Cash Flow Goals

These goals focus on improving a company's cash flow position. This can include goals related to reducing debt, improving collections, and increasing cash reserves.

Return on investment Goals

These goals focus on improving the return on investment (ROI) that a company generates from its operations. This can include goals related to increasing shareholder value, improving capital efficiency, and investing in high-return projects.

Copyrights 2023 Vocational Resources Australia. All Rights Reserved.

Financial/ Investment Decisions

Making sound finance and investment decisions can help organisations effectively allocate resources and achieve higher financial returns.

Here are some key considerations to keep in mind when making such decisions:

- Identify relevant metrics
  The first step is to identify the relevant metrics used to measure performance and return on investment (ROI).

  This could include profitability ratios, such as Return on Investment (ROI), Net Present Value (NPV), Internal Rate of Return (IRR) and Payback Period.

- Conduct market & industry analysis
  It is important to carefully assess market trends, demand patterns, competition movements, and regulatory factors before making investment decisions to ensure that the organisation will have sufficient market potential in which to sell its products or services.

- Determine investment risks
  Before investing in any new area, prudent attention should be paid to both project-specific risks and general financial market risks.

  Factors such as technological, economic, regulatory or environmental challenges may significantly impact the outcome of an investment decision.

Copyrights 2023 Vocational Resources Australia. All Rights Reserved.

- Consider capital allocation alternatives
  It is important to weigh the options when choosing whether or not to invest in a particular business venture or asset. Would it be more advantageous to allocate funding to high-growth opportunities, pay dividends to shareholders, or pay down debt?

  Proper allocation of capital ensures the best use of resources and helps the organisations increase its financial returns.

- Review and monitoring
  The evaluation of investments should continue throughout the lifespan of the investment/project. Results should be reviewed regularly to determine if the goals set out are being met, and corrective measures implemented if necessary.

- Maintain future flexibility
  Strategic finance and investment decisions should seek to position organisations with enough flexibility to adapt and change their plans should unforeseen market events occur.

  Properly positioning the organisation for change can ensure that it remains competitive even in difficult times.

Copyrights 2023 Vocational Resources Australia. All Rights Reserved.

Financial Management

Financial management is the process of managing an organisation's financial resources to achieve its goals and objectives effectively. It involves planning, organising, controlling, and monitoring financial resources to ensure that the organisation's financial goals are met.

Effective financial management involves several key elements, including budgeting, forecasting, financial analysis, and reporting *(all of the elements are discussed in detail in this chapter)*.

Best Practices in Financial Management

- Preparation and adherence to a budget.
  Creating and adhering to a realistic budget is one of the fundamental practices for financial management. The budget should be based on accurate financial data and forecasts, and a clear understanding of the organisation's financial goals and objectives.

- Regular financial reporting and analysis.
  Regular financial reporting and analysis can help identify trends, address financial issues and make informed decisions. Financial reports should be timely, accurate, and relevant to the decision-makers in the organisation.

- Effective cash flow management.
  Managing cash flow is essential for ensuring the financial solvency of an organisation. Organisations should have clear policies and procedures for managing cash, including invoicing, collections, and supplier payments.

Copyrights 2023 Vocational Resources Australia. All Rights Reserved.

- Efficient financial systems and processes.
  Efficient financial systems and processes are necessary for streamlining financial operations, reducing errors, and improving productivity. The use of technology, such as accounting software, can help automate financial operations, reduce manual errors and provide better visibility into financial data.

- Risk management.
  Effective risk management is critical to minimising financial risks and protecting the organisation against potential losses. Organisations should identify, measure, and prioritise financial risks and implement measures to minimise their impact.

- Compliance.
  Compliance with legal and regulatory requirements is essential to maintain the integrity of financial operations and protect the organisation from legal and financial penalties.

- Effective stakeholder engagement.
  Effective stakeholder engagement is crucial to building investor and customer confidence in the organisation's financial management. Key stakeholders, including investors, customers, and employees, need to be kept informed about the organisation's financial performance and future plans.

Copyrights 2023 Vocational Resources Australia. All Rights Reserved.

Role of Consultation in Financial Management

The role of consultation in organisational financial management is significant in ensuring the success of an organisation. Consulting ensures that the organisation has access to professional financial expertise, advice, and guidance. It also helps the organisation to manage its financial resources more effectively, which can lead to better decision-making, cost savings, and increased revenue.

Consulting can help organisations to identify financial opportunities & risks and develop strategies to manage them. This includes managing cash flow, budgeting, forecasting, and financial analysis. Through consultation, organisations can also gain insights into best practices for financial management, compliance, and risk management.

Consultants can also help organisations to identify inefficiencies in their financial processes and systems and recommend solutions to improve them. This can include implementing new technology platforms, streamlining financial workflows, and developing training programs to improve financial literacy among staff.

Copyrights 2023 Vocational Resources Australia. All Rights Reserved.

Financial Plans

Financial planning is an important process that helps organisations manage their finances, allocate resources, and achieve their goals. There are several types of financial plans that organisations can use to meet their financial objectives.

Benefits of a Financial Plan

- A financial plan involves evaluating your income and expenses.
- It can improve your understanding of your financial situation.
- It establishes short-term and long-term financial goals.
- It clarifies the actions required to achieve those goals.
- A financial plan can focus your attention on immediate priorities.
- It enhances the likelihood of achieving financial milestones and overall success.
- It provides a guide for monitoring progress over time.
- It can prevent financial difficulties and reduce stress and anxiety.

Types of Financial Plans

There are a few types of financial plans. The most common ones are discussed below:

Capital Budget Plan

A capital budget plan is a financial plan that outlines the organisation's capital investment strategy. This plan typically covers long-term investments, such as new buildings, equipment, or technology.

Copyrights 2023 Vocational Resources Australia. All Rights Reserved.

It includes details on the expected cost of the investment, the expected return on investment, and the financial impact of the investment on the organisation's operations.

Cash Flow Plan

A cash flow plan is a plan that outlines the organisation's expected cash inflows and outflows over a specific period. This plan is designed to help organisations manage their cash flow and ensure that they have sufficient cash reserves to meet their financial obligations.

Financial Contingency Plan

A financial contingency plan is a document that outlines a company's strategies for managing unexpected financial events or crises. It typically includes details on how the organisation will handle situations such as cash flow shortages, market downturns, and economic turbulence.

Financial contingency plans provide the foundation for mitigating business risk, speeding up disaster recovery and ensuring business continuity and resilience. The COVID-19 pandemic has put a new premium on companies establishing this resilience, in particular their supply chain resilience, according to analysts.

Contingency planning comes with a strong business case, because companies that can respond effectively to a crisis and quickly get back on their feet could gain a competitive advantage over other companies.

Staying solvent and maintaining near-normal business operations may be the most important benefits of a financial contingency plan, but there are other important advantages it

Copyrights 2023 Vocational Resources Australia. All Rights Reserved.

provides. One is the emotional benefit, since planning ahead can reduce stress and panic during an actual crisis. With a clear plan in place, your team can swiftly turn its focus to action in the midst of a challenging and often dynamic situation.

There is also the reputational benefit, as responding effectively in crisis reflects well on your company. Even if you never have to put the Plan B into action, the fact that you have a well-crafted financial contingency plan can make customers and other stakeholders more comfortable.

Financial contingency plans are not just for worst-case scenarios. They can also address best-case scenarios, like a flood of new online orders that you don't have the capacity to fill. In that way, financial contingency planning can also help companies fully capitalize on their success.

Key Steps in Developing the Financial Plan

1. Identify potential risks
   The first step is to identify potential risks that could impact the organisation's finances. This includes analysing market trends, industry developments, internal weaknesses, and external factors such as regulatory changes.

2. Define triggers
   Once potential risks have been identified, it's important to define specific triggers that would activate the contingency plan. These triggers could be based on metrics such as cash reserves, revenue declines, or key performance indicators.

Copyrights 2023 Vocational Resources Australia. All Rights Reserved.

3. Establish response strategies
   The financial contingency plan should include detailed strategies for responding to different scenarios. Depending on the risk involved, these responses may include reducing expenses, revising budgets, accessing emergency reserves, or seeking additional funding.

4. Assign responsibilities
   The plan should also clearly outline the roles and responsibilities of all involved parties throughout the implementation of the financial contingency plan.

   Team members' specific duties and authorities should be defined with regular check-ins to discuss areas of improvement or change.

5. Develop communication plan
   It is essential to establish a communication plan detailing who will be responsible for communicating with external stakeholders in response to potential crises. This may include shareholders, customers, vendors, banks, and regulatory bodies.

6. Review and update regularly
   As markets and industries continue to evolve, it's important to review and update the financial contingency plan regularly so it remains relevant and effective.

Copyrights 2023 Vocational Resources Australia. All Rights Reserved.

Expense Budget Plan

An expense budget plan is a plan that outlines the organisation's operating expenses for a specific period. This plan includes details on the organisation's expected expenses, such as salaries, rent, and supplies.

Operating Budget Plan

An operating budget plan is a plan that sets out the organisation's proposed revenues and expenses for a specific period. This plan is designed to help organisations manage their day-to-day cash flow and ensure that they can meet their financial obligations.

Revenue Budget Plan

A revenue budget plan is a plan that outlines the organisation's expected revenues for a specific period. This plan includes details on the organisation's expected sales, fees, and other sources of revenue.

Short-Term Financial Plan

A short-term financial plan is a plan that covers a period of less than one year. This plan typically includes details on the organisation's expected revenue, expenses, and cash flow for the coming months. It is designed to help organisations manage their day-to-day finances and address any short-term financial challenges.

Strategic Financial Plan

A strategic financial plan is a long-term plan that sets out an organisation's goals, objectives, and strategies for achieving financial success. This plan typically covers three to five years and includes details on revenue growth, cost reduction, and capital investments.

Copyrights 2023 Vocational Resources Australia. All Rights Reserved.

Financial Probity

Financial probity refers to the honesty, integrity, and soundness of financial management practices, including transparency, accountability, and adherence to ethical standards. It involves ensuring that financial statements, transactions, and dealings are accurate, complete, and above board.

The principle of financial probity is essential in maintaining the trust and confidence of stakeholders in public, private, and non-profit organisations. Fiscal transparency and good governance are the hallmarks of a financially stable and responsible organisation.

The following guidelines could be beneficial in achieving financial probity:

- Organisations must adopt and adhere to strong financial management policies and procedures.
- Create strong internal control systems to manage risk.
- Implement clear segregation of duties to reduce fraudulent activities.
- Ensure proper recording and reporting of all financial transactions.
- Regularly conduct independent audits and reviews.
- Establish effective anti-fraud and anti-corruption mechanisms.

Copyrights 2023 Vocational Resources Australia. All Rights Reserved.

- Encourage transparency and disclosure of relevant information.
- Appoint independent oversight or monitoring committees.

Misappropriation of Funds

Misappropriation of funds refers to the dishonest use or misuse of an organisation's funds or assets by an employee or a group of employees. This can include embezzlement, theft, or fraud.

To address the issue, it is important to establish internal controls and procedures to prevent such actions. This can include regularly monitoring financial records, conducting audits, implementing segregation of duties, and providing appropriate training to employees.

It is also important to investigate any suspected instances of misappropriation of funds promptly and take appropriate legal action if necessary. By establishing strong financial controls and responding quickly to suspected fraudulent activity, organisations can minimise the risk of misappropriation of funds.

Copyrights 2023 Vocational Resources Australia. All Rights Reserved.

Financial Recommendations

Financial recommendations typically refer to advice on how to manage a company's finances in a way that maximizes profits and minimises risk. This can include suggestions on budgeting, cash flow management, investment strategies, debt financing, and other financial matters related to the operation of a business.

Depending on the specific needs of your organisation, there may be various financial recommendations that could be beneficial.

Here are a few steps that are typically involved in preparing organisational financial recommendations:

1. Conduct a thorough analysis of the company's financial data, such as income statements, balance sheets, and cash flow statements. This will help you identify any areas where the company is experiencing financial difficulties or opportunities for improvement.

2. Identify the company's financial goals and objectives. This will help you understand what the company is trying to achieve financially and how you can help them get there.

3. Develop a range of financial strategies and recommendations that are tailored to the company's specific needs and objectives. This can include recommendations related to budgeting, cash flow management, investment strategies, debt financing, and other financial matters.

Copyrights 2023 Vocational Resources Australia. All Rights Reserved.

4. Evaluate the potential risks and benefits associated with each recommendation and determine its feasibility and impact on the company's financial performance.

5. Present the recommendations to the company's decision-makers, along with any supporting data or analysis. Be prepared to answer questions and provide additional information as needed.

6. Work with the company's financial team to implement the recommendations and monitor their effectiveness over time.

Supporting Staff in Implementation of Financial Recommendations

Supporting staff in implementation of financial recommendations typically involves a few key steps. First, it may involve providing training and resources to staff members so that they have the knowledge and skills needed to effectively implement the recommendations. This could include workshops, online training modules, or other types of training programs.

In addition to training, staff support may also involve providing ongoing guidance and coaching to individual staff members as they work to implement the recommendations. This could include regular check-ins, feedback sessions, and other forms of support to help staff members stay on track and make progress towards their goals.

Finally, financial recommendations often require changes to organisational processes, systems, and procedures, and so

Copyrights 2023 Vocational Resources Australia. All Rights Reserved.

supporting staff may also involve working with other teams or departments to ensure that these changes are implemented smoothly and effectively. This could include working with IT teams to update software systems, working with HR to update job descriptions and training programs, or other types of collaboration as needed.

Copyrights 2023 Vocational Resources Australia. All Rights Reserved.

Financial Resources

The financial resources of an organisation refer to the funds and assets utilised to finance its operations and investments. Financial resources are essentially the monetary means that enable a business to function, and there are various methods through which a business can acquire and employ its financial resources.

Financial management, also known as financial resource management (FRM), is the process by which an organisation plans, organises, directs, controls, and monitors its financial resources and activities to achieve its business goals.

Types of Financial Resources

There are different types of financial resources an organisation can have, such as:

Equity Financing

This is when a company raises funds by selling shares of ownership to investors. This type of financing can provide an organisation with a large sum of money but also means sharing ownership rights and profits with investors.

Debt Financing

In this type of financing, an organisation borrows money from lenders or financial institutions, which they then have to repay with interest. This can be a useful way to raise capital without giving up ownership, but it can also create financial burden if the organisation fails to make regular payments.

Grants

These are funds provided by governments, organisations or individuals for specific purposes or projects. Grants can

Copyrights 2023 Vocational Resources Australia. All Rights Reserved.

come with specific requirements, but they're a form of financing that doesn't have to be repaid.

Revenue

This is the money an organisation earns through the sale of goods or services. It can be used to fund ongoing operations and growth initiatives.

Donations

Similar to grants, donations are funds given to an organisation without the expectation of repayment. This type of financing is usually made by individuals, groups, or other organisations who support the cause of the recipient organisation.

Copyrights 2023 Vocational Resources Australia. All Rights Reserved.

Financial Risks

Organisational financial risks are a series of potential negative events or decisions that could negatively affect the financial health of an organisation.

The risks could arise from external factors like economic conditions, competition, changes in technology, regulatory requirements, or internal factors like poor managerial decisions or inadequate systems and processes.

Mitigation strategies for these risks could help to minimise losses and prevent long-term financial harm to the organisation.

Below are some common financial risks and their potential mitigation strategies:

Market Risk

This is when the value of an organisation's assets is affected by changes in market conditions. The mitigation strategy for this could involve reducing the reliance on one particular market, ensuring a diverse investment portfolio, and hedging against the risk using techniques like options or futures.

Credit Risk

Providing credit to other businesses for sales opportunities can expose a company to risks such as customers failing to make payments after receiving the products or services. This can lead to unexpected cash flow issues and put the company in a difficult position.

Copyrights 2023 Vocational Resources Australia. All Rights Reserved.

To recover from such situations, the company may need to increase sales or deny credit to other customers who rely on payment terms to purchase their products.

Self-Insurance

Self-insurance is a method that companies can use to mitigate credit risks, which involves creating a reserve fund to cover potential losses.

This approach can be compared to setting aside funds for a "rainy day." While this strategy may seem like a good idea, there are also some drawbacks to consider. For example, smaller companies may not have the resources to establish a bad-debt reserve.

Additionally, it is crucial to ensure that the reserve fund has sufficient funds to cover significant losses, such as a million-dollar deal with a company that fails to make payment.

Factoring

When businesses encounter customers who refuse to pay their debts, some opt to partner with factoring companies.

These companies purchase the invoices that businesses are unable to collect on, take a percentage of the margin after collecting on the invoice, and charge a fee. While this may seem like a viable solution for those facing cash flow issues, it comes with drawbacks.

Factoring companies charge fees and take a percentage of the invoice, so businesses will not be able to collect the full amount owed. Moreover, if the factoring company's

Copyrights 2023 Vocational Resources Australia. All Rights Reserved.

collection methods differ from those of the business, it could damage their customer relationships.

Letters of Credit

At first glance, requiring letters of credit may seem like the optimal solution for managing credit risk. By mandating letters of credit, customers are obligated to approach their bank and secure an agreement that guarantees payment in full by the due date.

For many accounts receivable departments, this appears to be an ideal solution. However, this approach can have negative consequences for the sales process.

Customers are required to go through an additional set of steps to apply for and obtain a letter of credit from their bank, which can be burdensome.

Furthermore, obtaining a letter of credit could count against their credit limit with the bank, potentially limiting their ability to make other purchases. As a result, implementing this approach in every sales opportunity could negatively impact total sales.

Trade Credit Insurance

Trade credit insurance functions similarly to other types of insurance policies. In the event that a customer defaults on payment, the policyholder can file a claim and receive reimbursement from the insurer. This straightforward process guarantees that the majority of unpaid accounts can be recovered by the accounts receivable department.

Copyrights 2023 Vocational Resources Australia. All Rights Reserved.

However, a disadvantage of this option is that, similar to traditional insurance policies, disputed accounts are usually not covered.

Consequently, your company must implement measures to significantly reduce invoice disputes.

Furthermore, when purchasing a trade credit insurance policy, it is critical to review the terms and conditions to ensure that the most common unpaid account scenarios are covered.

Liquidity Risk

This occurs when an organisation cannot meet its financial obligations due to cash shortages or lack of enough liquid assets to pay off debts. Mitigation strategies for liquidity risks could include developing a cash management plan, having reserves or borrowing arrangements in place, forecasting sales and cash flow accurately, and having contingencies in place to address any unexpected events.

Operational Risk

These are risks arising from internal business operations, such as employee fraud, errors or omissions, inadequate systems, or practices. Mitigation strategies could include internal controls, training employees on best practices, and implementing risk management procedures and regulatory compliance.

Regulatory Risk

This is the risk of non-compliance with changing government regulations, which may result in fines, legal action, or reputational damage. Mitigation strategies include close

Copyrights 2023 Vocational Resources Australia. All Rights Reserved.

monitoring of the regulatory environment, regular compliance checks, and maintaining proper documentation and record-keeping.

Copyrights 2023 Vocational Resources Australia. All Rights Reserved.

Reputational Risk

This is the risk of loss of reputation and credibility in the public eye, which can result from product recalls, lawsuits, or employee misconduct. Mitigation strategies could include regular customer satisfaction surveys, creating a robust corporate social responsibility program, and training employees to adhere to the organisation's standards and ethical practices.

Strategic Risk

Strategic risks arise when poor decision-making results in a significant financial loss. Mitigation strategies could include conducting strategic risk assessments, setting contingency planning into the decision-making process, or investing in robust business analytics to make informed decisions.

Copyrights 2023 Vocational Resources Australia. All Rights Reserved.

Financial Strategy

An organisational financial strategy is a plan that outlines how a company will manage its financial resources to achieve its objectives.

A comprehensive financial strategy takes into account a variety of factors, including market conditions, competition, operational costs, and revenue streams.

Key components of a financial strategy, including financial planning, budgeting, forecasting, risk management, and investment decisions.

The first component of an organisational financial strategy is financial planning.

Financial planning involves the development of short-term and long-term financial goals, and the strategies to achieve those goals. To develop a financial plan, companies must take into account their current financial situation, including cash flow, assets, liabilities, and capital structure.

The financial plan should also consider market conditions and trends, including interest rates, inflation rates, and economic growth. Companies must develop financial plans that are realistic, flexible, and adjustable to changes in the business environment.

The second component of an organisational financial strategy is budgeting.

Budgeting is the process of estimating future expenses and revenues and allocating resources accordingly. A budget is a

Copyrights 2023 Vocational Resources Australia. All Rights Reserved.

financial plan that details the expected revenue and expenses for a specific period, usually one year.

The budgeting process requires collaboration among various departments and stakeholders within the organisation. It involves setting financial targets, identifying the sources of revenue, estimating the cost of goods sold, and forecasting expenses.

The budgeting process should involve a review of historical data, trend analysis, and forecasting techniques to ensure that the budget is realistic and achievable.

A well-designed budget should also allow for flexibility and adjustments to changing market conditions or unexpected events.

The third component of an organisational financial strategy is forecasting. Forecasting is the process of estimating future trends and events based on past data and current market conditions.

Forecasting is essential for planning and decision-making, as it provides insights into future revenue and expenses. Forecasting techniques may include statistical models, trend analysis, and expert opinions. The forecasted data can be used for financial planning, resource allocation, and risk management.

The fourth component of an organisational financial strategy is risk management. Risk management is the process of identifying and mitigating financial risks that may impact the

Copyrights 2023 Vocational Resources Australia. All Rights Reserved.

company's financial performance. Financial risks include credit risk, market risk, operational risk, and liquidity risk.

The fifth and final component of an organisational financial strategy is investment decisions. Investment decisions involve the allocation of financial resources to various projects or initiatives that generate revenue or profits. Investment decisions must be based on a thorough cost-benefit analysis, considering the expected returns, risks, and opportunity costs. Investment decisions may involve capital expenditures, research and development, marketing campaigns, acquisitions, and divestitures.

Companies must evaluate investment opportunities based on their financial goals, market conditions, and competitive landscape.

Copyrights 2023 Vocational Resources Australia. All Rights Reserved.

Financial System

The financial system refers to a network of institutions, including banks, insurance companies, and stock exchanges, that enable the transfer of funds. These systems operate at various levels, including within firms, regions, and globally. Borrowers, lenders, and investors engage in the exchange of present funds to finance consumption or investment projects, with the aim of generating a return on their financial assets. Additionally, the financial system encompasses a collection of regulations and customs that borrowers and lenders follow to determine which projects are funded, who provides financing, and the conditions of financial transactions.

A financial system comprises a collection of institutions and practices, either global, regional, or firm-specific that are utilised to enable the transfer of funds. These systems can be organised based on market principles, central planning, or a combination of both. Institutions within the financial system range from banks, stock exchanges, and government treasuries, among others.

Similar to other industries, the financial system can be structured using market mechanisms, central planning, or a combination of the two. Financial markets typically involve borrowers, lenders, and investors negotiating loans and other transactions.

The economic goods exchanged on both sides usually involve some form of money, such as:

- current money (cash),
- claims on future money (credit), or

Copyrights 2023 Vocational Resources Australia. All Rights Reserved.

- claims on future income potential or
- The value of real assets (equity).

This also encompasses derivative instruments, such as commodity futures or stock options, which are financial instruments that are reliant on the performance of an underlying real or financial asset. In financial markets, these goods are traded between borrowers, lenders, and investors based on the laws of supply and demand.

In a centrally planned financial system, such as a single firm or a command economy, the financing of consumption and investment plans is determined by a manager or central planner rather than counterparties in a transaction. The planner decides which projects receive funding, who funds them, and whose projects receive funds, whether that planner is a business manager or a party boss.

Most financial systems incorporate both market mechanisms and top-down central planning. For instance, a business firm is a centrally planned financial system in terms of its internal financial decisions, but it typically operates within a broader market by interacting with external lenders and investors to carry out its long-term plans.

Moreover, all modern financial markets operate within some sort of government regulatory framework that places constraints on the types of transactions that are allowed. Financial systems are often strictly regulated because they directly impact decisions concerning real assets, economic performance, and consumer protection.

Copyrights 2023 Vocational Resources Australia. All Rights Reserved.

Financial Forecasting

Financial forecasting is the process of estimating future financial outcomes for a business or organisation. It involves analysing past financial data and using that information to make projections about future revenue, expenses, profits, and other financial metrics. Financial forecasting is an important tool for businesses because it can help them make informed decisions about budgeting, investment, and growth.

Financial Forecasting Methods

There are many methods and techniques for financial forecasting, including statistical modelling, trend analysis, and scenario planning.

Statistical Modelling

Statistical modelling involves using historical data to create mathematical models that can be used to predict future outcomes.

Trend Analysis

Trend analysis involves identifying patterns and trends in historical data to make predictions about future performance.

Scenario Planning

Scenario planning involves creating multiple projections based on different scenarios or assumptions.

Financial forecasting can be done for different time horizons, such as short-term (weeks or months), medium-term (one to three years), or long-term (three to five years or more). The time horizon chosen will depend on the business's needs and goals.

Copyrights 2023 Vocational Resources Australia. All Rights Reserved.

To create an accurate financial forecast, it is important to use reliable data and to consider all relevant factors that could impact the business's financial performance, such as economic trends, industry trends, and internal factors like changes in management or strategy.

Expenditure Forecasting

Expenditure forecasting is the estimation of future expenses based on historical data and assumptions. It is an important tool for businesses and organisations to plan and budget for their future expenses.

To begin with, expenditure forecasting requires historical data on expenses from previous periods. This data can be analysed to identify trends and patterns in spending. By examining the historical data, organisations can then make assumptions about future expenses.

There are different methods of forecasting future expenditure, including:

Trend analysis

This method involves analysing historical data to identify trends. By projecting the trend into the future, organisations can estimate future expenses.

Regression analysis

This method involves using statistical techniques to identify relationships between different variables. By analysing the relationship between expenses and other variables, such as revenue or GDP, organisations can forecast future expenses.

Copyrights 2023 Vocational Resources Australia. All Rights Reserved.

Time series analysis

This method involves analysing historical data to identify patterns in spending, such as seasonal variations. By projecting these patterns into the future, organisations can forecast future expenses.

In order to ensure the accuracy of expenditure forecasting, it is important to regularly review and adjust the assumptions made. This can involve revising assumptions based on changes in the business environment, such as changes in market conditions, policies, or regulations.

Difference between Financial Forecasting and Expenditure Forecasting

Financial forecasting and expenditure forecasting are two different types of forecasting that organisations often use in their financial planning.

Financial forecasting involves predicting an organisation's future financial performance, including revenue, expenses, profits, and cash flow. This type of forecasting typically takes a top-down approach, starting with the organisation's overall financial goals and working backwards to identify the specific actions that will help achieve those goals.

On the other hand, expenditure forecasting involves predicting an organisation's future expenditures, or spending. This type of forecasting typically takes a bottom-up approach, starting with individual departments or projects and working upwards to identify the total amount of spending the organisation will likely incur.

Copyrights 2023 Vocational Resources Australia. All Rights Reserved.

While both types of forecasting are important for financial planning, they serve different purposes. Financial forecasting is used to plan for overall financial performance, while expenditure forecasting is used to plan for specific spending needs.

By using both types of forecasting, organisations can gain a more comprehensive understanding of their financial situation and make better-informed decisions about resource allocation and budgeting.

Linking Forecast to Decision-Making

To increase the interest of decision-makers in the forecast, it is crucial to highlight the forecast's significance as a crucial element in the planning and budgeting process.

This entails promoting a long-term perspective in budgeting and emphasising financially sustainable choices.

The following financial policies might be particularly helpful for promoting interest in financial forecasting:

- A policy on reserves, which sets the target level of reserves to maintain, will necessitate the use of forecasting tools to determine if reserve levels will remain within desired limits considering future spending and revenues.
- A policy on maintaining structural balance involves ensuring that recurring expenditures are covered by recurring revenues. A forecast is necessary to determine if this will continue in the future, which helps in considering the long-term consequences of decisions.

Copyrights 2023 Vocational Resources Australia. All Rights Reserved.

- One policy that can promote interest in financial forecasting is a long-term financial planning policy, which urges decision-makers to consider the long-term implications of present decisions. Additionally, capital improvement plans should have a long-term planning horizon.

Forecasting Models

Some of the forecasting models are discussed below:

Extrapolation

Extrapolation involves using historical revenue data to predict future behaviour by projecting the trend forward. Trending, moving averages, and single exponential smoothing are commonly employed by forecasters.

Regression Analysis

Regression analysis is a statistical procedure based on the relationship between independent variables (factors that have predictive power) and a dependent variable (the revenue or expenditure being predicted).

By assuming a linear relationship between these variables, one or more independent variables can be used to predict future revenues or expenditures.

Hybrid Forecasting

Hybrid Forecasting is a popular approach that combines the forecaster's expert knowledge with quantitative forecasting techniques.

Copyrights 2023 Vocational Resources Australia. All Rights Reserved.

By leveraging both data-driven and judgment-driven approaches, hybrid forecasting can often produce more accurate and reliable forecasts.

This is because the forecaster's knowledge and experience can provide valuable insights into factors that may not be captured by statistical models, while quantitative methods can help identify patterns and relationships in historical data that may not be immediately apparent.

Overall, hybrid forecasting can be a powerful tool for organisations seeking to make informed decisions based on accurate and reliable forecasts.

Implementation Methods

The implementation methods involve both making the forecast using one or more of the previously described methods and utilising forecast ranges.

It is recommended to consider developing a range of potential forecast outcomes through the use of different scenarios, as multiple projections can be valuable in a well-planned and extensively discussed approach.

Copyrights 2023 Vocational Resources Australia. All Rights Reserved.

Forecasting Principles

Using a systematic and well-structured approach in judgmental forecasting helps to reduce the adverse effects of the limitations of judgmental forecasting, some of which we listed in the previous section. Whether this approach involves one individual or many, the following principles should be followed:

- Set the forecasting task clearly and concisely
  Care is needed when setting the forecasting challenges and expressing the forecasting tasks. It is important that everyone be clear about what the task is.

  All definitions should be clear and comprehensive, avoiding ambiguous and vague expressions. Also, it is important to avoid incorporating emotive terms and irrelevant information that may distract the forecaster.

  In the Delphi method that follows it may sometimes be useful to conduct a preliminary round of information gathering before setting the forecasting task.

- Implement a systematic approach
  Forecast accuracy and consistency can be improved by using a systematic approach to judgmental forecasting involving checklists of categories of information which are relevant to the forecasting task.

  For example, it is helpful to identify what information is important and how this information is to be weighted. When forecasting the demand for a new product, what factors should we account for and how should we account for them?

Copyrights 2023 Vocational Resources Australia. All Rights Reserved.

Should it be the price, the quality and/or quantity of the competition, the economic environment at the time, the target population of the product? It is worthwhile to devote significant effort and resources to put together decision rules that will lead to the best possible systematic approach.

- Document and justify
  Formalising and documenting the decision rules and assumptions implemented in the systematic approach can promote consistency, as the same rules can be implemented repeatedly.

  Also, requesting a forecaster to document and justify their forecasts leads to accountability, which can lead to reduced bias. Furthermore, formal documentation aids significantly in the systematic evaluation process that is suggested next.

- Systematically evaluate forecasts
  Systematically monitoring the forecasting process can identify unforeseen irregularities. In particular, keep records of forecasts and use them to obtain feedback when the corresponding observations become available.

  Although you may do your best as a forecaster, the environment you operate in is dynamic. Changes occur, and you need to monitor these in order to evaluate the decision rules and assumptions. Feedback and evaluation help forecasters learn and improve their forecast accuracy.

Copyrights 2023 Vocational Resources Australia. All Rights Reserved.

- Segregate forecasters and users
  Forecast accuracy may be impeded if the forecasting task is carried out by users of the forecasts, such as those responsible for implementing plans of action about which the forecast is concerned.

  We should clarify again that forecasting is about predicting the future as accurately as possible, given all of the information available, including historical data and knowledge of any future events that may impact the forecasts.

  Forecasters and users should be clearly segregated. A classic case is that of a new product being launched.

The forecast should be a reasonable estimate of the sales volume of a new product, which may differ considerably from what management expects or hopes the sales will be in order to meet company financial objectives. In this case, a forecaster may be delivering a reality check to the user.

It is important that forecasters communicate forecasts to potential users thoroughly. Users may feel distant and disconnected from forecasts and may not have full confidence in them.

Explaining and clarifying the process and justifying the basic assumptions that led to the forecasts will provide some assurance to users.

The way in which forecasts may then be used and implemented will clearly depend on managerial decision making. For example, management may decide to adjust a

Copyrights 2023 Vocational Resources Australia. All Rights Reserved.

forecast upwards (be over-optimistic), as the forecast may be used to guide purchasing and stock keeping levels. Such a decision may be taken after a cost-benefit analysis reveals that the cost of holding excess stock is much lower than that of lost sales.

This type of adjustment should be part of setting goals or planning supply, rather than part of the forecasting process. In contrast, if forecasts are used as targets, they may be set low so that they can be exceeded more easily. Again, setting targets is different from producing forecasts, and the two should not be confused.

Copyrights 2023 Vocational Resources Australia. All Rights Reserved.

Forecasting Process

Financial forecasting is the process of predicting future financial performance. It is a critical tool for businesses of all sizes, as it can help them make informed decisions about budgeting, planning, and growth.

There are many different methods of financial forecasting, but they all follow a basic process. The first step is to gather data. This includes historical financial statements, market research, and economic data. Once the data has been gathered, it needs to be analysed. This involves identifying trends, patterns, and relationships.

The next step is to make assumptions. This is where the forecaster uses their judgment to project future results. The assumptions should be based on the data that has been analysed, as well as the forecaster's knowledge of the industry and the company.

Once the assumptions have been made, the forecaster can begin to build a model. The model will be used to calculate future financial results. The model can be as simple or as complex as needed, depending on the accuracy and detail that is desired.

The final step is to review and revise the forecast. This is an important step, as it allows the forecaster to catch any errors and make adjustments as needed. The forecast should be reviewed regularly, as new information becomes available.

Financial forecasting is a complex process, but it is a valuable tool for businesses of all sizes. By following the

Copyrights 2023 Vocational Resources Australia. All Rights Reserved.

steps outlined above, businesses can gain valuable insights into their financial future.

Seven Steps to Financial Forecasting

1. Gather data
   The first step in financial forecasting is to gather data. This includes historical financial statements, market research, and economic data.

2. Analyse data
   Once the data has been gathered, it needs to be analysed. This involves identifying trends, patterns, and relationships.

3. Make assumptions
   The next step is to make assumptions. This is where the forecaster uses their judgment to project future results. The assumptions should be based on the data that has been analysed, as well as the forecaster's knowledge of the industry and the company.

4. Build a model
   Once the assumptions have been made, the forecaster can begin to build a model. The model will be used to calculate future financial results. The model can be as simple or as complex as needed, depending on the accuracy and detail that is desired.

5. Review and revise the forecast
   The final step is to review and revise the forecast. This is an important step, as it allows the forecaster to catch any errors and make adjustments as needed.

Copyrights 2023 Vocational Resources Australia. All Rights Reserved.

The forecast should be reviewed regularly, as new information becomes available.

6. Communicate the forecast
   Once the forecast has been finalised, it needs to be communicated to the appropriate stakeholders. This includes the company's management team, board of directors, and investors.

7. Use the forecast to make decisions
   The final step is to use the forecast to make decisions. This could include decisions about budgeting, planning, and growth.

Benefits

There are many benefits to financial forecasting. Some of the most important benefits include:

- Improved decision-making
  Financial forecasting can help businesses make better decisions about budgeting, planning, and growth. By projecting future financial results, businesses can identify potential problems and opportunities early on.

- Increased financial stability
  Financial forecasting can help businesses improve their financial stability. By identifying potential risks and challenges, businesses can take steps to mitigate them.

- Attract investors
  Financial forecasting can help businesses attract investors. By demonstrating that the business has a solid

Copyrights 2023 Vocational Resources Australia. All Rights Reserved.

financial plan, businesses can make themselves more attractive to potential investors.

- Improve communication
  Financial forecasting can help improve communication between the company's management team, board of directors, and investors. By sharing the forecast with these stakeholders, businesses can ensure that everyone is on the same page about the company's financial future.

Challenges

There are also some challenges associated with financial forecasting. Some of the most common challenges include:

- Data accuracy
  The accuracy of the forecast depends on the accuracy of the data that is used to build it. If the data is inaccurate, the forecast will be inaccurate.
- Assumptions
  The forecast is based on a number of assumptions. If these assumptions are incorrect, the forecast will be incorrect.

- External factors
  The forecast is also affected by external factors, such as the economy, the industry, and the competition. These factors can be difficult to predict, and they can make the forecast less accurate.

Copyrights 2023 Vocational Resources Australia. All Rights Reserved.

GST Requirements

Goods and Services Tax (GST) is a tax levied on most goods and services sold or consumed in Australia.

Any business that operates in Australia and has annual turnovers of $75,000 or more is required to:

- Register for GST
  Registration for GST is mandatory if your business's GST turnover (gross income minus GST) is $75,000 or more per financial year, or if you're a non-profit organisation with a GST turnover of $150,000 or more per financial year, or if you're a taxi driver or ride-sharing driver, regardless of your turnover.

  The due dates for lodging your BAS depend on your turnover.

  If your business has a turnover of $20 million or less, you can choose to lodge it monthly or quarterly, while those with a turnover over $20 million are required to report monthly.

- Charge GST
  Once registered, the business should charge GST at 10% on all goods and services sold to customers, unless the item is exempt or zero-rated.

- Lodge a Business Activity Statement (BAS)
  The business must lodge a BAS every quarter, which reports the amount of GST collected and paid, along with other tax obligations such as PAYG withholding and PAYG instalments.

Copyrights 2023 Vocational Resources Australia. All Rights Reserved.

- Claim Input Tax Credits (ITCs)
  The business can claim ITCs for GST paid on business purchases and expenses, such as goods and services used in the operation of the business. This can be claimed on the BAS.

- Keep accurate records
  The business must keep accurate records of all sales, purchases, and expenses, including GST.

- Comply with the ATO's reporting and payment requirements

The business must comply with the ATO's reporting and payment requirements for GST and any other taxes payable.

Copyrights 2023 Vocational Resources Australia. All Rights Reserved.

Income and Expenditure

Organisational income and expenditure are two critical components of any business, and they are essential in determining the financial health of an organisation. Income refers to all the money a business earns through its operations, while expenditure refers to the money a business spends on various activities such as salaries, rent, utilities, inventory, and other expenses.

The income of an organisation can come from a variety of sources, including sales, investments, donations, grants, and government subsidies. For most organisations, sales represent the primary source of income. In contrast, the other sources of income may be supplemental. Organisations that rely heavily on donations or government subsidies may be subject to fluctuations in funding, making it challenging to predict future income.

Organisations must also be mindful of their expenditure. They need to plan carefully to ensure that the money they spend aligns with their overall financial goals. Expenditure can be further divided into two categories: fixed and variable. Fixed expenses refer to expenses that do not change, regardless of the level of business activity. Rent, salaries, and insurance premiums typically fall into this category. Variable expenses, on the other hand, are expenses that fluctuate with the level of business activity. Examples of variable expenses include raw materials, inventory costs, and marketing expenses.

When it comes to managing organisational income and expenditure, it is essential to create a budget. A budget is a financial plan that outlines an organisation's expected

Copyrights 2023 Vocational Resources Australia. All Rights Reserved.

income and expenditure over a given period. By creating a budget, organisations can plan their operations more effectively, be prepared for future risks, and identify areas for cost savings.

Another aspect to consider when discussing organisational income and expenditure is financial reporting. Financial reports are critical because they provide a detailed picture of an organisation's financial health. Reports such as balance sheets, income statements, and cash flow statements provide valuable insights into an organisation's income and expenditure.

Organisations may also want to consider investing some of their income in revenue-generating activities. By investing in new products or services, an organisation can create new revenue streams and increase its overall income. However, they must be mindful of the risks associated with new investments and ensure they have a solid business plan in place.

Copyrights 2023 Vocational Resources Australia. All Rights Reserved.

Investment Decision-Making

Investment decision-making involves allocating financial resources based on an individual or firm's investment objectives, risk appetite, and expected returns.

For firms:

- capital budgeting is used to allocate limited resources towards long-term assets,
- while short-term investments are preferred for operational managers to ensure adequate liquidity and working capital.

Factors such as expected returns, risk levels, maturity periods, tax benefits, inflation rates, and volatility also play a crucial role in investment decision-making.

Investment decisions involve allocating financial resources to achieve the best possible returns, taking into account investment objectives, risk appetites, and the nature of the investor.

Investments can be classified as short-term or long-term, and can include strategic investments, capital expenditures, inventory investments, modernization, expansion, replacement, or new venture investments.

The investment process consists of several steps, including formulating investment objectives, determining risk profile, allocating assets, and monitoring performance.

Investment decisions are focused on maximising returns by allocating financial resources to the most suitable opportunities, while considering risks and returns.

Copyrights 2023 Vocational Resources Australia. All Rights Reserved.

These decisions are critical in financial management, as they involve significant funds and can have long-term impacts on both investors and businesses.

Investors and managers spend considerable time planning their investments and are often presented with various options such as securities, bonds, debentures, real estate, and more.

Investment Decision-Making Process

Investment decisions require patience and an analytical decision-making process.

The process involves five steps:

1. Analyse the current financial position of the company or individual.

2. Set investment objectives, including the duration of the investment and the level of risk.

3. Allocate assets among different asset classes such as stocks, bonds, and real estate.

4. Select specific investment products based on the asset allocation strategy.

5. Continuously monitor the performance of the portfolio and take prompt action if necessary.

Copyrights 2023 Vocational Resources Australia. All Rights Reserved.

Factors Affecting Investment Decision

An investment is a planned decision, and some of the factors that are responsible for these decisions are as follows:

- Investment objective
  The purpose behind investment drives short-term or long-term fund allocation.

- Return on investment
  Limited funds are invested in a profitable asset or security for a positive return.

- Return frequency
  Investors choose investments based on the frequency of returns needed, such as monthly, quarterly, semi-annual, or annual returns.

- Risk
  Every investment carries high, medium, or low risk, which requires risk analysis based on the investor or company's risk appetite.

- Maturity period
  Payback period is an essential factor influencing investor decisions.

- Tax benefit
  Tax liability associated with an asset or security is another critical deciding factor.

- Safety
  Assets or securities offered by companies with transparent financial disclosure and regulatory

Copyrights 2023 Vocational Resources Australia. All Rights Reserved.

frameworks are considered safe, while government-backed assets are the most secure.

- Volatility
  Market fluctuations significantly impact investment returns.

- Liquidity
  Investors consider the degree of liquidity an asset or security offers, specifically looking at withdrawal restrictions and penalties.

- Inflation Rate
  Investors seek investment opportunities where returns surpass the nation's inflation rate.

Financial Operations

Financial operations are the backbone of any company and are responsible for managing the company's financial resources effectively.

Some of the key aspects of financial operations are:

Accounting and Bookkeeping

Financial operations team must accurately record, classify, and maintain financial transactions of the company. This includes processes such as bookkeeping, accounts payable and receivable, payroll, tax management, and financial reporting.

Accuracy and Authorisation

Accuracy and authorization are two important requirements for organisational financial documents.

Copyrights 2023 Vocational Resources Australia. All Rights Reserved.

Accuracy refers to the requirement that financial documents must be complete, correct, and free from errors. This means that all financial information must be recorded accurately and in accordance with accounting standards and principles. Accuracy is essential to ensure that financial statements reflect a true and fair view of the organisation's financial position, performance, and cash flow.

To ensure accuracy, organisations must have appropriate financial controls in place, such as segregation of duties, regular reconciliations, and independent reviews. These controls help to prevent errors, fraud, and other financial irregularities.

Authorization refers to the requirement that financial documents must be approved and authorised by authorised personnel. This includes ensuring that all financial transactions are authorised by the appropriate individuals, such as managers or executives, and that all financial documents are signed or otherwise authenticated by authorised personnel.

Authorization ensures that financial transactions are conducted in accordance with organisational policies and procedures, and that financial documents are reliable and trustworthy. It also helps to prevent unauthorised transactions and financial irregularities.

To ensure authorization, organisations must have appropriate financial policies and procedures in place, such as approval limits, authorization matrices, and signature authority. These policies and procedures help to ensure that financial transactions are authorised by the appropriate

Copyrights 2023 Vocational Resources Australia. All Rights Reserved.

individuals and that financial documents are reliable and trustworthy.

Cash Management

Effective management of cash is critical for any company. The financial operations team must ensure that there is enough cash to meet the operating expenses of the business, pay off debts, and invest in growth opportunities. They also need to manage cash flow, forecast cash needs and ensure that there is enough liquidity to sustain operations.

Financial Controls

Maintaining strong financial controls helps prevent fraud, mismanagement of funds, and other financial irregularities. The financial operations team must establish and maintain effective financial control systems, such as internal audit, segregation of duties, and financial reporting systems to ensure compliance and prevent financial misstatements.

Financial Planning and Analysis

The financial operations team is responsible for forecasting and estimating financial outcomes, analysing business performance, and developing strategies for future growth. This involves creating budgets, developing business plans, analysing financial statements, evaluating investment opportunities, and forecasting cash flow.

Financial Reporting

The financial operations team is responsible for preparing financial statements that accurately represent the company's financial performance, position, and cash flows. They also

Copyrights 2023 Vocational Resources Australia. All Rights Reserved.

provide reports to management and other interested parties such as investors, shareholders, and regulatory agencies.

Risk Management

The financial operations team is responsible for managing risk associated with the financial operations of the business. They must identify and evaluate financial risks such as credit risk, market risk, and operational risk. They also need to ensure compliance with relevant regulatory requirements.

Copyrights 2023 Vocational Resources Australia. All Rights Reserved.

Accounting Procedures

Accounting procedures are the set of steps and processes that are used to record, classify, and summarise financial information. They are designed to ensure that financial data is accurate, complete, and reliable.

Accounting procedures can be manual or automated, and they typically include the following steps:

- Identifying transactions
  The first step is to identify all of the financial transactions that have occurred during a period of time. This includes sales, purchases, expenses, and other events that have affected the company's financial position.

- Recording transactions
  Once the transactions have been identified, they must be recorded in a journal. The journal is a chronological record of all of the company's financial transactions.

- Posting transactions
  After the transactions have been recorded in the journal, they must be posted to the ledger. The ledger is a more detailed record of the company's financial accounts.

- Preparing financial statements
  Once the transactions have been recorded and posted, they can be used to prepare financial statements. Financial statements provide a summary of the company's financial position and performance.

Accounting procedures are important for a number of reasons. They help to ensure that financial data is accurate,

Copyrights 2023 Vocational Resources Australia. All Rights Reserved.

complete, and reliable. They also help to identify and correct errors. Additionally, accounting procedures can help to prevent fraud and other financial irregularities.

Some of the key features of accounting procedures are listed below:

- Documented Policies and Procedures
  Organisational accounting procedures should be clearly documented to provide consistency and clarity in financial transactions.

- Internal Controls
  Accounting procedures should include effective internal controls to reduce the risk of errors and fraud, which includes segregation of duties, authorisation procedures, and monitoring controls.

- Compliance Assurance
  Procedures should ensure compliance with relevant accounting and tax standards, including regularly reviewing and updating procedures to ensure compliance.

- Adequate Record Keeping
  Accounting procedures should define record-keeping requirements, including maintaining accurate and complete records for financial transactions, invoices, and related documents.

Copyrights 2023 Vocational Resources Australia. All Rights Reserved.

- Accurate and Timely Reporting
  Procedures should outline the methods for producing timely financial reports and providing stakeholders with accurate financial information.

- Risk Assessment
  Accounting procedures should include regular risk assessment to identify areas of high risk to the organisation and implement appropriate controls.

- Ethical Considerations
  Procedures should outline ethical considerations in financial transactions, promoting honesty, transparency, and accountability in financial activities.

- Proper Authorisation and Approval
  Procedures should ensure that all financial activities are properly authorised and approved, with clear guidelines defining the levels of authority for different staff members.

- Communication
  Procedures should promote communication among staff members and management to raise awareness of financial activities and ensure compliance with accounting procedures.

- Continuous Improvement
  Procedures should include processes to continuously review and improve the efficiency and effectiveness of the accounting function, including employee training and use of technology.

Copyrights 2023 Vocational Resources Australia. All Rights Reserved.

Accounting Software

Accounting software is a type of computer program that helps companies manage their financial transactions. It is designed to automate many of the tasks involved in accounting, such as bookkeeping, invoicing, payroll processing, financial reporting, and tax preparation.

There are many different types of business accounting software available on the market, each with their own unique features and benefits. Some of the most popular accounting software packages include MYOB, QuickBooks, Xero, and Sage 50. These software packages are designed to be user-friendly and offer a range of features to help businesses manage their finances more effectively.

One of the key benefits of business accounting software is that it can help companies save time and reduce the risk of errors.

By automating many of the tasks involved in accounting, business owners and managers can focus on other important aspects of running their business, such as customer service, sales, and marketing.

Another benefit of business accounting software is that it can help companies make more informed financial decisions. With access to real-time financial data, business owners and managers can quickly identify trends and make adjustments to their operations to improve profitability and efficiency.

An accounting software is required to have following features as minimum:

Copyrights 2023 Vocational Resources Australia. All Rights Reserved.

- General ledger
  A general ledger serves as the foundation of any accounting software, recording all financial transactions and ensuring that debits and credits are balanced.

- Invoicing and billing
  Accounting software should allow businesses to create and send professional-looking invoices to customers, complete with custom branding, payment terms, and various payment options.

- Accounts Payable and Receivable
  The software should have features that enable businesses to manage vendor bills and track customer payments, making bookkeeping simpler and more efficient.

- Bank reconciliation
  Bank reconciliation is a critical feature of accounting software as it allows businesses to verify and reconcile transactions between their bank and accounting system.

- Financial reporting
  Accounting software should offer reporting capabilities, allowing businesses to generate financial reports such as balance sheets, income statements, cash flow statements, and reports tailored to specific business requirements.

- Budgeting and planning
  The ability to create budgets and forecast future cash flows is an essential feature of accounting software, as it

Copyrights 2023 Vocational Resources Australia. All Rights Reserved.

helps businesses make informed decisions about their financial resources.

- Payroll management
  Payroll management is a vital component of accounting software, allowing businesses to calculate employee salaries, taxes, and benefits, as well as stay compliant with payroll regulations.

- Inventory management
  For businesses that deal with inventory or stock, inventory management functionality allows businesses to keep track of stock levels, valuations, and reordering.

- Time tracking
  The ability to track and record employee time against specific projects, tasks or clients can help businesses manage labour costs and ensure accurate invoicing.

- Customisable Dashboards
  Customisable dashboards that feature visual representations of important financial metrics such as profit and loss, accounts payable, accounts receivable, and cash flow can help businesses monitor their financial health at a glance.

Copyrights 2023 Vocational Resources Australia. All Rights Reserved.

Accounting System

Accounting system refers to the set of processes and procedures that an organisation uses to manage its financial transactions and records. This includes the methods for recording and classifying transactions, creating financial statements, and tracking financial performance.

The system can include software, hardware, and personnel resources to ensure accurate and timely financial reporting. The goal of an organisational accounting system is to help the organisation understand its financial standing and make informed decisions based on accurate financial information.

An accounting system comprises of the following features:

- Bookkeeping
  Organisational accounting systems keep track of all financial transactions in the organisation, including expenses, income, assets, and liabilities.

- Financial statements
  Accounting systems generate financial statements, such as balance sheets, income statements, and cash flow statements, which convey the financial health of the company.

- Budgeting
  Accounting systems aid in the formulation and monitoring of the organisation's budgets.

- Cost accounting
  Accounting systems also calculate and assign costs of goods sold and other expenses.

Copyrights 2023 Vocational Resources Australia. All Rights Reserved.

- Regulatory compliance
  Accounting systems assist in maintaining records with regulatory bodies and ensure compliance with accounting standards and tax laws.

- Inventory management
  Accounting system help organisations manage and track inventory to monitor stock levels, turnover, and stock value.

- Data analysis
  Accounting systems can generate reports and insights on financial trends and performance, aiding decision-making processes.

- Payroll processing
  Many accounting systems can initiate payroll entries, manage employee records, monitor attendance, and calculate salaries, taxes, and insurance contributions.

- Electronic invoicing
  Accounting system make it easier to create and issue invoices and track payments owed.

- Security
  Accounting systems may include security features such as restricted access, password protection, and mandatory backups, safeguarding financial information.

Copyrights 2023 Vocational Resources Australia. All Rights Reserved.

Key Terminologies - Not discussed elsewhere in the chapter

Accruals

Accruals (ACCR) refer to revenues and expenses that a company has recognised but not yet recorded in their accounts. These transactions occur before an exchange of money has taken place. For instance, if a company hires an external consultant, the cost of that consultation would be recognised in an accrual, even if the consultant has not yet invoiced the company for their services. Accruals can take various forms, including accounts payable, accounts receivable, accrued costs (costs incurred but not yet resolved), and accrued expenses (expenses or liabilities incurred but not yet resolved).

Accrual Basis Accounting

Accrual basis accounting, also known as accrual accounting, is a method of accounting that records revenue- and expense-related items when they are earned or incurred, regardless of when the money is received or paid.

For example, if a customer buys a product on credit for $2,000, accrual accounting recognises the $2,000 in revenue on the date of the purchase, even if the money is not received until a later date. This is in contrast to cash basis accounting, which records revenue and expenses only when the money is actually received or paid.

While large businesses and publicly traded companies tend to favour accrual accounting, small businesses and individuals often use cash basis accounting.

Copyrights 2023 Vocational Resources Australia. All Rights Reserved.

Accounts Payable

Liabilities is a class of accounting entries that includes accounts payable (AP), which is used to track the money a company owes to creditors such as unpaid bills, invoices, bank loans, debts to suppliers or vendors, and credit card or line of credit debts. Sometimes, the term "trade payables" is used instead of "accounts payable."

Accounts Receivable

The tracking of money owed to a business or individual by debtors is called accounts receivable (AR), which is the opposite of accounts payable. Another term used for accounts receivable is "trade receivables." Typically, accounts receivable are generated from sales of products or services supplied on credit or without upfront payment.

Accountants consider accounts receivable as assets and keep track of them accordingly.

Accounting Period

The duration of a financial statement or operation is determined by the accounting period, which can be a fiscal year, calendar year, three-month calendar quarter, or even a month. Every accounting period covers an entire accounting cycle, which accountants utilise to monitor transactions during a specific period. Accountants use an eight-step system called the accounting cycle to track transactions during a specific period.

Ageing Summary

The Ageing Summary report is a financial statement that provides a snapshot of the outstanding balances on your company's accounts receivable. This report groups

Copyrights 2023 Vocational Resources Australia. All Rights Reserved.

outstanding customer invoices by the length of time they have been unpaid, which is referred to as their "ageing."

The Ageing Summary is typically broken down into columns that represent different aging periods, such as 0-30 days, 31-60 days, 61-90 days, and so on. The dollar amounts of unpaid invoices are listed in each column, so you can see at a glance how much money is owed to your company by customers in each aging category.

The Ageing Summary is useful for tracking how quickly your customers are paying their bills, and for identifying any problem areas where accounts are becoming excessively overdue. This can help your company take proactive steps to collect outstanding debts and improve cash flow.

Amortization

The process of allocating the cost of an intangible asset over its useful life. Intangible assets include patents, trademarks, copyrights, and franchise agreements that are essential to a company.

Assets

Assets are items that are owned by the business and have a monetary value. They are listed on the balance sheet in order of liquidity, which means that assets that can be easily converted into cash are listed first.

The main categories of assets include current assets and non-current assets.

Copyrights 2023 Vocational Resources Australia. All Rights Reserved.

Current assets include items such as cash, accounts receivable, inventory, and prepaid expenses that are expected to be converted to cash within one year.

Non-current assets, on the other hand, include items such as property, plant, equipment, and long-term investments that are expected to provide benefits to the company for more than one year.

Balance Sheet

A balance sheet is a financial statement that provides a snapshot of a business's financial position at a given point in time. It is one of the three critical financial statements used by businesses, along with the cash flow statement and income statement.

To assess a company's financial health, investors can rely on various ratios that can be calculated from its balance sheet, such as the debt-to-equity ratio and the acid-test ratio, among others. To obtain a comprehensive understanding of a company's finances, investors should also examine its income statement and statement of cash flows, as well as any accompanying notes or addenda in its earnings report that may reference the balance sheet.

The balance sheet follows a straightforward accounting equation where assets are placed on one side and liabilities and shareholder equity are positioned on the other, resulting in a balanced equation: Assets = Liabilities + Shareholders' Equity.

This equation is simple to comprehend because a company must fund all of its possessions (assets) either by borrowing

Copyrights 2023 Vocational Resources Australia. All Rights Reserved.

money (creating liabilities) or receiving investments from shareholders (issuing shareholder equity).

If a company obtains a $4,000 loan from a bank with a five-year repayment period, its assets, specifically the cash account, will increase by $4,000. Simultaneously, its liabilities, specifically the long-term debt account, will also rise by $4,000, balancing out the two sides of the equation. In case the company receives $8,000 from investors, its assets will increase by that amount, and its shareholder equity will also increase. All of the company's revenue that surpasses its expenses will go into the shareholder equity account. These revenues will be balanced on the assets side, appearing as cash, investments, inventory, or other assets.

Comparing a company's balance sheet with those of other businesses in the same industry is also crucial since different industries have their unique ways of financing.

It's essential to note that a company's balance sheet provides information about its assets, liabilities, and shareholder equity, and these three categories should always balance. This balance is the reason why the statement is called a balance sheet. When the balance is not correct, it could indicate errors in the data, inventory or exchange rate mistakes, or miscalculations.

Each category of assets, liabilities, and shareholder equity contains numerous smaller accounts that provide specific details about a company's finances. These accounts differ significantly across industries, and identical terms may have different interpretations depending on the company's nature

Copyrights 2023 Vocational Resources Australia. All Rights Reserved.

of business. Nonetheless, there are a few common elements that investors are likely to encounter.

Balance sheet assist in identifying the financial risks, securing capital, and providing important information to internal stakeholders such as management and shareholders.

Management can use the balance sheet to make informed decisions about resource allocation and investment opportunities. Shareholders can use the balance sheet to assess the financial performance of the company and make decisions about buying or selling stock.

Components of a Balance Sheet

Assets

In a balance sheet, current and non-current assets are listed in order of their liquidity, or ease of conversion into cash. Current assets can be converted into cash within a year or less, while non-current assets cannot. The order of accounts within current assets is typically as follows:

Cash and cash equivalents, which include items such as short-term certificates of deposit and Treasury bills, as well as hard currency.

Marketable securities, which are equity and debt securities that can be easily traded on a liquid market.

Accounts receivable (AR), which represent money that customers owe to the company. An allowance for doubtful

Copyrights 2023 Vocational Resources Australia. All Rights Reserved.

accounts may be included to account for customers who may not pay.

Inventory, which refers to goods that are available for sale and are valued at the lower of their cost or market price.

Prepaid expenses, which represent the value that has already been paid for items such as insurance, advertising contracts, or rent.

Long-term assets include the following:
The segment of the balance sheet that represents assets is divided into two categories: current assets and non-current assets.

Current assets, which can be converted to cash within a year or less, are listed in order of liquidity. They include cash and cash equivalents, marketable securities, accounts receivable, inventory, and prepaid expenses.

Non-current assets, on the other hand, include long-term investments, fixed assets, and intangible assets.

Long-term investments are securities that cannot be liquidated within a year, while fixed assets are physical assets such as land, buildings, and equipment.

Intangible assets, which are valuable but non-physical, include intellectual property and goodwill, and are only listed on the balance sheet if acquired, which can lead to their value being either understated or overstated.

Copyrights 2023 Vocational Resources Australia. All Rights Reserved.

Liabilities

Current liabilities are usually listed in the order of their due date and may include:

Current portion of long-term debt, which is the part of a long-term loan that must be paid within the next year.

Interest payable, which is the interest that has accumulated and is due to be paid, often as part of a past-due obligation like late property tax remittance.

Wages payable is the amount of money owed by the company to its employees for salaries, wages, and benefits, typically for the most recent pay period.

Customer prepayments refer to money received from a customer in advance for a product or service that has not yet been provided.

The company has an obligation to either provide the good or service or return the customer's money.

Dividends payable is the amount of dividends that a company has declared to be paid to its shareholders but has not yet paid out.

Current liabilities are due within one year and are arranged in order of their due date.

Among current liabilities are accounts payable, which are debts that a company owes to its suppliers and are usually paid within 30 days of receipt.

Copyrights 2023 Vocational Resources Australia. All Rights Reserved.

Other examples of current liabilities include interest payable, customer prepayments, and earned and unearned premiums, which are payments received by a company upfront for an agreement that has not yet been fulfilled.

Additionally, dividends payable refers to authorised dividend payments that have not yet been issued.

Long-term liabilities can include:
Long-term debt is a type of liability that includes both principal and interest payments on bonds issued by the company.

Pension fund liability is the obligation of a company to pay into its employees' retirement accounts as part of their compensation package.

Deferred tax liability refers to the taxes that a company has accrued but will not pay until a later date, usually due to differences in financial reporting and tax assessment methods.

Some liabilities are not included on the balance sheet and are known as off-balance sheet liabilities.

Shareholder Equity

Shareholder equity, also known as net assets, represents the portion of a company's total assets that is attributable to its owners or shareholders. It is calculated as the difference between a company's total assets and its liabilities, which is the debt it owes to non-shareholders.

Copyrights 2023 Vocational Resources Australia. All Rights Reserved.

Retained earnings are the net profits a company retains and reinvests in the business or uses to pay off debt. Any remaining amount can be distributed to shareholders in the form of dividends.

Treasury stock refers to the shares of a company's own stock that it has repurchased. These shares can be sold at a later date to raise cash or held in reserve to defend against a hostile takeover.

Some companies issue preferred stock, which is listed separately from common stock under shareholder equity. Preferred stock is assigned an arbitrary par value, similar to common stock, and its market value may not be related to its par value.

The total value of common stock and preferred stock is calculated by multiplying the par value by the number of shares issued.

Additional paid-in capital or capital surplus accounts for the excess amount that shareholders have invested beyond the par value-based common or preferred stock accounts. This amount is not necessarily related to a company's market capitalisation, which is determined by the current stock price. Instead, it represents the sum of equity that has been purchased at any price.

Par value, which is commonly set at a small amount such as $0.01, has no direct bearing on market value.

Copyrights 2023 Vocational Resources Australia. All Rights Reserved.

Capital

Capital can refer to any asset or resource that a business can use to generate revenue. Another meaning of capital is the level of investment made by the owner(s) in the business, adjusted for any gains or losses realised.

Accountants recognise different subcategories of capital, including working capital, which is the remainder after subtracting current liabilities from current assets; equity capital, which refers to money paid by investors in exchange for company stock; and debt capital, which covers money obtained through credit instruments like loans.

Capital Gain

A capital gain refers to the profit earned from selling an asset or investment at a higher value than its original purchase price. Conversely, if the asset is sold for a lower value than its purchase price, it results in a capital loss.

Capital Market

The capital market is a financial market where long-term debt or equity-backed securities are traded. It allows companies and governments to raise funds by selling securities to investors.

Capital markets are important for the economy because they help channel savings from households and financial institutions to businesses that need capital to grow their operations. The capital market also provides investors with opportunities to earn a return on their investment through capital gains or dividends.

Copyrights 2023 Vocational Resources Australia. All Rights Reserved.

Cash Basis Accounting

Cash basis accounting is a method of accounting where revenues and expenses are recorded when the actual exchange of money takes place. This method differs from accrual basis accounting, which recognises revenues and expenses when they are incurred, regardless of whether the cash has been exchanged.

Cash Journal

A cash journal is a special type of accounting journal that is used to record all cash transactions that occur within a business. Cash transactions include any exchange of cash for goods or services, as well as any payments made using cash. Cash journals are typically used by businesses that deal primarily in cash, such as retail stores, restaurants, and other cash-based businesses.

The purpose of a cash journal is to provide a detailed record of all cash transactions that occur within a business. This record is important for several reasons.

First, it allows the business to track its cash flow and ensure that it has enough cash on hand to cover its expenses.

Second, it provides a detailed record that can be used to reconcile the business's bank accounts and ensure that all transactions have been properly recorded.

Finally, it provides a record that can be used to identify any discrepancies or errors that may occur in the cash handling process.

Copyrights 2023 Vocational Resources Australia. All Rights Reserved.

Cash journals typically include several columns for recording different types of information, such as the date of the transaction, the name of the customer or vendor, the amount of the transaction, and any notes or comments related to the transaction. The columns may also include information about the type of transaction, such as whether it was a sale, a purchase, a refund, or a payment of expenses.

In addition to recording cash transactions, cash journals may also be used to record other types of transactions, such as checks and credit card payments. This allows businesses to keep a complete record of all financial transactions that occur within the business.

Compound Interest

Compound interest is a term that describes the interest earned on both the principal amount and any previously accumulated interest when investing or saving. It can help increase savings or investments, but it can also lead to higher debt when it is charged on the initial amount borrowed as well as any additional charges that accrue over time.

Depreciation

Depreciation refers to the reduction in the value of an asset over time. This accounting term is used to indicate the amount of an asset's value that a company has consumed or used up during a specific period.

EBITDA

EBITDA stands for Earnings Before Interest, Taxes, Depreciation, and Amortization, is a widely used metric to evaluate a company’s cash flow-generating capability. It is

Copyrights 2023 Vocational Resources Australia. All Rights Reserved.

calculated by summing up net profit, interest, taxes, depreciation, and amortization.

Equity

Equity represents the residual interest in the assets of the business after liabilities have been deducted. It includes items such as common stock, retained earnings, and additional paid-in capital.

Equity is listed on the balance sheet after liabilities.

Financial Transaction

A financial transaction refers to any exchange of money between two parties. This could be a payment made by a customer for goods or services, a transfer of funds between bank accounts, or an investment made by an individual or organisation. Financial transactions can take many forms, from simple cash payments to complex transactions involving securities, derivatives, and other financial instruments.

Financial Transaction Types

There are various types of financial transactions used in everyday money operations. Here are some of the most common ones:

- Accounts payable transactions
  Accounts payable transactions occur when a business owes money to a vendor or supplier. The business records the amount owed in their accounting system and pays the vendor or supplier at a later date, usually with interest.

Copyrights 2023 Vocational Resources Australia. All Rights Reserved.

- Accounts receivable transactions
  Accounts receivable transactions occur when a business is owed money from a customer. The business records the amount owed in their accounting system and waits for the customer to pay.

- Cash transactions
  These transactions are carried out with physical currency notes or coins. It can happen between two people or between a person and a business.

- Credit card transactions
  Credit card transactions are electronic payments made using credit cards issued by banks or other financial institutions. The transaction occurs instantly, and the payment is recorded on the cardholder's account.

- Debit card transactions
  Debit card transactions are similar to credit card transactions, but the payments are deducted instantly from the account linked to the debit card.

- Direct deposit
  Direct deposit is a secure electronic transfer of funds, and it is commonly used for payroll and other recurring payments. The funds are deposited directly into the recipient's bank account.

- International transactions
  International transactions involve sending or receiving money between two accounts located in different countries. It requires currency exchange and may take several days to complete.

Copyrights 2023 Vocational Resources Australia. All Rights Reserved.

- Investments and financing transactions
  Investment and financing transactions involve borrowing or lending money, issuing stocks or other securities, and investing in other companies or assets to grow the business and increase profitability.

- Mobile payments
  Mobile payments are transactions made using mobile apps, and they allow users to make payments and transfer money using their smartphones, tablets, or other mobile devices.

- Online transactions
  Online transactions are also known as electronic funds transfers (EFT) or online banking transfers. It involves transferring money between two accounts through the internet, and the transaction is usually completed within one business day.

- Payroll transactions
  Payroll transactions occur when businesses pay their employees for the work they have done. The payroll process includes calculating the employee's pay, accounting for any deductions, and issuing pay cheques or direct deposits.

- Purchasing transactions
  Purchasing transactions occur when businesses purchase goods or services from vendors or suppliers. The business records the purchase in their accounting

Copyrights 2023 Vocational Resources Australia. All Rights Reserved.

system, and the vendor or supplier is paid for the products or services.

- Sales transactions
  Sales transactions occur when a customer purchases goods or services from a business. The business records the sale in their accounting system, and the customer pays for the products or services.

- Tax transactions
  Tax transactions are related to paying taxes, filing tax returns, and managing tax obligations for the business. These transactions include sales tax, payroll tax, income tax, and other taxes that businesses are required to pay.

- Wire transfer
  Wire transfer is a transaction between banks where money is transferred from one account to another electronically. This process requires the sender to provide a beneficiary name, bank account number, and routing number.

Copyrights 2023 Vocational Resources Australia. All Rights Reserved.

Identifying Errors/ Discrepancies in Financial Transactions

There are several procedures you can use to check for errors or discrepancies in organisational financial transactions:

- Reconciling bank statements.
  This involves comparing the bank statement with the organisation's accounting records to ensure that all transactions match and that there are no errors or discrepancies.

- Reviewing financial statements.
  Reviewing financial statements, such as balance sheets, income statements, and cash flow statements, can provide valuable insights into the organisation's financial health and help identify any discrepancies or errors.

- Conducting internal audits.
  Performing internal audits can help identify any errors or discrepancies in financial transactions. This involves evaluating the organisation's internal controls and processes to ensure that they are working effectively.

- Performing variance analysis.
  Variance analysis involves comparing actual financial results with budgeted or expected results to identify any discrepancies or errors. This can help identify areas of concern and allow for corrective action to be taken.

Copyrights 2023 Vocational Resources Australia. All Rights Reserved.

- Conducting periodic inventory checks.
  Regular inventory checks can help identify any discrepancies or errors in inventory records, which can have a significant impact on financial statements.

Liabilities

Liabilities are debts that a company owes to others. They are listed on the balance sheet in order of maturity, meaning that those that are due to be paid first are listed first.

The main types of liabilities are current liabilities and long-term liabilities.

Current liabilities include items such as accounts payable, wages payable, and taxes payable that are due within one year.

Long-term liabilities include items such as long-term loans and bonds.

Ledger

The Ledger or general ledger is a central accounting record that contains all of the financial transactions of a business or organisation. It is the primary source of financial information for an organisation, and it provides a complete record of all financial transactions that have occurred over a specified period of time.

The general ledger is organised into accounts, which are used to classify and summarise financial transactions. Each account in the general ledger represents a specific type of financial transaction, such as sales, expenses, assets, liabilities, and equity. Each account has a unique account

Copyrights 2023 Vocational Resources Australia. All Rights Reserved.

number and name, and all financial transactions related to that account are recorded in that account.

The general ledger is typically divided into two main sections: the balance sheet accounts and the income statement accounts. The balance sheet accounts represent the assets, liabilities, and equity of the organisation, while the income statement accounts represent the revenues and expenses of the organisation.

The general ledger is updated on a regular basis as financial transactions occur. Each transaction is recorded in the appropriate account in the general ledger, and the account balances are adjusted accordingly. This process is known as posting, and it ensures that the general ledger always reflects an accurate and up-to-date picture of the organisation's financial position.

The general ledger is used to prepare financial statements, such as the balance sheet, income statement, and statement of cash flows. These statements provide a summary of the organisation's financial position, and they are used by stakeholders such as investors, creditors, and management to make financial decisions.

Liquidity

Liquidity refers to the ability of the company to meet its short-term obligations. A company's liquidity can be determined by analysing the current ratio, which is the ratio of current assets to current liabilities. A higher current ratio indicates that the company is more capable of meeting its short-term obligations.

Copyrights 2023 Vocational Resources Australia. All Rights Reserved.

Net Worth

To determine the net worth, you can subtract the liabilities from the assets. This calculation provides you with an understanding of your overall financial status.

PAYG

The term 'PAYG' is short for 'Pay As You Go', which refers to two distinct procedures implemented by the Australian Tax Office (ATO) for businesses in Australia: PAYG withholding and PAYG instalments.

Through the PAYG tax system, employers have the flexibility to adjust the amount of tax they withhold from their employees' payment instalments, setting aside a portion of it to anticipate the end-of-year tax liability. This helps avoid a large tax bill at the end of the financial year, as the instalments are spread out over the year, making it easier to meet taxation obligations.

PAYG Instalments

By using this system, individuals and businesses can fulfil their income tax responsibilities by making payments at the end of each quarter throughout the year.

These payments are used to cover the expected income tax obligation based on their business and investment income for the current financial year.

The ATO will notify taxpayers if they are required to make these payments, but typically it applies to those who earn a specific amount of individual, gross business, or investment income.

Copyrights 2023 Vocational Resources Australia. All Rights Reserved.

It should be noted that various business and company structures, trusts, primary producers, and consolidated groups may have special rules and exceptions regarding PAYG instalments. For example, if a company or super fund has a GST-registered organisation with an instalment rate greater than zero, it will be required to complete PAYG instalments.

PAYG Withholding

PAYG withholding is a tax system that involves the deduction of income tax from an employee/ contractor's earnings by the payer, who then remits the tax directly to the ATO on behalf of the employee or contractor. These tax payments are calculated based on the expected income level for the year and are taken into account when assessing the tax liability at the end of the financial year.

Your business is required to withhold tax if:

- you have employees
- you have other workers, such as contractors, and it has been agreed that you will withhold amounts from their payments
- you make payments to businesses that don't provide their Australian Business Number (ABN)

Registration is necessary before the day you need to start withholding amounts. This is a straightforward process that can be done online or by phone for businesses that have an ABN.

In case your business is structured as a sole trader or partnership and you withdraw amounts from it, those withdrawals are not considered as wages and hence may be

Copyrights 2023 Vocational Resources Australia. All Rights Reserved.

exempt from income withholding. To account for your income tax liability, you would need to make provisions for PAYG Instalments.

However, if your employee or contractor earns below the tax-free threshold, you don't need to exclude them from PAYG withholding. They can claim a refund for the amount withheld by your business at the end of the financial year while filing their individual tax return.

Reconciliation Report and Schedule of Accounts

A Reconciliation Report is a financial statement that shows the differences between two sets of records or accounts, and how those differences were resolved. It is used to ensure that all financial transactions are accounted for and properly recorded.

A Schedule of Accounts, on the other hand, is a document that lists all the accounts in a company's ledger, including the account numbers, account names, and balances. It is used to track the financial information of a business and to ensure that all the accounts are properly categorised and reported.

The process for preparation of reconciliation report and schedules of accounts involves the following steps:

Copyrights 2023 Vocational Resources Australia. All Rights Reserved.

1. Gather necessary information
   Collect all the necessary documentation, such as bank statements, invoices, receipts, and other financial records.

2. Review transactions
   Review all transactions entered into the accounts for the period under review. Ensure that all transactions are accurately recorded in the correct accounts.

3. Identify discrepancies
   Identify any discrepancies between the records of the organisation and external records, such as bank statements.

4. Investigate discrepancies
   Investigate any discrepancies found to identify the causes and make necessary corrections.

5. Prepare reconciliation statement
   Prepare a reconciliation statement summarising the differences between the organisation's internal records and external records, such as bank statements.

6. Prepare schedules of accounts
   Prepare schedules of accounts showing a detailed breakdown of the balances in each account, including any adjustments made due to discrepancies found.

Copyrights 2023 Vocational Resources Australia. All Rights Reserved.

7. Review and verify
   Review the reconciliation report and account schedules to ensure that they are correct and complete.

8. Finalise and present report
   Finalise the reconciliation report and account schedules, and present them to the relevant stakeholders, such as management, auditors, or regulatory bodies.

Return on Investment (ROI)

ROI is a financial metric used to assess the potential return of an investment by comparing its cost to the expected income or profit, usually expressed as a percentage.

It is a commonly used measure to evaluate the profitability and efficiency of a project or investment opportunity.

ROI can be calculated with the formula:
ROI = [(Income - Cost) / Cost] * 100

Solvency

Solvency refers to the ability of the company to meet its long-term obligations. It can be determined by analysing the debt-to-equity ratio, which reflects the proportion of debt to equity in the company's capital structure.

A high debt-to-equity ratio could indicate that the company is heavily reliant on debt financing.

Copyrights 2023 Vocational Resources Australia. All Rights Reserved.

Valuation

Valuation refers to the procedure of assessing the present value of an asset, company, or obligation. Although there are numerous methods to assess a business's value, regularly conducting this process can be beneficial in case you encounter an opportunity to merge or sell your company or seek financial support from external investors.

Copyrights 2023 Vocational Resources Australia. All Rights Reserved.

Managing Organisational Finances

Managing organisational finances is a critical aspect of running a successful business. It involves the allocation and management of financial resources, budgeting, financial forecasting, financial reporting, and financial risk management. This process helps organisations maintain financial stability and sustainability, avoid financial losses, and achieve long-term growth and success.

The first step in managing organisational finances is to create a budget. A budget outlines the projected revenue and expenses for the organisation and helps to identify potential areas of financial strain. The budget should be reviewed and revised regularly to reflect changes in the organisation's financial situation.

Financial forecasting is also an essential part of managing organisational finances. This involves analysing past financial data and trends to predict future revenue and expenses. The forecasting process helps organisations plan for the future and make informed decisions about investment opportunities, budget allocations, and pricing strategies.

Another critical aspect of managing organisational finances is financial risk management. This involves identifying potential financial risks and taking steps to mitigate them. Financial risks can include market fluctuations, economic downturns, and operational risks such as employee fraud or mismanagement.

Financial reporting is an essential tool for managing organisational finances. Accurate and timely financial reporting provides insights into the organisation's financial

Copyrights 2023 Vocational Resources Australia. All Rights Reserved.

performance and helps stakeholders make informed decisions about the organisation's future. Financial reporting includes financial statements such as balance sheets, income statements, and cash flow statements.

Evaluating Effectiveness of Financial Management

Following are the steps involved in evaluating the effectiveness of financial management processes:

1. Identify your financial goals and objectives
   Before you can evaluate the effectiveness of your financial management processes, you need to have clear goals and objectives in place. This will help you determine what metrics you need to track and how you will measure success.

2. Identify KPIs
   Identify the KPIs that will help you track progress towards your financial goals. Some common KPIs include profitability, liquidity, debt-to-equity ratio, cash flow, and return on investment (ROI).

3. Collect and analyse data
   Once you have identified your KPIs, you need to collect and analyse data to measure performance. This could involve reviewing financial statements, analysing sales data, or tracking expenses.

4. Compare actual performance to benchmarks
   After you have collected and analysed data, you need to compare actual performance to benchmarks. This will help you identify areas where you are falling short and areas where you are exceeding expectations.

Copyrights 2023 Vocational Resources Australia. All Rights Reserved.

5. Identify areas for improvement
   Based on your analysis, you can identify areas for improvement and develop strategies to address them. This might involve changing processes, investing in new technology, or improving communication between departments.

6. Monitor progress
   Monitor the progress towards your financial goals on an ongoing basis. This will help you identify emerging trends and make adjustments as needed.

Copyrights 2023 Vocational Resources Australia. All Rights Reserved.

Monitoring Expenditure

The main goal of monitoring expenses against income is to ensure that the expenses do not exceed the available income. Similar to monitoring expenses against a budget, the initial challenge is to determine which funding sources display significant surpluses or deficits.

Effective budget monitoring is essential for organisations to ensure that the financial, operational, and capital plans approved during the budget process are being implemented. It enables organisations to maintain accountability for expenditures and ensures that resources are being used efficiently.

Managers are required to:

- Approve and review expense reports of direct reports and ensure their team submits them on time.
- Approve and review invoice and payment requests and forward them to the Finance department.
- Monitor purchases in the respective area(s).
- Review vendor invoices and assess the necessity of the purchases.
- Submit invoices to the Finance department for processing promptly.
- Identify cost-saving opportunities and leverage purchasing power for recurring purchases. O Ensure purchases align with priorities.

Copyrights 2023 Vocational Resources Australia. All Rights Reserved.

Monitoring Actual Expenditure

This includes the following steps:

1. Determine the actual financial position by analysing the organisation's income and expenditure records.
2. Compare the actual financial position with the budget to identify any deviations.
3. Calculate the variances between the actual financial position and the budget.
4. Investigate and determine the reasons for the variances.
5. Take appropriate actions to address the variances and ensure that the budget is back on track.

Monitor Actual Income and Expenditure against Budgets

Monitoring actual income and expenditure against organisational budgets involves several steps. First, the budget must be established and agreed upon by the relevant stakeholders. This will involve setting financial targets for income and expenditure over a specified period, usually a fiscal year.

Once the budget has been established, actual income and expenditure must be tracked and recorded. This can be done using accounting software or other financial tracking tools. It is important to ensure that all income and expenditure is accurately recorded and categorised so that it can be easily compared to the budget.

Copyrights 2023 Vocational Resources Australia. All Rights Reserved.

Regular monitoring and reporting are essential to ensure that the organisation is staying on track with its financial goals. This may involve generating financial reports on a weekly, monthly, or quarterly basis. These reports should compare actual income and expenditure to the budgeted amounts, highlighting any areas where actual spending or income is significantly different from what was planned.

If there are significant deviations from the budget, it may be necessary to adjust the budget or take other steps to address the issue. This could include cutting expenses, seeking additional revenue sources, or making changes to organisational processes or systems.

Copyrights 2023 Vocational Resources Australia. All Rights Reserved.

Preparing Financial Recommendations

Preparing financial recommendations involve the following key steps:

1. Collecting and analysing financial data
   The first step in preparing financial recommendations is to gather all relevant financial data about the organisation. This includes financial statements, budgets, cash flow projections, and other financial metrics. Once these are collected, they must be analysed to identify trends, strengths, weaknesses, and opportunities.

2. Identifying financial goals
   Once the financial data has been analysed, it is important to identify the organisation's financial goals. These may include increasing profitability, reducing costs, improving cash flow, or investing in new projects. The goals must be specific, measurable, achievable, relevant, and time-bound.

3. Developing a financial plan
   With the financial data and goals in hand, the next step is to develop a comprehensive financial plan that outlines the steps needed to achieve the identified financial goals. The plan should include specific recommendations for investments, cost reductions, and other financial strategies.

4. Presenting recommendations
   Once the financial plan is developed, it must be presented to the decision-makers in the organisation. This may include the CEO, CFO, board of directors,

Copyrights 2023 Vocational Resources Australia. All Rights Reserved.

or other stakeholders. The recommendations must be clear, concise, and supported by data.

5. Implementing the plan
   Once the recommendations have been approved, they must be implemented. This may involve changes to the organisation's budget, investments, or other financial strategies. It is important to monitor the results of the plan and make adjustments as needed to ensure that the financial goals are being achieved.

Copyrights 2023 Vocational Resources Australia. All Rights Reserved.

Presenting Financial Data

There are various methods of presenting financial data, and choosing the appropriate method typically depends on the nature and complexity of the data, as well as the audience for which the financial data is being presented.

Here are some common methods to present different types of financial data:

Financial statements

Financial statements such as balance sheets, income statements, and cash flow statements are common methods used to present financial data.

These statements provide a comprehensive overview of a business's financial performance, including revenues, expenses, assets, liabilities, and equity.

Financial statements are typically prepared in accordance with accounting standards, making them a reliable and consistent source of information that is useful for a wide range of stakeholders.

Graphs and charts

Graphs and charts are useful for presenting complex financial data in a visually appealing and easily digestible format. They can be used to show trends over time, comparisons between different financial metrics, and other key takeaways.

Common types of graphs and charts used in financial reporting include line graphs, bar charts, pie charts, and tables.

Copyrights 2023 Vocational Resources Australia. All Rights Reserved.

Spreadsheets

Spreadsheets are versatile tools that can be used to present and analyse financial data, including budgeting, forecasting, and modelling data.

Spreadsheet software such as Microsoft Excel allows for the creation of customizable spreadsheets that can be tailored to a business's specific financial needs.

Summaries and dashboards

Summaries and dashboards are useful for presenting high-level financial data and key performance indicators (KPIs) in a concise and easy-to-understand format.

Dashboards typically display a collection of graphs, charts, and tables designed to highlight a business's financial performance metrics.

Written reports

Written reports can be used to provide a narrative summary of a business's financial performance, including its achievements, challenges, and strategies.

Reports can be prepared in different formats, including annual reports, financial reports, and management reports.

Copyrights 2023 Vocational Resources Australia. All Rights Reserved.

Quality Standards

There are several quality standards for organisational financial management. These standards are established to promote transparency, consistency, and accountability in financial management practices.

Some of them are discussed below:

Australian Accounting Standards

Australian Accounting Standards are adopted by the Australian Accounting Standards Board (AASB), and they provide a set of principles and practices for financial reporting. These standards ensure consistency and transparency in financial reporting across organisations.

Australian Auditing Standards

Australian Auditing Standards are developed by the Auditing and Assurance Standards Board (AUASB) and provide guidance to auditors in conducting an examination of financial statements. These standards ensure that the audit process is thorough, unbiased, and independent.

International Financial Reporting Standards (IFRS)

IFRS is a set of global accounting standards designed to ensure consistent accounting and financial reporting across the world. They provide a framework for decision-making, making financial statements transparent, and allowing investors to compare the performance of different organisations.

Treasury Management Standards

The Australian Government developed Treasury Management Standards to promote efficient and transparent

Copyrights 2023 Vocational Resources Australia. All Rights Reserved.

financial management practices across government agencies. These standards ensure that financial management practices are consistent with government policies and objectives.

Australian Prudential Regulation Authority Standards

The APRA Prudential Standards apply to financial institutions and aim to enhance the safety and stability of the Australian financial system. These standards are designed to ensure that financial institutions maintain adequate financial resources, manage risks effectively and comply with regulatory requirements.

National Governance Protocols

The National Governance Protocols are developed by the Australian Government and provide guidance on good governance practices for non-profit organisations. These protocols ensure that non-profit organisations adopt appropriate processes and procedures to manage their finances ethically, transparently and effectively.

Australian Accounting Standards

Some of the Australian Accounting Standards are:

AASB 101	Presentation of Financial Statements
AASB 102	Inventories
AASB 1031	Materiality
AASB 1048	Interpretation of Standards
AASB 1054	Australian Additional Disclosures
AASB 1055	Budgetary Reporting
AASB 1056	Superannuation Entities

Copyrights 2023 Vocational Resources Australia. All Rights Reserved.

AASB 1060	General Purpose Financial Statements - Simplified Disclosures for For-Profit and Not-for-Profit Tier 2 Entities
AASB 107	Statement of Cash Flows
AASB 108	Accounting Policies, Changes in Accounting Estimates and Errors
AASB 110	Events After the Reporting Period
AASB 111	Construction Contracts
AASB 112	Income Taxes
AASB 113	Fair Value Measurement
AASB 114	Segment Reporting
AASB 115	Revenue from Contracts with Customers
AASB 116	Property, Plant and Equipment
AASB 117	Leases
AASB 118	Revenue
AASB 119	Employee Benefits
AASB 120	Accounting for Government Grants and Disclosure of Government Assistance
AASB 121	The Effects of Changes in Foreign Exchange Rates
AASB 123	Borrowing Costs
AASB 124	Related Party Disclosures
AASB 125	Financial Instruments
AASB 126	Accounting and Reporting by Retirement Benefit Plans
AASB 127	Consolidated and Separate Financial Statements
AASB 128	Investments in Associates and Joint Ventures
AASB 129	Financial Reporting in Hyperinflationary Economies
AASB 130	Reporting of Comprehensive Income
AASB 131	Interests in Joint Ventures

Copyrights 2023 Vocational Resources Australia. All Rights Reserved.

AASB 132	Financial Instruments: Presentation
AASB 133	Earnings per Share
AASB 134	Interim Financial Reporting
AASB 136	Impairment of Assets
AASB 137	Provisions, Contingent Liabilities and Contingent Assets
AASB 138	Intangible Assets
AASB 139	Financial Instruments: Recognition and Measurement
AASB 140	Investment Property
AASB 141	Agriculture
AASB 142	Intangible Assets
AASB 143	Financial Instruments: Disclosures
AASB 144	Related Party Disclosures by Not-for-Profit Entities

Copyrights 2023 Vocational Resources Australia. All Rights Reserved.

Ratios

Financial ratios are quantitative measures that provide valuable insights into a company's financial health and performance. Here are some of the key financial ratios and what they indicate:

Asset Turnover Ratio

This measures an organisation's efficiency in using its assets to generate revenue - The higher the asset turnover, the more efficiently the company is utilizing its assets to generate revenue.

Balance Sheet Ratios

Balance sheet ratios are financial ratios that provide insight into a company's financial health and position.

There are several balance sheet ratios that are commonly used, including:

- current ratio *(discussed below)*
- quick ratio *(discussed below)*
- debt-to-equity ratio *(discussed below)*
- debt-to-asset ratio *(discussed below)*
- return on equity *(discussed below)*

Cash Conversion Cycle Ratio

This ratio measures the number of days it takes for a company to convert its inventory into cash. It is calculated by adding the average collection period to the average payment period and subtracting the average inventory holding period.

Copyrights 2023 Vocational Resources Australia. All Rights Reserved.

Cash Flow Coverage Ratio
This ratio is computed by dividing operating cash flows by total debt. A higher ratio suggests that a company has enough cash flow to cover its debt's scheduled principal and interest payments.

Cash Flow Margin Ratio
The cash flow-to-sales ratio is computed by dividing the cash flow generated from operating activities by the total sales revenue. Unlike net profit, this ratio provides a more accurate measure of the amount of cash generated per dollar of sales.

Cash Flow Ratios
Cash flow ratios are used to compare the cash flows of a company to other aspects of its financial statements. They provide valuable insight into a company's liquidity and ability to pay dividends to shareholders and are important tools for analysing a business.

Cash flow ratios become especially important when a company's reported profits do not align with its actual cash flows. There are several commonly used cash flow ratios that analysts use to evaluate a company's financial health.

Some of the commonly used cash flow ratios include:
- operating cash flow ratio *(already discussed in this section)*
- cash flow margin ratio *(already discussed in this section)*
- free cash flow ratio *(already discussed in this section)*
- cash conversion cycle ratio *(already discussed in this section)*

Copyrights 2023 Vocational Resources Australia. All Rights Reserved.

- cash return on assets ratio *(already discussed in this section)*

Cash Flow to Net Income

When the ratio is close to 1:1, it suggests that the organisation's reported earnings are in line with its actual cash flows, indicating that there is little or no manipulation of accounting numbers.

This ratio is particularly valuable to external analysts examining the financial performance of a reporting entity.

Current Liability Coverage Ratio

The ratio calculated by dividing cash flows from operations by current liabilities is a measure of a business's ability to meet its short-term obligations.

A ratio of less than 1:1 indicates that the company is not generating enough cash to cover its immediate financial obligations, putting it at a higher risk of insolvency.

Current Ratio

The current ratio is a measure of a company's ability to meet its short-term obligations with its current assets. This ratio is an indicator of a company's liquidity. A higher current ratio implies that the company can quickly generate cash to cover any unanticipated expenses without taking on debt.

To calculate the current ratio, divide the total current assets by total current liabilities. Current assets are those assets that a company expects to convert to cash or use within one year, while current liabilities are the debts that are due within

Copyrights 2023 Vocational Resources Australia. All Rights Reserved.

one year. Ideally, a company should have a current ratio of 1:1 or higher.

Current Ratio = Current Assets / Current Liabilities

Cash Return on Assets Ratio

This ratio measures the amount of cash generated by a company for each dollar of assets it owns. It is calculated by dividing operating cash flow by total assets.

Debt Service Coverage Ratio (DSCR)

Generating profits alone does not guarantee a company's success if it cannot generate enough cash to maintain liquidity.

This can occur if a company's profits are tied up in unpaid bills or excess inventory, or if it spends excessively on capital expenditures. As a result, investors and creditors need to determine if a company has enough cash to cover its short-term debts.

Analysts use the DSCR to assess whether a company can meet its current liabilities with the cash it generates from its operations.

Debt Service Coverage Ratio = Net Operating Income / Short-Term Debt Obligations (or Debt Service)

Although liquidity is an important metric, it doesn't provide a complete picture of a company's financial health. Having a lot of cash on hand may not necessarily indicate a company's long-term viability, as it may have obtained the cash by sacrificing its future growth potential, such as selling

Copyrights 2023 Vocational Resources Australia. All Rights Reserved.

off long-term assets or taking on unsustainable levels of debt.

Therefore, analysts and investors need to consider other financial metrics and ratios, such as profitability, efficiency, solvency, and market performance, in addition to liquidity, to make informed decisions and recommendations.

Debt-to-Asset Ratio

This ratio measures the amount of a company's assets that are financed by debt. It is calculated by dividing total liabilities by total assets. A higher debt-to-asset ratio indicates that a company is more heavily reliant on debt to finance its operations.

Debt-to-Equity Ratio

The debt-to-equity ratio is a measure of your business's reliance on debt. This ratio indicates the amount of equity available to cover debts. You can calculate this ratio by dividing your total liabilities by your total shareholder equity.

Debt-to-equity Ratio = Total Liabilities / Total Shareholder Equity

A lower debt-to-equity ratio is generally considered more favourable in most industries, although it can be challenging to compare ratios across different industries due to variations in business debt levels.

A higher ratio indicates a greater risk to shareholders, as the company is more dependent on borrowed funds to cover its financial obligations.

Copyrights 2023 Vocational Resources Australia. All Rights Reserved.

An example:
Suppose your business has a total of $40,000 in liabilities and $25,000 in shareholder equity. By dividing the total liabilities by the shareholder equity, you can determine the debt-to-equity ratio. In this case, the debt-to-equity ratio is 1.6:1, indicating that the business has $1.60 in debt for every dollar of equity.

Free Cash Flow Ratio
This ratio measures a company's ability to generate cash after accounting for capital expenditures. It is calculated by subtracting capital expenditures from operating cash flow.

Gross Profit Margin
This ratio evaluates a company's profitability by analysing its gross profit as a percentage of sales revenue. It provides an understanding of a company's ability to pass on cost increases to customers.

Income Statement Ratios
Income statement ratios, also known as profitability ratios, are financial metrics used to evaluate a company's ability to generate profits. Here are a few common income statement ratios:

- gross profit margin *(already discussed in this section)*
- operating profit margin *(already discussed in this section)*
- net profit margin *(already discussed in this section)*
- return on assets *(already discussed in this section)*
- return on equity *(already discussed in this section)*

Net Profit Margin
This ratio measures the percentage of sales that remain after deducting all expenses, including taxes. A higher ratio

Copyrights 2023 Vocational Resources Australia. All Rights Reserved.

indicates that the company is more efficient at generating profits.

Operating Cash Flow Ratio

This ratio compares a company's operating cash flow to its current liabilities. It measures a company's ability to pay off its short-term debt obligations with its operating cash flow.

Operating Profit Margin

This ratio measures the percentage of sales that remain after deducting the cost of goods sold and operating expenses. A higher ratio indicates that the company is generating more profit from its core operations.

Price-to-Earnings Ratio (P/E)

This ratio compares a company's stock price to its earnings per share. A high P/E ratio can indicate that investors expect future earnings growth.

Price to Cash Flow Ratio

The operating cash flow per share divided by the share price yields the price-to-operating cash flow ratio, which is considered superior to the price-to-earnings ratio because it is based on cash flows rather than earnings, making it less susceptible to manipulation by management.

Quick Ratio (Acid Test)

The quick ratio is another measure of a company's liquidity, similar to the current ratio, but it excludes inventory from the calculation. Inventory is not always easily convertible to cash at its book value, so some businesses prefer to remove it from the ratio. A quick ratio greater than one is generally

Copyrights 2023 Vocational Resources Australia. All Rights Reserved.

considered healthy. The formula for the quick ratio is as follows:

Quick Ratio = (Current Assets – Current Inventory) / Current Liabilities

Return on Assets (ROA)

This ratio assesses the profitability of a company by measuring how efficiently it uses its assets. It provides insight into how well a company generates earnings based on its total assets.

Return on Equity (ROE)

This ratio indicates how much return a shareholder earns for each dollar invested in the company. Higher ROEs can indicate better investment opportunities for shareholders and potentially stronger long-term performance.

Solvency Ratio

The solvency ratio is a useful tool to assess whether your business has enough cash flow to meet long-term debts while fulfilling other short-term obligations. By monitoring the solvency ratio regularly, you can detect potential financial issues before they escalate.

If the ratio consistently declines over time, it may indicate a problem with your business's financial health. Investors and creditors may also refer to the solvency ratio to evaluate the likelihood of your business's long-term survival.

Calculating the solvency ratio requires information from both your balance sheet and P&L statement.

Copyrights 2023 Vocational Resources Australia. All Rights Reserved.

To determine your total liabilities, you will need to refer to your balance sheet. However, to calculate your total net income and depreciation, you will need to refer to your P&L statement. Depreciation is the reduction in value of your assets over time.

To find your business's solvency ratio, use the formula below:

Solvency Ratio = (Total Net Income + Depreciation) / Total Liabilities

To calculate your solvency ratio, you will need both your balance sheet and P&L statement. Your total liabilities can be found on your balance sheet, while your total net income and depreciation can be found on your P&L statement.

If your business does not have any depreciation, you can still calculate your solvency ratio using your total net income and total liabilities.

A solvency ratio of 20% or higher is typically seen as favourable.

Solvency ratio example:
Suppose your business has a total net income of $25,000, $5,000 in depreciation, and $20,000 in total liabilities. Using the solvency ratio formula mentioned earlier, you can calculate your business's solvency ratio.

Solvency Ratio = ($25,000 + $5,000) / $20,000

Copyrights 2023 Vocational Resources Australia. All Rights Reserved.

Your business's solvency ratio is 1.5:1, or 150%. This means your business has a healthy cash flow to pay off its long-term debts and meet other financial obligations.

Working Capital

Working capital is the excess of your current assets over your current liabilities. It gives you an idea of how much money you have available for your day-to-day operations after paying off your short-term debts.

Calculating your working capital using the formula below can help you determine your company's ability to meet its short-term obligations.

Having a negative working capital means that your business may struggle to sustain its operations, while a positive working capital indicates that you have the financial flexibility to cover your expenses and pay off your debts. Investors and creditors often look at your working capital to assess your company's financial health.

If your current assets equal your current liabilities, your working capital is zero. To calculate your working capital, subtract your current liabilities from your current assets.

Working Capital = Current Assets – Current Liabilities

Working capital example:
Suppose your company has $40,000 worth of current assets and $20,000 in current liabilities.

Working Capital = $40,000 – $20,000

Copyrights 2023 Vocational Resources Australia. All Rights Reserved.

In this case, your working capital would be $20,000, indicating that you have $20,000 available to cover your day-to-day expenses and meet short-term obligations.

Copyrights 2023 Vocational Resources Australia. All Rights Reserved.

Record Keeping

Some of the financial record keeping requirements that Australian organisations need to comply with are listed below:

Accounting Records

An organisation needs to maintain accurate and complete accounting records that demonstrate its financial position, performance and cash flow. These accounting records must be kept for a minimum of 7 years and should include cash books, general ledgers, journals, trial balances, profit and loss statements, balance sheets, and other relevant documents.

Tax Records

The Australian Taxation Office (ATO) mandates that businesses keep accurate tax records as evidence of their income, expenses, and liabilities for tax purposes.

The ATO requires businesses to keep the following tax records:

- Income tax records
  Businesses should maintain records of all income earned through trading activities, investments, and other sources. This includes invoices, receipts, bank deposit records, and other documents that provide evidence of income.

- Expense records
  Expense records include invoices, receipts, bank or credit card statements, and other documents that provide evidence of expenditure.

Copyrights 2023 Vocational Resources Australia. All Rights Reserved.

These records should be detailed enough to support the nature, date, and amount of expenses.

Common business expenditures that should be recorded include rent, salaries, insurance, utilities, repairs and maintenance, travel expenses, and purchases of goods or services.

- Asset records
  Businesses should keep records of all assets and their corresponding values such as equipment, machinery, vehicles or property.

  Depreciation schedules are also necessary to track the value of any assets that have been used over time.

- GST records
  GST records should be maintained to satisfy the ATO's requirements. This includes records of all GST charged, paid and owed, including tax invoices and credit notes.

- Payroll Records
  Payroll records contain details of employee salaries, wages, allowances, leave entitlements, superannuation contributions, and taxes withheld.

These records should be kept for five years after the completion of the relevant year.

Copyrights 2023 Vocational Resources Australia. All Rights Reserved.

Stocktakes and Inventory Records

For businesses that carry stock or inventory, records should be kept showing the stock from opening to closing of the financial year.

Records should include details on the stock purchased, sales made, stock on hand at the end of the financial year, adjustments made during the year, and cost prices of each item.

Businesses must keep accurate records for at least five years after they are prepared or obtained, or for seven years for records involving capital assets.

Failure to keep proper records and lodge tax returns on time can result in penalties and legal consequences.

Therefore, it is important for businesses to maintain accurate records and comply with taxation regulations.

Some of the specifics are:

- Source documents
  An organisation must maintain accurate source documentation that supports its financial transactions.

  These documents include but are not limited to invoices, receipts, bank statements, credit card statements, cheque butts, purchase orders, and contracts.

  The source documents are crucial evidence to prove the validity and accuracy of the financial transactions.

Copyrights 2023 Vocational Resources Australia. All Rights Reserved.

- Payroll records
  An organisation needs to maintain payroll records that document employee salary, wages, deductions, and superannuation contributions.

  Payroll records must be kept for at least 7 years after they are made.

- Inventory records
  Companies dealing with stock or inventory are required to keep accurate inventory records that show the quantity and value of the stock or inventory.

  These records help organisations in preparing accurate financial statements and choosing tax accounting methods.

- Financial report preparation
  Organisations must prepare and lodge financial reports with regulatory authorities as required.

  This includes the preparation and filing of annual financial statements with the Australian Securities and Investments Commission (ASIC).

Copyrights 2023 Vocational Resources Australia. All Rights Reserved.

Reports

There are various types of financial reports e.g. ageing summary, balance sheet etc. Some of them have been discussed in the previous topics, and the rest are outlined below:

Financial Year Report

Financial year reports are an essential tool for businesses to determine their financial performance over the year. These reports provide an overview of a company's financial activities, including revenues earned and expenses incurred during the fiscal year.

A financial year report typically includes several key elements such as an income statement, balance sheet, cash flow statement, and notes to the accounts. The income statement shows the business's income and expenses over the year and provides a calculation of the company's net income. The balance sheet presents the company's assets, liabilities, and equity at the end of the year.

In addition to these financial statements, other key elements may be included in the report. For example, financial year reports may contain a management discussion and analysis section, which provides an overview of the company's performance over the year and its future prospects. This section may also discuss the company's internal controls, financial risks, and opportunities.

Another key component of financial year reports is the notes to the accounts section. This section provides detailed explanations of the company's financial statements, including any significant accounting policies and procedures

Copyrights 2023 Vocational Resources Australia. All Rights Reserved.

used by the company. It may also provide information on key business events that may impact the company's financial performance, such as mergers and acquisitions or significant capital expenditures.

Cash Flow Report

A cash flow report provides a detailed view of the inflow and outflow of cash within a business during a particular period. It captures all the money that comes in and goes out of the business, including revenue, expenses, investments, loans and other transactions that result in a cash inflow or outflow.

The main components of a cash flow report include operating activities, financing activities, and investing activities.

Operating activities cover the day-to-day operations of the business and include cash inflows from the sale of goods and services, payment of salaries, wages, and other expenses incurred in the course of conducting business.

Investing activities include the sales or purchase of long-term assets like property, plant, and equipment.

Financing activities reflect the inflows and outflows of cash from financing activities like loans, share issuances and repayments of debts.

A positive cash flow figure indicates that the business has more cash coming in than going out, while a negative cash flow figure implies that more cash is leaving the business than coming in.

Copyrights 2023 Vocational Resources Australia. All Rights Reserved.

Profit & Loss Statement / Income Statement/ Financial Operating Statement

A Profit and Loss (P&L) statement is a financial report that summarises the revenues, costs, and expenses incurred by a company over a particular period, typically a quarter or a fiscal year.

The statement provides valuable insights into the organisation's capacity to generate profits by either increasing revenue, reducing expenses, or both. P&L statements can be prepared on a cash or accrual basis.

Company executives and investors utilise P&L statements to evaluate the financial well-being of a business.

The P&L statement summarises the revenues, costs, and expenses incurred by a company during a specific period. Along with the balance sheet and cash flow statement, the P&L statement is one of the three financial statements that every publicly traded company issues quarterly and annually. The combination of the P&L statement, balance sheet, and cash flow statement offers a comprehensive view of a company's overall financial performance.

P&L statements can be prepared using either the cash method or accrual method of accounting.

Comparing P&L statements from different accounting periods is crucial as changes over time can be more informative than the actual figures themselves.

Copyrights 2023 Vocational Resources Australia. All Rights Reserved.

Comparing P&L Statements

To evaluate a company's financial health, it is essential to compare income statements from various accounting periods. This is because changes in revenues, operating costs, research and development (R&D) spending, and net earnings over time carry more significance than the absolute figures.

For instance, although a company's revenues may increase consistently, its expenses could be growing at a much faster pace. Moreover, comparing the P&L statement of a company with that of a similar-sized company in the same industry can provide further insights into its financial performance. By doing so, investors can determine which company is more effective at managing expenses and has better growth prospects.

Assessing Reasons for Previous Profits or Losses

To assess the reasons for losses or profits identified from previous financial reports, one could start by analysing the financial statements, including the income statement, balance sheet, and cash flow statement.

Next, it may be helpful to identify any significant changes in revenue, expenses, or other financial metrics, and investigate the causes of those changes. This could involve looking into external factors such as changes in market conditions, competition, or economic trends, as well as internal factors such as operational inefficiencies, changes in management or staffing, or product development strategies.

Copyrights 2023 Vocational Resources Australia. All Rights Reserved.

Once the causes of the losses or profits have been identified, strategies can be developed to either mitigate losses or enhance profits in the future.

Establishing & Reviewing Profits or Losses

To establish and review profits and losses from financial statements, you should follow a process of analysing financial statements that involves the following steps:

1. Collect the relevant financial statements, including the income statement, balance sheet, and cash flow statement.

2. Review the income statement, which summarises the company's revenues and expenses for a specific period.

3. Examine the balance sheet, which shows the company's assets, liabilities, and equity at a specific point in time.

4. Analyse the cash flow statement, which tracks the inflow and outflow of cash over a specific period.

5. Calculate the company's net profit or loss by subtracting its total expenses from its total revenue.

6. Evaluate the company's profitability by calculating its gross profit margin, operating profit margin, and net profit margin.

Copyrights 2023 Vocational Resources Australia. All Rights Reserved.

7. Review the financial statements periodically to identify any trends or changes in the company's financial performance.

Preparation Methods

There are two methods used to prepare a P&L statement: the cash method and the accrual method.

Cash Method

The cash method, also known as cash accounting, only recognises transactions when cash is received or paid out of the business. It is a straightforward approach that records revenue when cash is received and liabilities when cash is used to pay bills or other obligations. This method is popular with smaller businesses and individuals who want to manage their personal finances.

Accrual Method

In contrast to the cash method, the accrual accounting method records revenue when it is earned, regardless of whether the company has received payment or not. For instance, if a company delivers a product or service to a customer, it records the revenue on the P&L statement even if it hasn't received payment yet. The accrual method also accounts for liabilities before the company has actually paid for any expenses.

Copyrights 2023 Vocational Resources Australia. All Rights Reserved.

Risk Analysis

Financial risk analysis refers to the process of identifying, assessing, and quantifying risks that an organisation faces in its financial operations. This analysis helps organisations to develop a risk management strategy that minimises potential financial losses and ensures the sustainability of the organisation.

Some of the important factors organisations should consider when conducting financial risk analysis include:

- Understanding the organisation's operations and objectives.
  The financial risk analysis process should be tailored to the specific needs and goals of the organisation.

- Stakeholder engagement
  The involvement of key stakeholders in the financial risk analysis process can enhance the quality of analysis and increase support for the resulting mitigation strategies.

- Regular reviews.
  To keep the risk management strategy relevant and effective, the financial risk analysis process should be reviewed and updated regularly to ensure that the organisation is not taking unnecessary risks and that the risk management strategy is still viable.

- Resources.
  Organisations should allocate sufficient resources, including staff and technology, to carry out financial risk analysis and implement preventive measures.

Copyrights 2023 Vocational Resources Australia. All Rights Reserved.

Risk Analysis - Steps

1. Identify Financial Risks
   The first step is to identify the risks that an organisation faces in its financial operations. These risks may include market risk, credit risk, liquidity risk, currency risk, interest rate risk, and operational risk.

2. Quantify Financial Risks
   The next step is to quantify the risks identified. This can be achieved through data analysis, modelling, and scenario analysis. For example, a market risk analysis might involve modelling different market scenarios to estimate potential losses.

3. Evaluate Financial Risks
   Once risks have been identified and quantified, the next step is to evaluate the level of risk an organisation faces. Evaluation involves considering the likelihood of each risk event and its potential impact on the organisation.

4. Develop a Risk Management Strategy
   With knowledge of the risks and their potential impact, the organisation then needs to develop a risk management strategy. This strategy may include risk mitigation, risk transfer, or risk avoidance options.

5. Implement the Risk Management Strategy
   The final step is to implement the risk management strategy. This often involves the development of policies, procedures, and controls to manage the identified financial risks.

Copyrights 2023 Vocational Resources Australia. All Rights Reserved.

Risk Analysis - Tools & Techniques

There are several tools and techniques used in organisational financial risk analysis. Below are some commonly used tools and techniques:

SWOT Analysis

SWOT analysis is a strategic planning tool that helps an organisation to identify its strengths, weaknesses, opportunities, and threats. It can be used to identify and assess financial risks and opportunities.

Risk Assessment Matrix

A risk assessment matrix is a tool used to evaluate the likelihood and impact of financial risks. The matrix involves assigning scores to the likelihood and impact of risks to identify high-risk areas that require immediate attention.

Scenario Analysis

Scenario analysis involves modelling different scenarios to assess the potential impact of external factors on an organisation's financial operations. It helps organisations to prepare for potential risks and opportunities.

Sensitivity Analysis

Sensitivity analysis involves testing the impact of changes in specific variables on an organisation's financial performance. For example, sensitivity analysis can be used to assess the impact of changes in interest rates or currency fluctuations on the organisation's revenue.

Copyrights 2023 Vocational Resources Australia. All Rights Reserved.

Stress Testing

Stress testing involves modelling extreme scenarios to assess the ability of an organisation to withstand financial shocks. It can be used to identify potential weaknesses in an organisation's financial operations and develop mitigation strategies.

Monte Carlo Simulation

Monte Carlo simulation is a statistical model used to simulate various outcomes of a particular event. It can be used to assess the probability of various financial risks and opportunities.

Techniques for Calculating and Analysing Financial Data

These are several techniques for calculating and analysing organisational financial data. It's important to choose the right techniques for your organisational needs, and to use the data to inform strategic decision-making.

Some of them are outlined below:

Financial Ratio Analysis

This technique involves calculating and analysing financial ratios, such as liquidity ratios, profitability ratios, and debt ratios. Financial ratio analysis can provide insight into an organisation's financial health. It also helps in identifying areas of strength and weakness.

Please refer to "Ratios" section in this chapter for further details.

Copyrights 2023 Vocational Resources Australia. All Rights Reserved.

Budgeting and Forecasting

Budgeting and forecasting involve creating a financial plan for the organisation, typically for the upcoming year. This helps organisations plan for expenses and revenue and make informed decisions about investments and growth opportunities.

Please refer to "Budgeting" and "Forecasting" sections in this chapter for further details.

Cash Flow Analysis

Cash flow analysis involves assessing the inflow and outflow of cash in an organisation. This can help an organisation identify potential cash flow problems, as well as opportunities to improve cash management.

Here are the general steps to follow to use cash flow analysis:

1. Collect financial data
   Gather all the necessary financial data, such as revenue, expenses, and investments for the period under analysis. This information can be obtained from financial statements, bank statements, and other financial documents.

2. Record cash inflows
   Record all cash inflows during the period under analysis, including sales, loans, and investments.

Copyrights 2023 Vocational Resources Australia. All Rights Reserved.

3. Record cash outflows
   Record all cash outflows during the period under analysis, including expenses, loan payments, and investments.

4. Calculate net cash flow
   Subtract total cash outflows from total cash inflows to find your net cash flow for the period.

5. Analyse cash flow
   Analyse your cash flow statement to identify any areas where your business could improve cash flow. This could include reducing expenses or increasing revenue.

6. Make decisions
   Use your analysis to make informed financial decisions, such as investing in new equipment or reducing your debt.

7. Monitor and adjust
   Regularly monitor and adjust your cash flow analysis to ensure your business remains financially healthy and on track to meet its goals.

Copyrights 2023 Vocational Resources Australia. All Rights Reserved.

Variance Analysis

Variance analysis involves comparing actual financial performance to expected financial performance. This can help identify areas where an organisation is underperforming, and opportunities for improvement.

Here are the general steps to follow to use variance analysis:

1. Define the budget
   The first step is to define the budget for the period you want to analyse. This will provide a baseline against which you can compare actual performance.

2. Collect financial data
   Gather all the relevant financial data for the period under analysis. This should include actual revenues, expenses, and other costs incurred during the period.

3. Calculate the variances
   Calculate the difference between the actual financial performance and the budgeted financial performance. This will allow you to identify where your business has performed better or worse than expected.

4. Analyse the variances
   Analyse the variances to identify the causes behind them. For example, a favourable variance may be due to higher sales or lower costs, while an unfavourable variance may be due to unexpected expenses or lower-than-expected sales.

Copyrights 2023 Vocational Resources Australia. All Rights Reserved.

5. Take corrective action
   Use the results from your analysis to take corrective action. If you have identified favourable variances, you may want to continue the activities that led to these results. If you have identified unfavourable variances, you may need to adjust your budget or take steps to reduce costs.

6. Monitor and adjust
   Regularly monitor and adjust your variance analysis to ensure your business remains on track to meet its financial goals.

Copyrights 2023 Vocational Resources Australia. All Rights Reserved.

Cost Analysis

Cost analysis involves assessing the costs associated with specific products or services, as well as the overall cost structure of the organisation. This can help identify areas where costs can be reduced, and where investments should be made.

Here are a few steps to help you get started:

1. Identify your cost drivers
   Cost drivers are the activities or factors that cause your costs to increase or decrease. Common drivers include materials, labour, and overhead costs.

2. Collect data
   Collect data on your costs, including direct and indirect costs. This data can be found in your financial statements, accounting software, and other sources.

3. Allocate costs
   Allocate your costs to specific cost drivers. This will help you understand which drivers have the greatest impact on your costs.

4. Analyse your data
   Analyse your data to identify trends and patterns. Look for areas where you can reduce costs or improve efficiency.

5. Develop action plans
   Use your analysis to develop action plans to reduce costs and improve efficiency. This may involve changes to your processes, technology, or workforce.

Copyrights 2023 Vocational Resources Australia. All Rights Reserved.

14 Human Resources Management

For Australian Vocational Education readers:
Some of the topics in this chapter has been mapped to the following Units of Competency:

BSBCRT511, BSBHRM411, BSBHRM412, BSBHRM413, BSBHRM415, BSBHRM521, BSBHRM523, BSBHRM524, BSBHRM525, BSBHRM527, BSBHRM613, BSBHRM614, BSBRM615, BSBLDR301, BSBLDR521, BSBLDR522, BSBOPS502, BSBPEF501, BSBPMG424, BSBPMG633, BSBPMG814, BSBSTR801, BSBSTR601, BSBTWK301, BSBXTW401, and TAELED803.

Copyrights 2023 Vocational Resources Australia. All Rights Reserved.

Chapter 14: Human Resources Management

Human Resource Management

HRM is the strategic and coordinated approach to managing an organisation's employees. It involves the recruitment, training, development and management of employees in order to achieve the organisational goals. HRM aims to ensure that organisations have the right people with the right skills, knowledge, and abilities in the right place at the right time. This includes activities such as job analysis, workforce planning, talent acquisition, performance management, employee engagement, and employee retention.

The ultimate goal of HRM is to create a productive and positive work environment that supports the organisation's mission and values while meeting the needs of its employees.

HR Philosophies

Some of the modern HR philosophies are discussed below:

- Diversity and inclusion
  The philosophy that promotes equality and fairness in the workplace, valuing and respecting individual differences to create a diverse and inclusive work environment.

- Employee engagement
  The philosophy that focuses on creating job satisfaction, positive morale, and employee commitment to the organisation by involving employees in decision-making, providing opportunities for growth and development, and recognising employee contributions.

Copyrights 2023 Vocational Resources Australia. All Rights Reserved.

- Talent management
  The philosophy that recognises the importance of identifying, developing, and retaining top talent within the organisation, ensuring that employees have the necessary skills and abilities to succeed.

- Work-life balance
  The philosophy that aims to support employees in balancing their work and personal lives, recognising the importance of personal well-being to job satisfaction and productivity.

- Constant learning and development
  The philosophy that encourages continuous learning and development for employees by providing them with opportunities to learn, grow, and develop their skills and knowledge.

- Agile HR
  The philosophy that emphasises flexibility, adaptability, and responsiveness in HR management to keep up with the changing needs of the organisation and its employees.

- Data-driven HR
  The philosophy that uses data and analytics to make HR decisions based on evidence and objective information, thus improving the effectiveness of HR practices.

Copyrights 2023 Vocational Resources Australia. All Rights Reserved.

Relevant Legislations

Some of the relevant legislations are:

- Age Discrimination Act 2004
- Anti-Discrimination Act 1977 (NSW)
- Anti-Discrimination Legislations
- Australian Human Rights Commission Act 1986
- Charter of Human Rights and Responsibilities Act 2006
- Disability Discrimination Act 1992
- Equal Opportunity Act 2010
- Fair Work Act 2009
- Fringe Benefits Assessment Act 1986
- Income Tax Assessment Act 1997
- Occupational Health & Safety Act 2004 (VIC)
- Privacy Act 1988
- Racial & Religious Tolerance Act 2001
- Racial Discrimination Act 1975
- Sex Discrimination Act 1984
- State Superannuation Act 1988 (VIC)
- Taxation Administration Act 1997
- Work Health & Safety Act 2011
- Workers Compensation Act 1987
- Workers Compensation Regulation 2010
- Workplace Injury Management and Workers' Compensation Act 1998
- Workplace Injury Rehabilitation and Compensation Act 2013

Copyrights 2023 Vocational Resources Australia. All Rights Reserved.

Relevant Policies

Some of the relevant policies are:

- Anti-Discrimination and Harassment Policy
- Bullying, Harassment and Discrimination Policy & Procedures
- Code of Conduct
- Complaint Handling Policy & Procedures
- Conflict Management Policy & Procedures
- Discipline and Termination Policy
- Drug and alcohol Policy
- Equal Opportunity Policy
- Grievance Handling Policy
- Health and Safety Policy
- Injury Management Policy
- Internet and Email Policy
- Learning and Development Policy and Procedures
- Leave Policy & Procedures
- Mobile Phone Policy
- Non-smoking Policy
- Performance & Development Policy
- Performance Management Policy
- Privacy & Confidentiality Policy
- Professional Development Policy
- Recruitment Policy & Procedures
- Reward and Recognition Policy
- Risk Management Policy & Procedures
- Training & Development Policy
- Work Health & Safety Policy & Procedures

Copyrights 2023 Vocational Resources Australia. All Rights Reserved.

Key Elements of Recruitment Policy

They recruitment policy is a document that outlines the processes and procedures that an organisation will follow to attract, select, and hire new employees. Here are some elements that should be included in a recruitment policy:

- Recruitment goals
  The policy should outline the organisation's recruitment goals and objectives, such as diversity and inclusion, talent acquisition, or employee retention.

- Recruitment process
  The policy should describe the steps the organisation will take to recruit and select candidates, including the job posting process, candidate screening, interview process, and reference checking.

- Job descriptions
  The policy should provide guidance on how to create accurate and thorough job descriptions that accurately reflect the duties and responsibilities of the position.

- Candidate screening
  The policy should specify the qualifications and competencies required for each position and describe the screening process for assessing candidate skills and experience.

- Interview process
  The policy should define the interview process, including the types of questions that will be asked, the interview format, and the evaluation and selection criteria.

Copyrights 2023 Vocational Resources Australia. All Rights Reserved.

- Candidate selection
  The policy should outline the selection process, including the factors that will be considered when evaluating candidates and making final hiring decisions.

- Background checks
  The policy should include information about the types of background checks that will be conducted, such as criminal history, credit history, and reference checks.

- Job Offers
  The policy should provide guidance on how job offers will be made, including the terms and conditions of employment, salary, benefits, and any other relevant details.

- Compliance
  The policy should ensure compliance with all applicable laws and regulations, such as equal employment opportunity laws, and include procedures for addressing discrimination or harassment allegations.

- Evaluation and Improvement
  The policy should specify how the recruitment process will be evaluated and improved over time, based on feedback from employees, hiring managers, and other stakeholders.

Copyrights 2023 Vocational Resources Australia. All Rights Reserved.

Key Elements of Onboarding Policy or Procedures

An onboarding policy is a document that outlines the processes and procedures that an organisation will follow to help new employees integrate into the workplace and become productive members of the team.

Here are the key elements that should be included in an onboarding policy:

- Welcome message
  The policy should include a welcoming message from the organisation's leadership, which sets the tone for the new employee's experience and emphasises the importance of their role.

- New hire orientation
  The policy should describe the new hire orientation process, including the schedule, topics covered, and the roles and responsibilities of the employees responsible for conducting the orientation.

- Employee handbook
  The policy should provide a copy of the employee handbook, which outlines the organisation's policies, procedures, and expectations for behaviour and performance.

- Job training
  The policy should describe the training that will be provided to help the new employee develop the knowledge and skills required to perform their job effectively.

Copyrights 2023 Vocational Resources Australia. All Rights Reserved.

- Performance expectations
  The policy should define the expectations for job performance, including goals, objectives, and key performance indicators (KPIs).

- Mentorship program
  The policy should describe any mentorship or coaching programs available to the new employee, which provide guidance and support as they navigate the organisation.

- Communication channels
  The policy should describe the various communication channels available to the new employee, such as email, instant messaging, and team meetings.

- Benefits and compensation
  The policy should provide information about the organisation's benefits and compensation packages, including health insurance, retirement benefits, and paid time off.

- Company culture
  The policy should describe the organisation's culture, values, and mission, which help the new employee understand the organisation's purpose and priorities.

- Evaluation and feedback
  The policy should describe the process for evaluating the new employee's performance and providing feedback on their progress, including regular performance reviews and opportunities for professional development.

Copyrights 2023 Vocational Resources Australia. All Rights Reserved.

Reviewing/ Updating the Policies

Here are some key considerations to keep in mind when reviewing and updating recruitment policies:

- Compliance with laws and regulations
  It is important to ensure that the recruitment policies are compliant with all the applicable laws and regulations.

- Diversity and inclusion
  Diversity and inclusion are critical considerations in modern recruitment policies. The policies should ensure fair hiring practices and provide equal opportunities to all candidates regardless of their race, gender, age, religion, or other protected characteristic.

- Job descriptions
  Effective recruitment starts with clear and accurate job descriptions. The policies should require up to date job descriptions that accurately reflect the duties, responsibilities, and qualifications required for each position.

- Sourcing channels
  The policies should specify the sourcing channels used to attract candidates - including job postings, social media, networking events, and employee referrals.

- Screening and selection criteria
  The policies should establish screening and selection criteria that are based on the job description and required qualifications. The policies should also define the interview and selection process, including the use of pre-employment tests and background checks.

Copyrights 2023 Vocational Resources Australia. All Rights Reserved.

- Employer branding
  Recruitment policies should take into account the organisation's employer brand, messaging, and value proposition. This can help attract the right candidates who align with the company's culture and mission.

- Candidate experience
  The policies should also focus on providing a positive candidate experience to every applicant, regardless of whether or not they are ultimately selected for the position. This includes clear communication, timely feedback, and a respectful and professional hiring process.

Communicating & Educating the Policies

Policies and procedures are essential for maintaining order and ensuring that everyone in the workplace is on the same page.

Here are some ways policies & procedures should be communicated to the staff:

- Employee handbook
  Create an employee handbook that outlines all the policies and procedures in a clear and concise manner. Make it easily accessible to all staff members.

- Training sessions
  Conduct training sessions to educate staff members about the policies and procedures. This will ensure that everyone understands the policies and knows how to follow them.

Copyrights 2023 Vocational Resources Australia. All Rights Reserved.

- Communication channels
  Use various communication channels such as emails, newsletters, and bulletin boards to keep staff members informed about policy updates and changes.

- Regular reminders
  Regularly remind staff members about the policies and procedures to ensure that they remain top of mind.

Obtaining Stakeholders' Support

Here are a few strategies I can suggest to obtain stakeholders' support in the review of recruitment policy:

- Communicate the benefits
  Clearly explain to stakeholders how reviewing the recruitment policy can benefit the organisation, such as better hiring practices, increased efficiency, and cost savings.

- Involve stakeholders in the process
  Consult with stakeholders from different departments and levels of the organisation to gain their input, address their concerns, and ensure that the revised recruitment policy meets their expectations.

- Provide training
  Offer training to stakeholders on the updated recruitment policy and how it aligns with the organisation's goals and objectives. This can also help stakeholders understand how to implement the changes in their day-to-day activities.

Copyrights 2023 Vocational Resources Australia. All Rights Reserved.

- Demonstrate transparency
  Provide transparency throughout the review process and explain the reasons behind any changes made to the recruitment policy. This can help build trust and support among stakeholders.

- Use data
  Use data and analytics to back up the need for changes to the recruitment policy. This can provide stakeholders with a clear understanding of the rationale behind the changes and make it easier for them to support the updated policy.

Support Services

HR support services are a range of services that can be provided by a third-party to help businesses with their human resources (HR) needs. These services can include:

- Recruitment and selection
  This can involve sourcing and screening candidates, conducting interviews, and making hiring decisions.

- Onboarding
  This can involve orienting new employees to the company's culture, policies, and procedures.

- Performance management
  This can involve setting goals, providing feedback, and managing performance.

- Compensation and benefits
  This can involve designing and administering compensation and benefits programs.

Copyrights 2023 Vocational Resources Australia. All Rights Reserved.

- HRIS (Human Resource Information System) support
  This can involve providing access to HR data and reports, and developing HR-related software applications.

- Employee Assistance Programs (EAPs)
  EAPs provide confidential counseling and support to employees facing personal or work-related problems.

- Health and wellness programs
  These programs help employees to improve their health and well-being through initiatives such as fitness classes, nutrition counseling, and stress management programs.

- Diversity and inclusion programs
  These programs promote a workplace that is welcoming and inclusive of all employees, regardless of their race, ethnicity, gender, sexual orientation, or other personal characteristics.

- Employee engagement programs
  These programs help to create a workplace where employees feel connected to their work and their colleagues.

- Learning and development
  These programs provide employees with the skills and knowledge they need to do their jobs effectively and to advance their careers.

- Talent management
  These programs help to identify and develop high-performing employees.

Copyrights 2023 Vocational Resources Australia. All Rights Reserved.

- Succession planning
  These programs help to ensure that the organisation has the right people in the right positions to meet its future needs.

- Compensation and benefits programs
  These programs help to attract and retain top talent by providing competitive salaries, benefits, and other rewards.

- Employee relations
  These programs help to resolve employee disputes and to maintain a positive work environment.

Copyrights 2023 Vocational Resources Australia. All Rights Reserved.

Awards

Modern awards are official documents that establish the minimum wage rates and employment terms and conditions applicable to various industries or occupations in Australia.

They are legal instruments that specify the minimum pay rates and employment terms and conditions for employees and employers, based on their industry and job type. They apply to various industries and contain information about the employees who are covered under them. These awards establish the lowest standards that employers are permitted to pay for specific work in their industry.

They are legally binding and provide all employees in an industry or workplace with the same wages and employment terms. The primary purpose of awards is to safeguard employees' wages and working conditions.

Fair Work Australia is the organisation responsible for determining awards, and it is a government-established tribunal.

Copyrights 2023 Vocational Resources Australia. All Rights Reserved.

Disciplinary Action

Disciplinary action against an employee is a process that an employer may use to address and correct unacceptable behaviour or performance in the workplace. This can range from a verbal warning to a written warning, suspension, or even termination of employment. The purpose of disciplinary action is to promote a safe and respectful work environment and to ensure that employees are meeting the expectations and standards set by their employer.

Disciplinary Action Process

The process of disciplinary action against an employee involves several steps.

1. First, the employer must investigate the alleged misconduct or poor performance by the employee. This investigation should be thorough and objective, with all relevant evidence and witnesses considered.

2. Once the investigation is complete, the employer should inform the employee of the allegations against them and provide them with an opportunity to respond. The employee should also be given access to any evidence that was gathered during the investigation.

3. If the employer determines that disciplinary action is necessary, they should communicate this to the employee in writing, outlining the reasons for the decision and the specific disciplinary measures that will be implemented. The employee should also be given the opportunity to respond to this decision.

Copyrights 2023 Vocational Resources Australia. All Rights Reserved.

4. The employer must ensure that any disciplinary action taken is fair and reasonable, taking into account the severity of the alleged misconduct or poor performance, the employee's past performance and conduct, and any mitigating circumstances.

5. Finally, the employer should follow up with the employee to ensure that they understand the disciplinary action taken and what is expected of them going forward. This may involve setting specific goals for improvement and providing additional support or training if needed.

Copyrights 2023 Vocational Resources Australia. All Rights Reserved.

Diversity

Diversity in the workplace is crucial for a number of reasons. Some of them are outlined below:

- It allows for a wider range of perspectives, experiences, and skills to be utilised. This more varied pool of input and insight can lead to more creative and innovative solutions.

- Research has shown that diversity leads to increased employee engagement, retention, and job satisfaction.

- A diverse workplace can better serve a diverse customer base and lead to improved business outcomes.

- Having a diverse workforce is simply the right thing to do. By embracing and celebrating differences, we can create a more inclusive and equitable workplace for all.

Types

Understanding the different types of diverse individuals and groups is key to promoting inclusivity and creating a welcoming environment for everyone.

Here are some examples of diverse individuals and groups that may be found in the workplace:

- People with different ethnic and cultural backgrounds This includes individuals who come from different countries or regions, have different religions or belief systems, speak different languages, or have different customs and traditions.

Copyrights 2023 Vocational Resources Australia. All Rights Reserved.

- People with different genders and sexual orientations
  This includes individuals who identify as male, female, transgender, genderqueer, or non-binary, as well as those who identify as gay, lesbian, bisexual, or asexual.

- People with disabilities
  This includes individuals who may have physical, sensory, intellectual, or mental health disabilities, and may require accommodations in the workplace to help them perform their job duties.

- People with different ages
  This includes individuals of all ages, from younger employees just starting out in their careers to older workers who may be nearing retirement.

- People with different education levels
  This includes individuals with different levels of education, from those who have completed high school to those with advanced degrees.

- People with different socio-economic backgrounds
  This includes individuals from different socio-economic backgrounds, who may have different levels of income, education, and social status.

Copyrights 2023 Vocational Resources Australia. All Rights Reserved.

Factors and their Impact on Workforce

There are various factors which may an impact on workplace and work arrangements. Some of them are outlined below:

- Gender
  Research suggests that women may experience lower levels of engagement due to gender bias, unequal pay, and limited opportunities for advancement. On the other hand, creating a diverse and inclusive workplace culture can positively impact engagement among all employees.

- Race
  Race can be a factor in workforce engagement, with people of colour often reporting lower levels of engagement due to systemic racism, stereotypes, and discrimination. Organisations that prioritise diversity and inclusion can help mitigate these issues and promote engagement among all employees.

- Age
  Age can also impact workforce engagement, with younger workers often prioritizing development opportunities and work-life balance, while older workers may value stability and job security. Organisations can support engagement across age ranges by offering a variety of development opportunities, work-life balance options, and other benefits.

- Disability
  Disability can also affect workforce engagement, with individuals with disabilities often facing barriers to employment and workplace accommodations. Organisations that prioritise accessibility and inclusion

Copyrights 2023 Vocational Resources Australia. All Rights Reserved.

can help support the engagement and success of employees with disabilities.

- Sexual orientation
  Sexual orientation can impact engagement, with LGBT employees facing discrimination and harassment in the workplace. Creating a safe and inclusive workplace culture can help support the engagement of all employees, regardless of sexual orientation or gender identity.

- Engagement Type
  Form of work engagement, such as part-time or full-time employment, can also impact engagement levels. Studies suggest that part-time workers may be less engaged than full-time workers, but offering flexible work arrangements can promote engagement among all employees.

  Flexible work arrangements, such as telecommuting and flexible schedules, can boost engagement by offering employees more control over their work-life balance and reducing stress.

  However, organisations must ensure that all employees have access to these benefits, regardless of gender, race, age, or other factors.

Copyrights 2023 Vocational Resources Australia. All Rights Reserved.

Promoting Workforce Diversity

Engaging and integrating a diverse workforce is key for building a culture of inclusivity and productivity. Here are some strategies, tools, and techniques that you can use to achieve that goal:

- Create a diversity and inclusion task force
  The task force can help you identify potential barriers to diversity and inclusion, and can create strategies to address them. Include employees from different backgrounds, job levels, and functions to create a well-rounded team.

- Implement diversity training
  Providing diversity training to all employees can help them understand the importance of diversity, how to work with people from different backgrounds, and how to recognise and address unconscious biases.

- Celebrate cultural differences
  Celebrating cultural differences can help employees feel valued and included. You can hold cultural events, organise potlucks, or create a diversity calendar to recognise different holidays and celebrations.

- Foster mentorship and sponsorship
  Pairing employees from different backgrounds, job levels, and functions can help to build relationships, develop skills, and promote diversity and inclusion within the workplace.

Copyrights 2023 Vocational Resources Australia. All Rights Reserved.

- Evaluate hiring practices
  Evaluate your hiring practices to ensure they are free from bias. This can include blind screening, setting diversity targets, and using structured interviews to reduce bias.

- Use Employee Resource Groups (ERGs)
  ERGs are employee-led groups that focus on different diversity and inclusion topics. They can help to create a sense of community within the workplace and provide support for employees from different backgrounds.

- Create a culture of inclusion
  This means creating an environment where everyone feels welcome, respected, and valued, regardless of their background.

- Create opportunities for employees to network and get to know each other.
  This can help to break down barriers and build relationships between employees from different backgrounds.

- Conduct diversity audits
  Regularly conduct diversity audits to track your progress and identify areas that need improvement. This can help you understand how well you are engaging and integrating a diverse workforce.

Copyrights 2023 Vocational Resources Australia. All Rights Reserved.

Barriers

Some common barriers include:

- Unconscious bias
  This is a natural tendency to gravitate towards people who look and think like us. It can lead to overlooking or undervaluing individuals who are different from us.

- Lack of awareness
  Many people simply don't recognise the importance of diversity and inclusion in the workplace. They may not understand the benefits of having a diverse team or may not be aware of how their actions or language can create barriers to inclusion.

- Systemic barriers
  There may be structural or systemic barriers that prevent certain groups of people from accessing opportunities or advancing in their careers. For example, if a company only recruits from Ivy League schools, it may inadvertently exclude individuals from other backgrounds.

- Stereotyping
  Stereotyping involves making assumptions about individuals based on characteristics such as their gender, race, or religion. This can result in people being unfairly judged or excluded from opportunities.

- Lack of resources
  Organisations may not allocate adequate resources towards promoting diversity and inclusion, including training and development opportunities for employees from underrepresented groups.

Copyrights 2023 Vocational Resources Australia. All Rights Reserved.

Biases and Assumptions

Biases and assumptions can have a significant impact on communication in a diverse workforce. When people communicate with each other, they often bring their own biases and assumptions to the table. These biases can influence how they interpret what others are saying, how they respond to others, and how they make decisions.

In a diverse workforce, people from different backgrounds may have different experiences, values, and ways of communicating. This can lead to misunderstandings and conflict. For example, someone from a collectivist culture may be more likely to value harmony and consensus, while someone from an individualistic culture may be more likely to value directness and individual achievement. These different communication styles can clash, leading to misunderstandings and conflict.

Biases and assumptions can also lead to discrimination. For example, someone who holds negative stereotypes about a particular group of people may be less likely to listen to or trust members of that group. This can make it difficult for people from underrepresented groups to succeed in the workplace.

There are a number of things that organisations can do to address the impact of biases and assumptions on communication in a diverse workforce. These include:

- Training employees on unconscious bias.
  This training can help employees to become aware of their own biases and how they might be affecting their communication.

Copyrights 2023 Vocational Resources Australia. All Rights Reserved.

- Encouraging employees to be mindful of their language.
  Employees should be careful not to use language that is offensive or discriminatory.

- Creating a culture of inclusion.
  Employees should feel comfortable speaking up if they feel that they have been treated unfairly.

Copyrights 2023 Vocational Resources Australia. All Rights Reserved.

Developing Work Plan

Here are some steps you can take to develop a work plan to accommodate diversity:

- Assess your current diversity landscape.
  What is the makeup of your workforce in terms of race, ethnicity, gender, sexual orientation, age, disability, and other factors? What are your strengths and weaknesses in terms of diversity?

- Set goals for diversity and inclusion.
  What do you want to achieve in terms of diversity and inclusion in your workplace? Do you want to increase the representation of certain groups in your workforce? Do you want to create a more inclusive workplace culture?

- Develop strategies to achieve your goals.
  What specific steps can you take to increase diversity and inclusion in your workplace? These steps could include things like:

  Reviewing your hiring and recruitment practices to ensure that all candidates are considered fairly.

  Providing training on diversity and inclusion for all employees

  Creating a more inclusive workplace culture by celebrating diversity and promoting respect for all employees.

  Consult relevant stakeholders to ensure everyone is involved.

Copyrights 2023 Vocational Resources Australia. All Rights Reserved.

- Measure your progress and make adjustments as needed.
  It is important to track your progress towards your diversity and inclusion goals. This will help you to identify areas where you need to make adjustments to your strategies.

Qualifying & Quantifying Source of Workforce Diversity

Qualifying and quantifying the source of workforce diversity is an important aspect of diversity and inclusion in the workplace. It involves recognising and measuring the different factors that contribute to the diversity of a company's workforce, such as age, gender, ethnicity, education, and socio-economic background, among others.

To qualify the source of workforce diversity, organisations need to understand where their employees come from, what their unique backgrounds and experiences are, and how these factors contribute to the overall diversity of the workforce. This can include collecting data on employee demographics, conducting surveys to gain insights into their experiences, and analysing the results to identify trends and patterns.

Quantifying the source of workforce diversity involves measuring the extent to which different factors contribute to the overall diversity of the workforce. This can be done through statistical analysis to identify the percentage of employees who fall into different demographic categories, or by assessing the skills, knowledge, and experience of employees to identify areas of strength and potential for growth.

Copyrights 2023 Vocational Resources Australia. All Rights Reserved.

Qualifying and quantifying the source of workforce diversity is important because it helps organisations to better understand their workforce and to identify ways to leverage diversity to achieve their goals. For example, diverse teams are often more innovative and can bring different perspectives to problem-solving, leading to better outcomes for the organisation. Understanding the different sources of workforce diversity can also help organisations to develop more effective diversity and inclusion strategies, policies, and training programs.

Relevant Legislations

Some of the relevant legislations are:

- Racial Discrimination Act 1975 - prohibits discrimination based on race, colour, descent, or national or ethnic origin in various areas, including employment.
- Sex Discrimination Act 1984 - prohibits discrimination based on gender or sexual orientation in various areas, including employment.
- Disability Discrimination Act 1992 - prohibits discrimination based on disability in various areas, including employment.
- Age Discrimination Act 2004 - prohibits discrimination based on age in various areas, including employment.
- Fair Work Act 2009 - includes provisions on workplace diversity and preventing discrimination, harassment, and bullying in the workplace.

Copyrights 2023 Vocational Resources Australia. All Rights Reserved.

- Workplace Gender Equality Act 2012 - requires certain employers to report on and promote gender equality in the workplace.

- Migration Act 1958 - prohibits discrimination based on a person's immigration status in employment and other areas.

- Public Service Act 1999 - requires the Australian Public Service to promote workplace diversity and prevent discrimination.

- Australian Human Rights Commission Act 1986 - establishes the Australian Human Rights Commission, which is responsible for promoting and protecting human rights, including in the workplace.

Relevant Policies

Here are some organisational policies relevant to diversity in the workplace:

- Diversity and inclusion policy
  This policy should state the organisation's commitment to creating a diverse and inclusive workplace. It should also outline the organisation's procedures for preventing and addressing discrimination and harassment.

- Recruitment and hiring policy
  This policy should ensure that all employees are considered for employment opportunities regardless of their race, ethnicity, gender, sexual orientation, age, disability, or other protected characteristics.

Copyrights 2023 Vocational Resources Australia. All Rights Reserved.

- Training and development policy
  This policy should ensure that all employees have access to training and development opportunities that will help them grow and develop their skills. This is important for creating a more diverse and inclusive workforce, as it can help to break down barriers and create a more level playing field for all employees.

- Performance management policy
  This policy should ensure that all employees are evaluated fairly and that their performance is not influenced by their race, ethnicity, gender, sexual orientation, age, disability, or other protected characteristics.

- Compensation and benefits policy
  This policy should ensure that all employees are compensated fairly and that they have access to the same benefits, regardless of their race, ethnicity, gender, sexual orientation, age, disability, or other protected characteristics.

- Workplace conduct policy
  This policy should set out the organisation's expectations for employee behaviour in the workplace. It should also outline the consequences for employees who violate the policy.

- Grievance procedure
  This policy should outline the process for employees to file a grievance if they believe they have been discriminated against or harassed.

Copyrights 2023 Vocational Resources Australia. All Rights Reserved.

Employment Contract

An employment contract is a legal agreement between an employer and an employee that outlines the obligations and rights of each party. The contract is signed voluntarily by both parties, making it legally enforceable.

To form a contract, both parties must agree to provide something of value to each other. In the case of an employment contract, the employer agrees to pay the employee for performing specific work-related duties. The contract is prepared by the employer, usually using a template, and the employee accepts the terms as a condition of their employment.

There is no standard employment contract as the terms and provisions can vary based on the company's business nature, internal policies, and the offered position. A contract for a senior executive will likely be more comprehensive than an agreement for an entry-level position.

Despite the variations, most employment contracts contain fundamental provisions that are commonly included. These standard clauses ensure that both parties understand their rights and responsibilities. Some of them are discussed below:

- Terms of employment
  The terms of employment typically pertain to the duration of the job that one agrees to undertake. While some roles may have an open-ended term of employment, others with fixed start and end dates are considered short-term positions.

Copyrights 2023 Vocational Resources Australia. All Rights Reserved.

- Employee responsibilities
  To ensure that you are meeting your obligations as an employee, it is crucial to have a clear understanding of the specific duties that are expected of you. Generally, an employee's responsibilities will encompass several aspects, such as the regular work location and schedule, a comprehensive outline of the services or tasks that the employee is expected to deliver, the individual within the management hierarchy to whom the employee must report, and any relevant prerequisites for maintaining the employee's professional license(s).

  The level of specificity regarding your job responsibilities listed in your employment agreement may vary depending on your role. Nevertheless, it is essential to have a clear comprehension of your duties to determine if you are fulfilling them appropriately. Failing to understand what your employer expects from you can be detrimental to your job performance. Additionally, it is equally crucial to recognise which tasks lie beyond your area of responsibility to avoid being burdened with work that is outside the scope of your position.

- Performance expectations and requirements
  In numerous professions, particularly in industries like sales, employers establish definite performance objectives that their staff must attain. Along with fulfilling the fundamental requirements of the job, employees may be expected to meet other specific targets as well. For instance, while your primary responsibility may be to perform certain tasks, you could also be tasked with acquiring new clients for the company. Alternatively, you may be required to participate in philanthropic or

Copyrights 2023 Vocational Resources Australia. All Rights Reserved.

community service initiatives that the company organises, as positive publicity is deemed crucial for the overall success of the organisation.

Irrespective of whether your employer evaluates your job performance based on monetary figures or other measurable criteria, it is imperative to have a clear understanding of the expected outcomes from the beginning. For instance, if you are hired to enhance a particular aspect of the organisation, the division may still incur losses in the short-term, regardless of your performance. However, if you devise innovative ideas that will eventually turn the situation around, you could exceed expectations, even if the balance sheet shows otherwise. Failing to establish these benchmarks as part of your employment agreement could impede your ability to justify a raise or promotion, or even to retain your job.

- Employee benefits and premiums
  The benefits package provided by your employer is often just as significant, if not more so, than your salary. A comprehensive benefits package for full-time employees typically encompasses health insurance, life insurance, disability coverage, and contributions towards retirement plans. In addition to these, some companies may also offer stock options and profit-sharing as part of their benefits package.

  It is crucial to have a clear comprehension of the scope of your employee benefits. For instance, if your health insurance plan has an annual deductible, you will be responsible for paying that amount out of pocket every year.

Copyrights 2023 Vocational Resources Australia. All Rights Reserved.

You also need to ascertain if the company's benefits package includes dental and vision coverage and find out the co-pay amounts for doctor visits. Additionally, it is essential to know the restrictions and limits for out-of-network care. These are critical inquiries that will affect you and your family if you opt for one of the company's health plans, and therefore, you should seek answers to these questions beforehand.

- Employment Absence

  While it may not appear significant initially, it's important to note that not all types of days off are equivalent. Employee absence policies can vary widely across different companies. Some organisations provide their employees with a fixed number of sick days, personal days, and vacation time each year, while others offer a specific number of paid time off (PTO) days annually that employees can use for any reason.

  For individuals who seldom miss work, it is crucial to determine if unused days off accumulate and carry over to future periods. Different companies have varying policies regarding carrying over days off.

  Some firms allow employees to carry over a fixed number of days annually, while others permit carryover of days per quarter. In contrast, some companies have a policy of not allowing carryover of any days at all. Alternatively, some organisations compensate employees for unused days. It is essential to clarify the details of time off policies before commencing work.

Copyrights 2023 Vocational Resources Australia. All Rights Reserved.

- Dispute Resolution
  It is a reality that not all working relationships conclude with a celebratory gathering and gifts. In case of a disagreement between you and your employer, a dispute resolution clause in your employment contract will outline the process to be followed for resolving the conflict.

  When it comes to resolving disputes, there are typically three options available. For minor conflicts within lower levels of management, the company may have an internal policy to address and resolve the issue, at least initially. For more significant disputes, the company may either opt for an arbitration process to keep the matter out of court or specify a particular jurisdiction where all legal claims must be filed and litigated.

  It's important to understand that agreeing to an arbitration clause that restricts your legal actions against the company can be a complex legal matter. For instance, such a clause might limit your ability to file a sexual harassment claim against your employer. While this may shield companies from negative publicity by keeping claims confidential, it raises concerns about transparency and accountability. Additionally, arbitration can avoid the risk of a large jury verdict against an employer that could result from litigation.

- Non-Disclosure Agreements
  A non-disclosure agreement, or NDA, is a legal contract that prohibits an employee from disclosing confidential or valuable information about the company. This information may include business strategies, client information, internal policies and procedures, and trade secrets.

Copyrights 2023 Vocational Resources Australia. All Rights Reserved.

NDA may have a set timeframe specified in the employment contract, which is generally enforceable. However, if the agreement doesn't mention any time limit, it is considered indefinite, meaning it could last indefinitely. Courts usually uphold NDA's if the terms are reasonable and understood by both parties. It's important to carefully examine the language to avoid restricting future job opportunities in the same industry.

- Non-Compete clause
  A non-compete clause, also called a covenant not to compete, and is a provision in a contract that limits an employee's ability to compete against their former employer. This clause aims to prevent the employee from utilising the company's proprietary information, client list, or other trade secrets to start a competing business or work for a direct competitor.

  Non-compete clauses are generally considered valid if they are reasonable. For example, it might be reasonable to prohibit a former employee from starting a similar business within a certain radius of their former employer. However, it would not be reasonable to restrict an employee from starting any kind of business within a large geographical area. The clause should also be limited to direct competition. If you previously worked at an auto repair shop and then open an ice cream parlour nearby, it would be difficult for your former employer to argue that your ice cream parlour is in direct competition with their shop, even if there was a non-compete clause in place.

Copyrights 2023 Vocational Resources Australia. All Rights Reserved.

- Ownership agreement
  The idea behind an ownership agreement is straightforward: any work or product you create while employed by the company belongs to the company. For instance, if you work on a production line, any finished products that come out of that line automatically belong to the company.

  The ownership agreement becomes more complex when an employee creates something of significant value such as a product, process or idea. In such cases, the company owns the creation regardless of its potential profitability, and the employee is only entitled to the compensation outlined in their employment contract. These protections may even extend to intellectual property that has not yet been developed. For instance, a Texas court required a former Alcatel employee to surrender a software algorithm to the company, despite the fact that it only existed as a theoretical concept in the employee's mind during their employment.

- Employment opportunity limitations
  An employment opportunity limitations clause can be included in an employment agreement to prevent an employer from harming an employee's future job prospects. When an employee leaves a job, they would not want their previous employer to sabotage their potential opportunities. This clause prevents the former employer from contacting the new employer and saying negative things about the employee to interfere with their new job.

Copyrights 2023 Vocational Resources Australia. All Rights Reserved.

In essence, this clause ensures that your current employer does not impede your job search with a new company, regardless of whether you are fired or leave voluntarily. However, it is essential to note that these contractual provisions can present issues because leaving a job can sometimes result in difficult situations and ill feelings between both parties.

- Termination clauses
  Having a well-defined employment contract is crucial for employees, as it specifies the reasons for termination. Even in "at-will" employment states where employers can terminate employees at any time, an employment contract can offer certain protections. Without an employment contract, an employer could terminate an employee without any legal repercussions, even for a trivial reason like the colour of their shoes. However, to ensure that employees are fully protected, the grounds for termination must be clearly and unambiguously outlined in the contract.

- Severance terms
  Severance pay refers to the compensation and benefits that an employee may be entitled to receive after their employment term has ended.

  Severance pay can be granted in various situations such as downsizing, early retirement incentives, or outsourcing of employee duties to another location. In some cases, an employer may offer severance pay to an employee who resigns or is fired, as a gesture of goodwill to prevent potential litigation or other negative consequences. Although companies may offer severance

Copyrights 2023 Vocational Resources Australia. All Rights Reserved.

pay voluntarily, they are not necessarily obligated to do so. Without clear provisions in your employment contract, you may not be able to compel your employer to provide severance pay.

It's important to pay close attention to the details of employment contracts. Even if you feel pressured to sign, don't be afraid to take the time to review the contract, seek legal advice, ask questions, and suggest changes to ensure that it's fair and protects your rights. Remember that the employer wants you to be a happy and productive employee, so you may have more bargaining power than you think. It's worth taking the time to negotiate and ensure that your employment contract is a good fit for you and your new role.

Copyrights 2023 Vocational Resources Australia. All Rights Reserved.

Enterprise Agreements

An enterprise agreement is a type of agreement that outlines the terms and conditions of employment, including wages, at the enterprise level. This is usually in place where Unions have an effective role in the organisation, and they were able to negotiate favourable employment conditions for the workers.

An enterprise agreement is a legally binding document that outlines the terms and conditions of employment, including wages, at the enterprise level. It is required to have a nominal expiry date within four years, but it can continue to be in effect after that date until it is replaced by a new enterprise agreement or terminated by the Fair Work Commission.

The Fair Work Act lays out guidelines for bargaining for a proposed enterprise agreement. This refers to an agreement that is being negotiated with the intention of being approved by the Commission as an enterprise agreement. For example, a group of employees may put forth a series of claims through their bargaining representatives to negotiate with their employer and reach a proposed enterprise agreement as defined by the Fair Work Act.

Types of Enterprise Agreements

Under the Fair Work Act, there are two primary types of enterprise agreements that can be created:

Single Interest Employers

A single-enterprise agreement is an agreement made between an employer, or multiple employers that have a

Copyrights 2023 Vocational Resources Australia. All Rights Reserved.

single interest, and the employees who are currently employed and will be affected by the agreement.

To be considered as single interest employers, two or more employers must meet one of the following criteria:

- They are involved in a joint venture or common enterprise.
- They are related bodies corporate.
- They are specified in a single interest employer authorisation that applies to the proposed enterprise agreement.

A joint venture refers to a group of individuals or organisations who come together for a specific financial endeavour, such as trading, commercial, or mining activities, with the intention of sharing in the profits.

Participants in a joint venture often contribute money, property, or skills to the venture.

Multi-Enterprise Agreement

Employers who are not considered single interest employers can still create an enterprise agreement with their employees who are employed during the agreement's creation and covered by it. If low-paid employees who have not been involved in enterprise-level collective bargaining before want to create a multi-enterprise agreement, they can utilise a special bargaining stream.

The Fair Work Commission can authorize access to this stream through low paid authorizations.

Copyrights 2023 Vocational Resources Australia. All Rights Reserved.

Differences between single and multi-enterprise agreements

To initiate bargaining for a multi-enterprise agreement, it is necessary for two or more employers to agree to bargain together voluntarily. It should be noted that a majority support determination cannot be used for a multi-enterprise agreement except for in the low-paid bargaining stream. Therefore, unless using the low-paid bargaining stream, multi-enterprise bargaining can only occur if employers agree to bargain together voluntarily.

In the case of multi-enterprise agreements, bargaining orders cannot be applied for by bargaining representatives except for in the low-paid bargaining stream. However, both single-enterprise agreements and multi-enterprise agreements must adhere to the good faith bargaining requirements.

It is possible to replace a multi-enterprise agreement with a single-enterprise agreement prior to the nominal expiry date of the former.

According to the general rule, a new enterprise agreement does not apply to an employee until an earlier enterprise agreement that applies to the employee has passed its nominal expiry date. Nevertheless, a single-enterprise agreement may replace a multi-enterprise agreement prior to the nominal expiry date of the latter.

Copyrights 2023 Vocational Resources Australia. All Rights Reserved.

External HR Consultant

An HR Consultant is a skilled professional who specializes in human resources management. They provide consulting services to businesses as an external party, offering advice on employee matters and compliance with employment law. In addition to providing tools and advice for HR management, they can also provide mediation, review, performance metrics, and management training. Some HR Consultants are generalists, covering most aspects of HR management, while others are specialists, focusing on areas such as Work Health and Safety, Recruitment, Mediations, and more.

HR Professionals work with other businesses as advisers, providing external HR management tools and advice. They become the HR Department for their customers, becoming trusted advisors. In some cases, even In-house HR departments may require the services of an independent HR consultant. Sometimes, having a second opinion is a good idea, especially if the matter could lead to legal implications with significant consequences.

A business should hire a HR Consultant to ensure they meet mandatory compliance with employment legislation with their employees. As soon as a business has employees, they must ensure they meet their obligations. A short project can ensure the right documentation, pay, and conditions are in place. As a business grows and hires more people, the need for the services of a HR Consultant increases. Issues can arise in a business with any number of employees, including casuals. Thus, having the skills of a HR Consultant at hand becomes vital.

Copyrights 2023 Vocational Resources Australia. All Rights Reserved.

A business with good HR practices and a sound business model will see improvement in profit. This makes it easier to attract great employees to their business. Therefore, it is essential to work with a HR Consultant to ensure that HR management is in line with the business's needs, goals, and objectives. Whether you require an independent opinion or ongoing consulting services, a HR Consultant can provide valuable guidance and support to help you manage your human resources effectively.

HR Professionals can provide consulting services on a range of employee issues including:

- Performance management
- Underperformance
- Attitude
- Attendance and punctuality
- Significant absences
- Work Health and Safety
- Conflict resolution
- Bullying and Harassment
- Managing difficult employees
- Pay and conditions (Payroll, Reward and Recognition, Work life balance, etc.)
- Performance incentives
- Key performance metrics

HR Consultants can offer various services, but one of the most significant is providing up to date advice on employment legislation. By doing so, they become a trusted advisor to both the management and employees.

Copyrights 2023 Vocational Resources Australia. All Rights Reserved.

Expectations from a HR Consultant

A competent HR Consultant possesses in-depth knowledge of employment legislation, including industry-specific and regional requirements, as well as diverse industries and roles. They should be capable of setting clear expectations and boundaries in the workplace while being respectful and advocating for compliance with employment legislation. Aligning the workforce with the company's profitability is critical, and HR Consultants ensure that pay, conditions, and rewards are appropriate to attract and retain top talent. They also establish and manage talent acquisition processes.

When looking for an HR Consultant, it is critical to find one that is a good fit for your business. Take the time to research and speak with several consultants to determine their skills and approach. A good match is essential, given the sensitive nature of the relationship. There are various HR Consulting firms available, from large to small boutique firms, each with unique skills and costs.

HR Consultants can be invaluable in times of crisis, such as the pandemic. Finding a consultant who can serve as a trusted advisor is critical to navigating such situations. The consultant's expertise, approach, and compatibility with your company can make a significant difference in achieving positive outcomes.

Copyrights 2023 Vocational Resources Australia. All Rights Reserved.

Human Resource Functions

Human resource functions play a vital role in the success of any organisation. They are responsible for managing and taking care of the employees of the organisation.

The core HR functions are discussed below:

Recruitment and Selection

Recruitment and selection is one of the primary functions of HR. It involves attracting, screening, and selecting the most suitable candidate for the job position. HR is responsible for creating job descriptions, job postings, and conducting interviews and assessments to find the best fit for the organisation.

Further details are available under "Recruitment", as well as "Onboarding" topics of this chapter.

Training and Development

Training and development is another critical function of HR. They are responsible for providing training and development programs to enhance the skills and knowledge of the employees. It helps in improving the quality of work and productivity of the employees.

Further details are available under "Staff Development" topic of this chapter.

Performance Management

The topic has been discussed under separated heading in detail, in this chapter.

Copyrights 2023 Vocational Resources Australia. All Rights Reserved.

Compensation and Benefits

HR is responsible for designing and implementing the compensation and benefits plans for the employees. It includes salary packages, bonuses, health insurance, retirement plans, and other perks that attract and retain the employees.

Employee Relations

HR is responsible for maintaining a healthy relationship between the employees and the employer. They mediate disputes between employees and provide counselling to the employees. It helps in maintaining a productive and positive work environment.

Compliance

HR is responsible for ensuring that the organisation complies with all the legal and regulatory requirements. They keep up to date with the employment laws and regulations and ensure that the organisation complies with them.

Health and Safety

HR is responsible for ensuring the safety and health of the employees. They provide safety training, maintain a safe work environment, and provide medical assistance when required.

Employee Engagement

The topic has been discussed under separated heading in detail, in this chapter.

Diversity and Inclusion

HR is responsible for promoting diversity and inclusion in the workplace. They develop programs to attract a diverse pool

Copyrights 2023 Vocational Resources Australia. All Rights Reserved.

of candidates and ensure that the workplace is inclusive and free from discrimination.

Succession Planning
The topic has been discussed under separated heading in detail, in this chapter.

Copyrights 2023 Vocational Resources Australia. All Rights Reserved.

Human Resource Levelling

Human resource levelling, also known as job leveling or job grading, has become an essential aspect of modern organisations.

Human resource leveling is a strategic process that helps organisations to achieve their goals and objectives. It is essential because it helps to ensure that employees are fairly compensated for their skills and contributions, and that they have a clear path for professional growth and development within the organisation.

It also helps organisations to attract and retain top talent by providing competitive compensation and benefits packages.

Furthermore, it helps to create a transparent system for determining pay, benefits, and career advancement opportunities for employees.

Benefits

There are several benefits of human resource leveling for organisations. Some of the benefits include:

- Improved retention rates
  Human resource leveling helps to ensure that employees are fairly compensated for their skills and contributions. This, in turn, helps to improve retention rates by reducing turnover rates.

  When employees feel that they are being compensated fairly, they are more likely to stay with the organisation for the long term.

Copyrights 2023 Vocational Resources Australia. All Rights Reserved.

- Attracting top talent
  Human resource leveling helps to create a transparent system for determining pay, benefits, and career advancement opportunities for employees. This, in turn, helps to attract top talent to the organisation. When potential employees see that the organisation has a fair and transparent system for determining compensation and benefits, they are more likely to consider working for the organisation.

- Improved employee morale
  Human resource leveling helps to improve employee morale by ensuring that employees are compensated fairly for their skills and contributions. This, in turn, helps to create a positive work environment where employees feel valued and appreciated.

- Increased productivity
  Human resource leveling helps to increase productivity by providing employees with a clear path for professional growth and development. When employees see that there are opportunities for career advancement within the organisation, they are more likely to be motivated to work hard and increase their productivity.

Copyrights 2023 Vocational Resources Australia. All Rights Reserved.

Challenges

While human resource leveling has many benefits, it also has several challenges that organisations need to be aware of.

Some of the challenges include:

- Subjectivity
  Human resource leveling involves a certain degree of subjectivity. Different people may have different opinions on what constitutes a fair and transparent system for determining compensation and benefits. This can lead to disagreements and conflicts within the organisation.

- Cost
  Human resource leveling can be costly, particularly if the organisation decides to use an external consultant to conduct the job evaluation process. This can be a significant expense for small organisations with limited resources.

- Time-Consuming
  Human resource leveling can be a time-consuming process, particularly if the organisation has a large number of job positions that need to be evaluated. This can be a drain on the organisation's resources and can lead to delays in implementing the new compensation and benefits packages.

Copyrights 2023 Vocational Resources Australia. All Rights Reserved.

Methods

There are several different methods for conducting human resource leveling. Each method has its strengths and weaknesses, and organisations may choose the method that best fits their needs.

Some of the commonly used methods include:

Point-Factor Analysis

Point-factor analysis involves breaking down each job into individual factors or components, such as skill level, complexity, and responsibility, and assigning points to each one based on its importance.

This method is commonly used in organisations that have a large number of job positions with varying levels of responsibility and complexity.

It is also useful for organisations that need to create a uniform job evaluation system that can be applied across different departments and functions.

Job Evaluation

Job evaluation is a methodical process used to determine the comparative value of different jobs within an organisation, with the ultimate aim of creating a fair and equitable pay structure for all employees. HR departments, in collaboration with worker unions and other stakeholders such as commercial consultants, typically develop job evaluations.

One of the advantages of job evaluation is that it focuses solely on the characteristics of the job itself, rather than the

Copyrights 2023 Vocational Resources Australia. All Rights Reserved.

individual who holds the position. In this way, the relative value of a job can be assessed irrespective of the qualities of the job holder. A ranking system is typically used to determine the relative worth of each job, which corresponds to basic pay brackets or scales, also known as wage grids.

While personal qualities of the job holder, such as seniority, education level, and tenure, may impact their entitlement to higher steps within the applicable pay bracket, they are not taken into account during the job evaluation process.

Job evaluation relies on job analysis to gather accurate and relevant information about the duties, responsibilities, and requirements of each job. The information gathered from job analysis, such as job descriptions, is then used to evaluate the relative value and importance of each job within the organisation. This evaluation is based on various factors, such as the skills and knowledge required to perform the job, the level of responsibility, and the impact on the organisation's goals and objectives.

Once the jobs have been evaluated, they can be added to the organisation's pay structure, which ensures that each job is compensated fairly and equitably, based on its relative worth. This helps to promote pay transparency and equity, and can also help to prevent discrimination based on gender, ethnicity, or other factors.

Job Evaluation Methods

Job evaluation is the process of determining the relative value of different jobs within an organisation. The goal is to establish a fair and equitable pay structure that reflects the contributions of employees in different roles and positions.

Copyrights 2023 Vocational Resources Australia. All Rights Reserved.

There are several methods used for job evaluation, each with its unique advantages and disadvantages.

Here are a few of the most common ones:

Job Ranking

This is a simple method that involves ranking jobs from most to least important based on their overall significance to the organisation. While this method is easy to use and understand, it can be subjective and may not provide a detailed analysis of the various factors that contribute to job value.

Job Grading

This method involves assigning jobs to predetermined grades or levels based on predetermined criteria such as skill level, education, and experience. This method is more objective than job ranking, but it can also be inflexible and may not take into account the unique characteristics of individual jobs.

Point Factor

This method assigns points to different aspects of a job, such as skill level, responsibility, and working conditions. The total points for a job determine its overall value relative to other jobs within the organisation. This method is more comprehensive than the previous two methods and provides a more detailed analysis of job value. However, it can also be complex and time-consuming to implement.

Factor Comparison

This method is similar to point factor but involves comparing jobs to benchmark jobs to determine their relative value. The

Copyrights 2023 Vocational Resources Australia. All Rights Reserved.

benchmark jobs are chosen based on their importance to the organisation and the market value of their skills. This method is more flexible than point factor and can be adapted to changing organisational needs.

Market Pricing

Market pricing involves looking at external factors such as market demand, supply and demand of labour, and compensation trends for similar jobs in the industry.

This method is useful for organisations that want to ensure that their compensation packages are competitive with other organisations in the same industry. It is also useful for organisations that want to attract and retain top talent by offering competitive compensation and benefits packages.

Copyrights 2023 Vocational Resources Australia. All Rights Reserved.

Induction

When starting a new job, new employees can feel overwhelmed by the amount of information they need to learn in the first few weeks. To make the onboarding process smoother, it's important to develop a personalised induction program that helps new staff feel more at ease in their new work environment and gain a clearer understanding of the business and their role expectations.

An effective induction process plays a crucial role in familiarizing new employees with their job and the company. It's an opportunity to welcome new hires and support them as they adjust to their new role. Providing a well-designed induction program is considered a best practice to ensure that new employees understand the company's expectations, performance standards, and culture. This can contribute to higher employee retention rates and productivity, as new employees are able to contribute to the business more quickly. By completing a structured induction program, employees gain a better understanding of the company's operations.

The induction process typically consists of three stages:

- the pre-induction process,
- the induction, and
- the post-induction process or follow-up and ongoing development.

For employers an induction process can:

- Promotes a positive workplace culture by helping new employees' transition and assimilate into the workplace.

Copyrights 2023 Vocational Resources Australia. All Rights Reserved.

- Saves time and money for employers by allowing employees to partially self-educate through online learning modules.
- Encourages employee retention, reduces turnover, and saves on recruitment costs by making new hires feel welcome and valued.
- Ensures operational efficiency and increases productivity by giving employees a comprehensive understanding of the company and their role.
- Educates employees on compliance with company policies, procedures, and workplace health and safety.
- Enhances company reputation by creating a professional impression.

The benefits of employee induction for new staff are:

- The induction process accelerates new employees' adaptation to their role.
- New hires gain a deeper understanding of their role and its integration into the organisation.
- New starters feel appreciated, respected, and accepted into the team by their colleagues.
- New employees acquire a better comprehension of company processes and workplace policies and procedures.
- New staff receive important information about organisational culture and behavioural standards to assist with assimilation.
- The induction process facilitates effective communication with managers and team members.

Copyrights 2023 Vocational Resources Australia. All Rights Reserved.

Induction Checklist

An induction program serves the purpose of helping new employees settle into their new role at a company, business, or organisation. To ensure the success of the induction program, it's important to create a checklist that outlines all the documents and information new staff will receive on their first day of the job.

This checklist need not be extensive, but the induction should at least cover the following:

- An introduction to the business, colleagues, and important stakeholders, such as the team leader.
- An overview of the organisational history, structure, vision, culture, and values.
- A briefing on the employee handbook and reference to the code of conduct.
- A job description that includes the employee's title, roles, and responsibilities.
- A roster or work schedule.
- Copies of the employment agreement, company handbook, and HR manual.
- Work Health and Safety information, including the layout of premises, fire exits, first aid facilities, and an overview of WHS policies.
- Induction and setup of the workstation and systems.
- An overview of upcoming key dates and events.
- Provision of tools of trade, such as ID, keys, name badge, swipe card, phone, etc.
- A contact list of staff members.

At the conclusion of the induction, it's advisable to ask the employee if they have any queries or concerns that they

Copyrights 2023 Vocational Resources Australia. All Rights Reserved.

would like to address. Its best practice to provide the employee with ample written material that they can refer to later to refresh their understanding.

For compliance purposes, you should also ask the new employee to provide you with copies of the following documents:

- Signed employment contract
- Tax file declaration
- Choice of superannuation form
- Bank details (including bank, BSB, and account number)
- Emergency contact details (including name, address, phone number, and relationship)
- Licence, passport, and visa (if applicable)

Encouraging Social Interaction

Integrating new staff members into an established work environment can be a challenging task. It is recommended that on the new employee's first day, a tour of the workplace is given and introductions are made to other team members. Consider assigning a main point of contact from the team to offer guidance and support.

In addition to the customary introductions, the following activities may help foster social interaction:

- Conducting a group meeting and allowing everyone to introduce themselves to the new member

- Encouraging the team to create a "welcome card" or other written introduction

Copyrights 2023 Vocational Resources Australia. All Rights Reserved.

- Hosting an informal team lunch If your business is active on social media, consider welcoming the new team member with a brief online description or profile within your social media network.

It is essential to maintain efforts to encourage the new employee's social interaction even after the first few days.

Some individuals may require more time to become comfortable in their new environment. As a result, it is recommended to space out the above activities over several days to prevent overwhelming the employee.

Following Up

Managers can use the follow-up process to determine whether employees have successfully integrated, identify any additional resources or necessary changes, and assess whether further training is needed. The insights gained from this process can inform improvements to induction programs for future new hires.

After completing the formal induction, it is advisable to schedule regular meetings with the new employee to check on their progress and provide them with an opportunity to voice any concerns confidentially. It is important to address any issues promptly, whether they relate to job requirements, conflicts with colleagues, or negative experiences with customers, to ensure the employee's success and retention within the company.

Copyrights 2023 Vocational Resources Australia. All Rights Reserved.

Industrial Relations

Industrial relations refer to the relationship between employers and employees in the workplace. It involves the management of the employment relationship, including issues such as wages, working conditions, workplace safety, and employee rights.

It also includes the negotiation of collective bargaining agreements between employers and labour unions, as well as the resolution of disputes that may arise between the two parties.

In recent years, industrial relations have evolved significantly due to changing economic, social, and technological trends.

Here are some of the key trends that are shaping the future of industrial relations:

- Globalisation
  The globalisation of the economy has resulted in the expansion of cross-border trade, investment, and competition. This has contributed to the growth of multinational corporations that operate in multiple countries, creating new challenges for industrial relations.

- Technological advancements
  The emergence of new technologies such as artificial intelligence (AI) and automation is transforming the nature of work and the skills required by employees. This is leading to changes in the types of jobs available and the way work is organised, which can affect the employment relationship.

Copyrights 2023 Vocational Resources Australia. All Rights Reserved.

- Demographic changes
  The aging of the population, along with shifts in immigration patterns and family structures, is changing the composition of the workforce. This has implications for workplace diversity, inclusion, and the need for flexible work arrangements.

- Environmental concerns
  The increasing awareness of environmental issues is leading to demands for sustainable business practices. This can affect the employment relationship by creating new opportunities for green jobs and requiring employers to adopt environmentally responsible policies and practices.

- Political developments
  Changes in the political landscape, such as shifts in government policies and the rise of populism, can impact industrial relations by creating uncertainty and instability in the business environment.

Copyrights 2023 Vocational Resources Australia. All Rights Reserved.

Job Description

A job description is a document that outlines the primary tasks, responsibilities, and requirements of a particular job. It typically includes information about the position's title, the level of experience required, and the qualifications and skills needed to perform the job effectively.

A job description can include information about the duties and responsibilities that come with the role, as well as any specific requirements like certifications, licenses, or education. It can also provide information about the physical demands of the job, such as standing for extended periods or lifting heavy objects.

Overall, a job description provides a clear and detailed understanding of what is expected of someone in a certain role. It helps both the employer and the employee to have a shared understanding of the job's demands and requirements, which can lead to a smoother hiring and onboarding process.

Developing a Job Description

Here are the steps involved in developing a job description:

1. Conduct a job analysis
   Start by identifying the key tasks, responsibilities, and requirements of the position. Collect data through observation, interviews, and surveys to determine what the job entails.

2. Determine the job title
   The job title should be concise, accurate, and reflect the position's seniority level.

Copyrights 2023 Vocational Resources Australia. All Rights Reserved.

3. Write a job summary
   It should provide a brief overview of the role, its purpose, and how it contributes to the organisation.

4. List job duties
   Describe the specific tasks and responsibilities of the position. Use action verbs to make it clear what the job entails.

5. Specify job qualifications
   List the knowledge, skills, experience, education, and certifications required for the position.

6. Define physical requirements
   Describe the physical demands of the job, such as standing for long periods, lifting heavy objects, and working in hazardous conditions.

7. Include salary range
   Provide a salary range that is competitive and commensurate with the job responsibilities and requirements.

8. Get input from others
   Have relevant stakeholders, such as employees who currently hold the position, review and provide feedback on the job description.

9. Review and revise
   Make any necessary changes based on feedback and ensure that the job description is accurate, clear, and compliant with relevant laws and regulations.

Copyrights 2023 Vocational Resources Australia. All Rights Reserved.

Ensuring Compliance

Ensuring that a job description complies with legislation and other compliance requirements is important for any organisation. Here are some steps that can help:

- Check for relevant legislation
  The first step is to identify the relevant legislation that applies to the job. For example, there may be laws governing discrimination, the minimum wage, or working conditions. Check with your local government agency or legal counsel to identify the applicable legislation.

- Review job duties and responsibilities
  Once you have identified the relevant legislation, review the job duties and responsibilities to ensure they comply with the legislation. For example, if the job description includes physical requirements, ensure they comply with any disability discrimination laws.

- Avoid discriminatory language
  It's important to ensure that the job description does not include any discriminatory language that could be construed as discriminatory. Avoid language that could be seen as discriminatory based on race, gender, age, or any other protected characteristic.

- Use accurate job titles
  Ensure that the job title is accurate and reflects the actual job duties and responsibilities. This can help avoid any confusion or misinterpretation of the role.

Copyrights 2023 Vocational Resources Australia. All Rights Reserved.

- Set appropriate qualifications and requirements
  Ensure that any qualifications or requirements listed in the job description are necessary for the job and do not discriminate against any protected characteristic. For example, if a job requires a college degree, ensure that it is necessary for the job and not a way to discriminate against individuals who may not have had the opportunity to attend college.

- Include equal opportunity statement
  It is also important to include an equal opportunity statement in the job description. This statement expresses that the employer provides equal employment opportunities to all employees and applicants for employment without regard to race, colour, religion, sex, national origin, age, disability, or any other characteristic protected by law.

Copyrights 2023 Vocational Resources Australia. All Rights Reserved.

Motivation

Motivation refers to the process of encouraging and inspiring employees to work hard and contribute to the success of the organisation. It involves creating a positive work environment, recognising and rewarding good performance, providing opportunities for growth and development, and fostering a sense of purpose and belonging among team members. Motivated staff are more likely to be productive, engaged, and committed to achieving organisational goals.

Motivation is the driving force behind human actions and refers to the reason why a person engages in a certain activity. It is a process that triggers, guides, and sustains goal-oriented behaviours, such as losing weight or aiming for a job promotion. Motivation involves various factors, including biological, emotional, social, and cognitive forces that stimulate human behaviour.

Although not always directly observable, motivation directs and maintains goal-directed actions. To understand people's motives, we must often infer their reasons based on observable behaviours.

There are different types of motivation that we use in our daily lives. If you feel like you have lost motivation, there are ways to develop or enhance your self-motivation levels.

Having an understanding of motivation can:

- enhance your productivity while working towards your objectives;

Copyrights 2023 Vocational Resources Australia. All Rights Reserved.

- urge you to take necessary actions; inspire you to adopt health-promoting behaviours;
- prevent you from engaging in harmful or unproductive activities such as addiction or risk-taking;
- provide a sense of control over your life; and promote your overall well-being and happiness.

Likewise, employee motivation is crucial for the success of any organisation, as it determines the level of commitment, drive, and energy that employees bring to their roles on a daily basis. Without motivation, companies may suffer from reduced productivity, lower output levels, and failure to achieve important goals. However, tracking and maintaining employee motivation can be challenging, as not all tasks may be inherently interesting. Therefore, companies must find ways to keep their employees engaged and motivated, while also monitoring and nurturing their motivation levels.

An employee with low work motivation tends to work slowly, avoid tasks, and spend time on their phones. Their lack of focus and energy can be a waste of resources and may also affect the productivity of other employees. This can lead to the company failing to meet important targets or producing work of a lower quality. On the other hand, motivated employees are enthusiastic, driven, and take pride in their work. They complete tasks efficiently, take initiative, and strive to do their best for themselves and the company. Therefore, regardless of whether a company is already successful or working towards success, employee motivation plays a vital role. If motivation declines, revenue and productivity may soon follow suit.

Copyrights 2023 Vocational Resources Australia. All Rights Reserved.

Some specific advantages of motivation are:

- Higher productivity levels
  It's widely acknowledged that implementing motivation techniques for employees leads to better productivity and improved financial outcomes. However, what's often overlooked is that increased productivity also results in a better overall employee experience, leading to higher job satisfaction.

- More innovation.
  Motivation and rewards in the workplace also foster a culture of innovation, as employees who feel valued and supported by their organisation are more inclined to push themselves and take risks.

  Therefore, the significance of motivation in the workplace cannot be overstated, as it drives growth. Additionally, managers who understand which benefits motivate their teams tend to see the most positive outcomes.

- Lower levels of absenteeism.
  Recognising the significance of motivation in management means that leaders understand that supportive and non-critical management is the key to getting the best out of their teams. Managers who show care towards their teams' workload and wellbeing tend to experience lower levels of absence, as employees feel less stressed and overwhelmed.

- Lower levels of staff turnover.
  The correlation between employee benefits and motivation is evident, as they work in conjunction to

Copyrights 2023 Vocational Resources Australia. All Rights Reserved.

promote high retention rates. Offering employees additional perks and incentives to rewards is a strong motivator that can deter them from seeking employment elsewhere, particularly if the compensation package is superior to other companies.

Moreover, when organisations prioritise employee motivation, they often create a positive reputation and internal brand. This reputation takes time to establish and requires data-driven strategies that rely on feedback from employees. With a strong internal brand, businesses can retain and attract top talent, creating brand ambassadors who are happy and motivated within the workplace.

Improving Your Motivation

Everyone experiences changes in their level of motivation and determination. At times, you may feel inspired and intensely motivated to achieve your objectives, while at other times, you may feel lethargic or uncertain about your goals or how to reach them.

If you find yourself lacking motivation, there are steps you can take to boost your drive. To increase or enhance your motivation, you can do the following:

To boost your motivation when it's low, there are various steps you can take.

For instance:

- You can adjust your goals to concentrate on what's truly significant to you, rather than things that are of low importance.

Copyrights 2023 Vocational Resources Australia. All Rights Reserved.

- If a task feels too daunting, you can divide it into smaller, more achievable steps.
- Additionally, confidence is linked to motivation, so you can improve your self-confidence to enhance your ability to attain your objectives.
- Furthermore, reflecting on your accomplishments and strengths from the past can help you overcome self-doubt.
- Lastly, you can work on developing your skills and abilities in areas where you feel insecure to build your confidence.

Types of Motivation

Motivation is often classified into two main types: extrinsic and intrinsic.

Extrinsic motivation comes from external factors, such as receiving a reward, prize, or praise.

On the other hand, intrinsic motivation comes from within the individual and is driven by personal satisfaction, enjoyment, or fulfillment. An example of intrinsic motivation is solving a difficult crossword puzzle for the sheer satisfaction of completing it.

According to some research, there exists a third type of motivation called family motivation, which refers to the motivation to engage in certain behaviours in order to support one's family financially or otherwise. For instance, going to work even when one is not intrinsically motivated to do so.

Copyrights 2023 Vocational Resources Australia. All Rights Reserved.

Components of Motivation

Simply desiring to achieve a goal is not enough; persistence and endurance are necessary to overcome obstacles. Researchers have identified three main components of motivation: activation, persistence, and intensity. These components are essential for getting and staying motivated.

Activation refers to the initial decision to start a behaviour. An example of activation could be making the decision to enrol in psychology courses in order to earn a degree.

Persistence is the ability to continue making efforts towards a goal even in the face of challenges and obstacles. An example of persistence would be regularly attending your psychology class, even when feeling tired after staying up late the previous night.

Intensity refers to the amount of effort and concentration a person puts into pursuing a goal. For instance, one student might attend classes and complete assignments without much enthusiasm, while another student might actively participate in class discussions, seek out additional resources, and invest significant effort into their coursework. This greater level of engagement reflects higher intensity in pursuing their academic goals.

Each of the three components of motivation - activation, persistence, and intensity - play a crucial role in determining whether or not you will achieve your goals. A high level of activation will help you get started on pursuing your goal, while persistence and intensity are important for maintaining your motivation and continuing to work toward the goal even in the face of obstacles or setbacks. In other words, the

Copyrights 2023 Vocational Resources Australia. All Rights Reserved.

strength of each of these components will determine how much effort you put into achieving your goal and whether you ultimately succeed.

Causes of Low Motivation

There are some factors that can harm or limit your motivation levels. These include:

- Adopting an all-or-nothing mindset.
  If you believe that you must be perfect to achieve your goals, any small mistake or setback may demotivate you.

- Chasing after quick fixes.
  If you expect to reach your goals quickly, you may become demotivated when you realise that success takes time and effort.

- Assuming that one approach suits everyone.
  What works for someone else might not work for you, and trying to apply a method that does not fit your personality or style may reduce your motivation. If you don't feel motivated, consider exploring other approaches that might suit you better.

Copyrights 2023 Vocational Resources Australia. All Rights Reserved.

Motivation and Mental Health

Low motivation can certainly have a significant impact on our mental health. When we lack motivation, it can be challenging to get out of bed in the morning, follow through on goals or responsibilities, or engage in activities that we typically enjoy. This can lead to feelings of apathy, low mood, anxiety, and even depression.

Additionally, when we don't feel motivated, we may start to feel like we are not living up to our potential, or that we are not accomplishing the things we want to in life. This can have a negative impact on our self-esteem and overall sense of worth.

On the other hand, when we feel motivated and engaged in the things we do, we tend to feel more fulfilled, productive, and satisfied with life. This can have a positive impact on our mental health, boosting our self-esteem, and overall sense of well-being.

If you are struggling with low motivation, there are many ways to address this issue. Engaging in regular exercise, setting achievable goals, practicing mindfulness, and seeking support from a mental health professional can all be helpful strategies.

Copyrights 2023 Vocational Resources Australia. All Rights Reserved.

Theories of Motivation

Over the years, various theories have been put forward by psychologists to shed light on what drives human behaviour. The following are some of the major motivation theories.

Instinct Theory

According to the instinct theory of motivation, behaviour is driven by innate and fixed patterns of behaviour called instincts. Prominent psychologists such as William James, Sigmund Freud, and William McDougall have proposed various basic human drives or instincts that motivate behaviour. These include biological instincts that are crucial for an organism's survival, such as fear, cleanliness, and love.

Drives and Needs Theory

Biology plays a significant role in motivating behaviours such as eating, drinking, and sleeping. These behaviours are driven by our biological needs for food, water, and rest, which are crucial for our survival. According to the drive reduction theory of motivation, people have these basic biological drives, and our actions are motivated by the need to satisfy these drives. Another theory, proposed by Abraham Maslow, is the hierarchy of needs theory, which states that once we meet our basic physiological needs, our motivation expands to other needs such as safety, socialisation, self-esteem, and self-actualisation.

Arousal Theory

According to the arousal theory of motivation, individuals are motivated to participate in activities that help them maintain their optimal level of arousal. For example, those with low arousal needs may prefer relaxing activities such as reading

Copyrights 2023 Vocational Resources Australia. All Rights Reserved.

a book, while those with high arousal needs may seek out exciting and adventurous activities like motorcycle racing.

Improving the Motivation Levels

To enhance employee satisfaction, it's crucial to start with improving their motivation levels.

Here are the top ten measures you can take to keep your employees engaged and invested in their work:

- Lead with a vision.
  Having a clear vision for the company is crucial in motivating employees. Knowing the next step and what success looks like gives direction and purpose to their efforts. A well-defined destination can inspire and drive employees to work towards achieving it.

- Make sure everyone understands the 'why'.
  It is important to ensure that your employees understand the purpose behind the tasks they are performing. While they may know what needs to be done, you should also communicate the "why" behind each task, which is the company's overall mission. When employees understand how their individual actions can contribute to the company's overall goal, it brings a sense of intrinsic motivation to even the most basic tasks.

- Set frequent clear targets.
  While it's important to have big targets, smaller goals can be more motivating for employees. These smaller goals should contribute to the overall target, but breaking them down into achievable chunks can make them feel less daunting. When employees consistently meet these

Copyrights 2023 Vocational Resources Australia. All Rights Reserved.

smaller goals, it creates a sense of accomplishment and satisfaction that can motivate them to continue working towards the next set of goals.

- Recognise and reward great work.
  Showing appreciation and recognition for employees' hard work is crucial in boosting their motivation and team morale. A recognition platform can be a helpful tool in celebrating star performers who embody the company's values.

  In addition to this, supporting employees throughout the year with team-building exercises, wellbeing schemes, secondment opportunities, and EAP programs can also boost motivation. However, for special occasions such as work anniversaries or employee of the month, it's recommended to go the extra mile and provide rewards.

  Rewards don't always have to be monetary, and gestures like giving them a day off can be equally effective. Rewards are excellent motivators and can significantly enhance job satisfaction, encouraging employees to go the extra mile in their work.

- Give your team autonomy.
  Having control over their time and energy is crucial for employees to feel motivated. If they feel like they are constantly under pressure and have no flexibility in their work schedule, it can lead to a drop in motivation.

  One way to address this issue is to provide some level of freedom in the workplace, such as flexible working hours or unlimited time off. When employees are trusted to

Copyrights 2023 Vocational Resources Australia. All Rights Reserved.

manage their own time, they feel more satisfied and motivated to do their best work. This sense of control also contributes to a greater sense of achievement and fulfilment when they complete tasks or meet targets.

- Create a welcoming workplace environment.
  Creating a positive work environment is crucial for employee motivation. A workplace with a friendly culture, comfortable break areas, and opportunities for leisure activities can make employees excited to come to work.

  The idea of "work hard, play hard" is relevant here. A negative mood can impact productivity and motivation, so it's important to foster a positive and enjoyable atmosphere in the workplace.

- Offer impressive benefits.
  Creating a positive work environment is crucial for maintaining employee motivation. To achieve this, companies can offer employee benefits and perks that aim to improve their employees' lives both in and outside of work. This includes perks platforms that offer a wide range of benefits, as well as fringe benefits that are tailored to meet employees' specific needs. For example, if employees live in London, they may require a London weighted allowance. Providing such benefits can boost employee morale and foster a sense of loyalty to the company.

- Encourage teamwork.
  Encouraging collaboration between teams within the company can lead to the development of better ideas. Working alongside colleagues with different skill sets can

Copyrights 2023 Vocational Resources Australia. All Rights Reserved.

result in more innovative and creative outcomes. When individuals are part of a team, they can feel supported and motivated by their colleagues, helping to boost their own motivation levels.

- Create a career path.
  It's natural for individuals to seek growth and development in their career. To keep your employees motivated, it's important to have open conversations with them about their career aspirations and goals. By collaborating on designing a clear career path and outlining the necessary steps to achieve it, employees will have a sense of direction and purpose. This will help create the drive to progress within the company, and feel fulfilled by a long and productive journey ahead.

- Support staff motivation by supporting employee wellbeing.
  When it comes to implementing strategies to boost employee motivation or incentives, companies often neglect the importance of employee well-being. While it is true that offering rewards can be a powerful motivator, employees who are experiencing fatigue or stress may not be able to perform their best, no matter how hard they try.

  Therefore, it is crucial for companies to adopt a comprehensive approach to employee well-being, which includes addressing their mental, emotional, and physical health needs, in order to ensure that they remain healthy, happy, and productive.

Copyrights 2023 Vocational Resources Australia. All Rights Reserved.

Measuring Employee Motivation

there are several methods to measure employee motivation.

Here are some of them:

- Surveys
  Conducting surveys is a common method to measure employee motivation. You can either create your own survey questions or use a pre-made survey tool. Surveys can help you collect data on what motivates employees, what demotivates them, and how satisfied they are with their work environment.

- Feedback sessions
  Feedback sessions can also be used to measure employee motivation. By having one-on-one discussions with employees, you can gather information on how motivated they are, what they are passionate about, and what changes could improve their motivation.

- Performance reviews
  Performance reviews can provide valuable insights into employee motivation. By reviewing an employee's performance, you can understand how motivated they are, what motivates them, and what areas they need to improve.

- Goal setting
  Setting goals and tracking progress is an effective way to measure employee motivation. When employees have clear goals to work towards, they can remain motivated and engaged. You can track their progress towards these goals and adjust as needed.

Copyrights 2023 Vocational Resources Australia. All Rights Reserved.

- Recognition and rewards
  Recognising and rewarding employees for their hard work and achievements can be a motivational boost. This can include bonuses, promotions, or even just public recognition for a job well done.

Copyrights 2023 Vocational Resources Australia. All Rights Reserved.

Onboarding

The onboarding process is a critical stage in any organisation's talent management strategy. A well-structured onboarding program can help new hires feel confident, engaged and ready to contribute to the organisation's success.

A positive onboarding experience can lead to increased employee satisfaction, engagement, and motivation. It can also reduce the time it takes for new hires to become productive, thereby enhancing the organisation's bottom line.

There are several key benefits of an effective onboarding process, such as:

- Improved retention rates.
  Research shows that effective onboarding can significantly improve retention rates. According to a study by Glassdoor, organisations with a strong onboarding process improve new hire retention rates by 82%.

- Increased productivity.
  An effective onboarding process can significantly reduce the time it takes for new hires to become productive. This can lead to increased efficiency and improve the organisation's bottom line.

- Enhanced employee engagement.
  A positive onboarding experience can improve employee engagement by fostering a sense of belonging and connection to the organisation.

Copyrights 2023 Vocational Resources Australia. All Rights Reserved.

- Improved employer branding.
  A well-designed onboarding program can help organisations establish a positive employer brand by showcasing the organisation's culture, values, and mission.

Best Practices

Some of the best practices in onboarding are:

- Define clear goals and objectives
  Before designing an onboarding program, it's essential to define clear goals and objectives. This includes establishing the desired outcomes of the onboarding process, such as improved retention rates or increased productivity.

- Involve key stakeholders
  Involve key stakeholders in the design and implementation of the onboarding program. This can include HR, managers, and other team members who will be responsible for supporting new hires.

- Customise the onboarding process
  Customise the onboarding process to meet the needs of each new hire and their role. This includes tailoring the training and development program to meet the specific needs of each employee.

- Leverage technology
  Leverage technology to streamline the onboarding process and provide new hires with access to necessary resources and tools. This can include using an HR information system (HRIS) to automate onboarding tasks

Copyrights 2023 Vocational Resources Australia. All Rights Reserved.

and provide new hires with access to necessary information.

- Measure and evaluate
  Measure and evaluate the effectiveness of the onboarding program regularly. This includes tracking retention rates, productivity, and employee engagement. Use this feedback to continuously improve the onboarding process and ensure that it remains effective.

Key Elements

Pre-onboarding

The pre-onboarding stage involves preparing new hires for their first day and setting expectations for the onboarding process. This includes sending pre-boarding materials, such as an employee handbook, welcome letter, and information about the company's culture, values, and mission.

Orientation

The orientation stage involves introducing new hires to the organisation's culture, values, and mission. This includes providing a tour of the workplace, introducing new hires to their colleagues, and providing an overview of the organisation's history, structure, and goals.

Training

This topic has been discussed in detail under "training & Development" section.

Feedback and Evaluation

The feedback and evaluation stage involves providing new hires with regular feedback and evaluation to ensure that

Copyrights 2023 Vocational Resources Australia. All Rights Reserved.

they are meeting the organisation's expectations. This can include regular performance reviews, coaching, and feedback from peers and supervisors.

Ongoing support

The ongoing support stage involves providing new hires with ongoing support to help them succeed in their role. This can include mentoring, coaching, and development opportunities.

It also involves providing new hires with opportunities to connect with colleagues and become involved in the organisation's culture.

Methods

There are several onboarding methods that companies use. Some of them are outlined below:

- Formal orientation
  This is a common method used by companies to introduce new hires to the company culture, mission, and policies. Formal orientation includes presentations on company values, policies, and benefits, and often includes a tour of the office or facilities.

- Buddy system
  The buddy system pairs a new employee with a more experienced employee who can help them learn the ropes of the company culture, policies, and procedures. This method allows the new hire to get personalised attention and guidance.

  It also helps them form a connection with someone in the company.

Copyrights 2023 Vocational Resources Australia. All Rights Reserved.

- Self-directed learning
  With this method, new hires are given access to company resources such as manuals, videos, and online courses to learn about the company's policies and procedures. This method allows the new hire to take responsibility for their own learning and can also be cost-effective for the company.

- E-Learning
  E-learning is a form of self-directed learning that uses technology to deliver training and education. Online courses, webinars, and videos are popular forms of e-learning, and they can be accessed from anywhere with an internet connection.

- On-the-job training
  This method involves new employees learning on the job by shadowing experienced employees and gradually taking on more responsibilities. This method allows the new hire to learn in a hands-on, real-world environment, and can help them build relationships with their colleagues.

Copyrights 2023 Vocational Resources Australia. All Rights Reserved.

Performance Management

Performance management is a process used by organisations to measure, monitor, and improve the performance of their employees. It aims to improve organisational effectiveness by aligning individual and team goals with the overall objectives of the organisation. In this essay, we will discuss performance management in detail.

Performance management can be defined as a continuous and systematic process that involves setting goals, measuring progress, providing feedback, and making adjustments to improve performance. It is a proactive and ongoing process that is designed to enhance the performance of individuals, teams, and the organisation as a whole.

Performance management has several benefits for both employees and employers. These benefits include:

- Improved performance
  Performance management helps to improve the performance of employees by setting clear goals, providing regular feedback, and supporting employees to achieve their potential.

- Increased motivation
  Performance management helps to increase motivation levels among employees by providing them with clear expectations, feedback, and recognition for their work.

- Enhanced communication
  Performance management promotes communication between employees and employers, which helps to build

Copyrights 2023 Vocational Resources Australia. All Rights Reserved.

stronger relationships and promotes a positive work culture.

- Better decision making
  Performance management provides employers with valuable information on employee performance, which can be used to make better decisions regarding promotions, rewards, and training.

- Employee development
  Performance management helps to identify the training and development needs of employees, which can be used to provide them with the necessary support to improve their skills.

Components of Performance Management

Performance management consists of several components that work together to achieve the desired outcomes.

These components include:

Goals

Goals provide a framework for employees to work towards and achieve.

Goals can help to:

- Align employee efforts with the company's overall objectives.
  When employees know what the company is trying to achieve, they can focus their efforts on contributing to those goals.

Copyrights 2023 Vocational Resources Australia. All Rights Reserved.

- Increase motivation and engagement.
  Employees are more likely to be motivated and engaged in their work when they have clear goals to work towards.

- Provide a sense of direction and purpose.
  Goals can help employees feel like they are part of something bigger than themselves and that their work is making a difference.

- Track progress and identify areas for improvement.
  Goals can be used to track employee progress and identify areas where they need to improve. This information can then be used to provide feedback and development opportunities.

- Make performance reviews more objective.
  When goals are clearly defined, performance reviews can be more objective and fair. This is because the focus is on whether or not the employee has achieved their goals, rather than on their personal qualities or characteristics.

Overall, goals are an essential part of employee performance management. They can help to improve employee motivation, engagement, and performance.

Here are some additional benefits of goal setting in the context of employee performance management:

- Improved communication
  Goal setting can help to improve communication between employees and managers. When employees know what is expected of them, they are more likely to communicate

Copyrights 2023 Vocational Resources Australia. All Rights Reserved.

openly and honestly with their managers about their progress.

- Increased accountability
  Goal setting can help to increase accountability among employees. When employees have specific goals to work towards, they are more likely to take responsibility for their own performance.

- Enhanced teamwork
  Goal setting can help to enhance teamwork among employees. When employees are working towards common goals, they are more likely to collaborate and support each other.

- Improved decision-making
  Goal setting can help to improve decision-making among employees. When employees have a clear understanding of the company's goals, they are more likely to make decisions that are aligned with those goals.

- Increased productivity
  Goal setting can help to increase productivity among employees. When employees are focused on achieving their goals, they are more likely to work efficiently and effectively.

Copyrights 2023 Vocational Resources Australia. All Rights Reserved.

Performance Measurement

Performance measurement involves tracking progress against the set goals. It can be done through regular performance reviews, self-assessment, peer assessment, and other methods.

Role of KPIs in Performance Measurement

Key Performance Indicators (KPIs) are measurable values that track the progress of an employee towards their goals. They can be used to measure a variety of things, such as productivity, quality, customer satisfaction, and safety.

KPIs play an important role in employee performance measurement because they provide a way to track progress over time and identify areas where improvement is needed. They can also be used to compare the performance of different employees or teams.

When choosing KPIs, it is important to select metrics that are relevant to the employee's role and goals.

The KPIs should also be measurable, so that progress can be tracked over time. In addition, the KPIs should be specific, so that it is clear what is being measured.

Once KPIs have been selected, they need to be tracked on a regular basis. This will help to ensure that the employee is on track to meet their goals. If the KPIs are not being met, then corrective action can be taken.

KPIs can be a valuable tool for improving employee performance. By tracking progress over time and identifying areas where improvement is needed, KPIs can help

Copyrights 2023 Vocational Resources Australia. All Rights Reserved.

employees to achieve their goals and contribute to the success of the organisation.

Here are some of the benefits of using KPIs in employee performance measurement:

- Improved goal setting
  KPIs can help employees to set clear and measurable goals. This can lead to increased focus and motivation.

- Increased accountability
  KPIs can help to hold employees accountable for their performance. This can lead to improved performance and productivity.

- Improved feedback
  KPIs can provide employees with regular feedback on their performance. This can help them to identify areas where they can improve and develop their skills.

- Increased motivation
  KPIs can help to motivate employees by providing them with a sense of accomplishment and recognition. This can lead to increased job satisfaction and productivity.

Here are some examples of KPIs that can be used to measure employee performance:

- Productivity
  Number of units produced, number of sales calls made, number of customer service tickets resolved.

Copyrights 2023 Vocational Resources Australia. All Rights Reserved.

- Quality
  Number of defects, number of customer complaints, number of accidents.

- Customer satisfaction
  Customer satisfaction surveys, customer feedback.

- Safety
  Number of lost-time accidents, number of near misses.

These are just a few examples, and the specific KPIs that are used will vary depending on the role of the employee and the goals of the organisation.

It is important to note that KPIs should not be used in isolation. They should be used in conjunction with other performance management tools, such as performance reviews, to get a complete picture of an employee's performance.

Feedback

Feedback is an essential part of employee performance management. It allows managers to assess employee performance, identify areas for improvement, and provide guidance on how to achieve goals. Feedback can also help to motivate employees and boost morale.

There are many benefits to providing regular feedback to employees. Here are a few of the most important:

- Improves performance
  Feedback can help employees to identify areas where they can improve their performance. By providing

Copyrights 2023 Vocational Resources Australia. All Rights Reserved.

specific, actionable feedback, managers can help employees to set goals and develop strategies for achieving them.

- Increases motivation
  Feedback can help to motivate employees by showing them that their work is valued and that they are making a contribution to the team or organisation. When employees feel appreciated and valued, they are more likely to be motivated to perform at their best.

- Boosts morale
  Feedback can help to boost morale by creating a positive and supportive work environment. When employees feel like they are part of a team and that their contributions are important, they are more likely to be happy and engaged in their work.

There are a few things to keep in mind when providing feedback to employees.

- First, it is important to be specific and provide examples to illustrate your points.

- Second, it is important to be constructive and offer suggestions for improvement.

- Finally, it is important to be timely and provide feedback as soon as possible after the event or behaviour that you are commenting on.

Giving and receiving feedback can be a challenging task, but it is an essential part of employee performance

Copyrights 2023 Vocational Resources Australia. All Rights Reserved.

management. By providing regular, constructive feedback, managers can help employees to improve their performance, increase motivation, and boost morale.

Here are some tips for giving feedback:

- Be specific and provide examples
  Don't just say "good job" or "you need to improve." Instead, give specific examples of what the employee did well or what they could do better.

- Be constructive
  Focus on the employee's behaviour, not their personality. Offer suggestions for improvement, but don't be critical.

- Be timely
  Don't wait until the end of the year to give feedback. Provide feedback as soon as possible after the event or behaviour that you are commenting on.

Here are some tips for receiving feedback:

- Be open-minded
  Don't be defensive when you receive feedback. Instead, listen to what the person has to say and try to see things from their perspective.

- Ask questions
  If you don't understand something, ask for clarification.

- Be willing to change
  If the feedback is constructive, be willing to make changes. Thank the person for their feedback. Feedback

Copyrights 2023 Vocational Resources Australia. All Rights Reserved.

can be helpful, but it can also be difficult to hear. Thank the person for their feedback and let them know that you appreciate their input.

Rewards and Recognition

Reward and recognition are important components of employee performance management. They can help to motivate employees, improve performance, and create a positive work environment.

Rewards can be tangible or intangible. Tangible rewards include things like bonuses, raises, and promotions. Intangible rewards include things like verbal praise, public recognition, and opportunities for professional development.

Recognition is the act of acknowledging and appreciating an employee's contributions. It can be done informally, such as through a quick thank-you note or a public shoutout, or it can be done more formally, such as through a company award or a public ceremony.

Rewards and recognition can be used to:

- Motivate employees
  When employees are rewarded for their good performance, they are more likely to continue to perform well. Rewards can also help to motivate employees to achieve goals.

- Improve performance
  Rewards and recognition can help to improve employee performance by providing feedback and motivation.

Copyrights 2023 Vocational Resources Australia. All Rights Reserved.

When employees know that their good work is being noticed, they are more likely to continue to do good work.

- Create a positive work environment
  A positive work environment is one where employees feel appreciated and valued. Rewards and recognition can help to create a positive work environment by showing employees that their work is important and that they are making a contribution to the team or organisation.

It is important to note that not all rewards and recognition programs are created equal. For a program to be effective, it must be:

- Well-designed
  The program should be aligned with the organisation's goals and objectives. It should also be fair and equitable, and it should be communicated effectively to employees.

- Consistent
  The program should be consistently applied to all employees.

- Meaningful
  The rewards and recognition should be meaningful to the employees.

By following these guidelines, organisations can create reward and recognition programs that are effective in motivating employees, improving performance, and creating a positive work environment.

Copyrights 2023 Vocational Resources Australia. All Rights Reserved.

Here are some examples of rewards and recognition programs:

- Bonuses
  Bonuses are a common form of financial reward. They are typically paid out based on individual or team performance.

- Raises
  Raises are another form of financial reward. They are typically given out annually, based on performance and other factors.

- Promotions
  Promotions are a form of non-financial reward. They provide employees with new opportunities and responsibilities.

- Verbal praise
  Verbal praise is a form of informal recognition. It can be given by managers, peers, or customers.

- Public recognition
  Public recognition is a form of formal recognition. It can be given at company meetings, in newsletters, or on social media.

- Opportunities for professional development
  Opportunities for professional development are a form of recognition that can help employees improve their skills and knowledge. They can include things like tuition reimbursement, training programs, and conferences.

Copyrights 2023 Vocational Resources Australia. All Rights Reserved.

Performance Improvement Plans (PIPs)

PIP is a tool used by employers to help employees improve their performance and meet the organisation's expectations. It is a formal document that outlines specific goals and objectives for the employee to achieve within a certain timeframe.

The plan is used when the employee's performance is not meeting the required level and the employer wants to give them the opportunity to improve before taking any disciplinary action.

The PIP typically includes the following components:

- Background information
  This includes details about the employee's role, responsibilities, and performance issues that led to the need for a PIP.

- Goals and objectives
  The PIP should list SMART goals and objectives.

- Action steps
  The plan should also outline specific actions that the employee should take to achieve the goals and objectives. These may include training, coaching, shadowing, or other interventions.

- Timeline
  The PIP should include a specific timeline for achieving the goals and objectives. This should be a reasonable timeframe, usually ranging from 30 to 90 days.

Copyrights 2023 Vocational Resources Australia. All Rights Reserved.

- Monitoring and feedback
  The PIP should outline how progress will be measured and monitored. This may include regular check-ins with a supervisor or manager, progress reports, or other feedback mechanisms.

The purpose of the PIP is to give the employee a clear understanding of what is expected of them, and what actions they need to take to improve their performance. It is important that the PIP is communicated clearly and effectively to the employee so that they understand the requirements and feel supported in achieving the goals.

When developing a PIP, it is important to focus on the areas where improvement is needed, and to be specific about the actions that the employee needs to take to improve. The goals should be achievable, but also challenging enough to motivate the employee to improve their performance.

It is also important to provide support to the employee during the PIP process. This may include training, coaching, or mentoring, as well as regular feedback and check-ins. The supervisor or manager should be available to answer questions and provide guidance as needed.

At the end of the PIP timeframe, the employee's performance should be evaluated to determine whether they have met the goals and objectives outlined in the plan.

If the employee has successfully improved their performance to meet the required level, the PIP can be closed. If the employee has not met the goals and objectives, further

Copyrights 2023 Vocational Resources Australia. All Rights Reserved.

action may be required, such as additional coaching or disciplinary action.

Performance Appraisal

Performance appraisal is a systematic evaluation of an employee's job performance and productivity within an organisation. It is a crucial process that helps to identify an employee's strengths, weaknesses, areas for improvement, and overall contribution to the organisation.

Performance appraisal is typically conducted annually, although some organisations may conduct it bi-annually or quarterly.

Performance appraisal has several benefits for both the employee and the organisation. It helps to:

- Identify employee strengths and weaknesses
- Improve employee performance
- Provide feedback to employees
- Align employee goals with organisational objectives
- Track employee progress
- Identify training and development needs
- Provide a basis for employee rewards and recognition.

Steps

1. Goal setting
   The first step in the performance appraisal process is setting up SMART goals. The employee and the manager should work together to set goals that align with the organisation's overall objectives.

Copyrights 2023 Vocational Resources Australia. All Rights Reserved.

2. Performance monitoring
   Once the goals are set, the employee's performance is monitored throughout the year. The manager should provide regular feedback on the employee's performance and provide guidance on areas for improvement.

3. Self-evaluation
   The employee should also evaluate their own performance and provide input on their strengths and weaknesses.

4. Performance review
   Discussed in detail as a sub-heading on following pages.

5. Performance improvement plan
   Discussed in detail as a sub-heading on following pages.

6. Performance appraisal documentation
   All performance appraisal information should be documented and stored in the employee's personnel file. This documentation includes the employee's goals, performance evaluations, and any performance improvement plans.

Copyrights 2023 Vocational Resources Australia. All Rights Reserved.

Methods

There are several methods available for performance appraisal. Commonly used ones are discussed below:

Rating scales

This method evaluates an employee's performance using a numerical rating system. The employee is rated on various job-related criteria, such as quality of work, productivity, and attendance.

360-degree feedback

This method involves collecting feedback from the employee's supervisor, peers, subordinates, and customers. The feedback is used to provide a comprehensive evaluation of the employee's performance.

Behavioural observation

This method involves observing the employee's behaviour on the job and evaluating their performance based on specific job-related behaviours.

Narrative method

This method involves writing a narrative description of the employee's performance. The narrative includes specific examples of the employee's strengths and weaknesses.

Copyrights 2023 Vocational Resources Australia. All Rights Reserved.

Performance Management Cycle

The performance management cycle is a process that organisations use to evaluate and improve the performance of their employees. It typically consists of several stages, including:

- Planning
  This stage involves setting goals and objectives for each employee or team. These goals should be specific, measurable, achievable, relevant, and time-bound (SMART).

- Monitoring
  During this stage, managers and employees track progress toward their goals and objectives. This can include regular check-ins, performance metrics, and other tools to evaluate performance.

- Developing
  If an employee is not meeting their goals, this stage involves identifying areas for improvement and developing a plan to address these issues. This may include training, coaching, or other interventions.

- Rating
  At the end of the performance cycle, managers typically assign a rating or score to each employee based on their performance. This rating can help inform decisions about promotions, bonuses, and other rewards.

- Rewarding
  The final stage of the performance management cycle involves rewarding employees for their performance. This

Copyrights 2023 Vocational Resources Australia. All Rights Reserved.

can include bonuses, promotions, or other incentives for meeting or exceeding their goals.

Performance Management Process

The performance management process consists of several stages, including:

- Planning
  The planning stage involves setting goals and expectations for the employee. It includes defining the key performance indicators (KPIs) that will be used to measure progress.

- Monitoring
  The monitoring stage involves tracking the progress of the employee against the set goals. It can be done through regular performance reviews, self-assessment, or other methods.

- Feedback
  The feedback stage involves providing regular feedback to the employee. It can be done through one-on-one meetings, performance reviews, or other methods.

- Evaluation
  The evaluation stage involves assessing the performance of the employee against the set goals. It helps to identify areas where the employee has performed well and areas where improvement is needed.

Copyrights 2023 Vocational Resources Australia. All Rights Reserved.

- Development
  The development stage involves identifying the training and development needs of the employee. It can be done through training, coaching, or other methods.

Performance Management within a Team

Performance management within a team is a critical component of achieving organisational goals and objectives. It involves the process of identifying, measuring, and developing the performance of individuals within a team to ensure that they are meeting their goals and contributing to the success of the team as a whole.

When every team member is working towards a common goal, the team can achieve more than any individual could on their own.

Performance management allows for the identification of KPIs that are essential to achieving team goals. It also ensures that each team member is aware of their role in achieving those goals and has access to the resources and support needed to succeed.

Strategies for Effective Performance Management

There are several strategies that can be used to effectively manage team performance. These include:

- Communication
  Open and honest communication is essential for effective performance management. Regular communication helps team members stay informed about team goals, progress, and challenges.

Copyrights 2023 Vocational Resources Australia. All Rights Reserved.

- Collaboration
  Encouraging collaboration helps team members work together effectively towards a common goal. Collaboration can help identify new ideas, approaches, and solutions to problems.

- Recognition and rewards
  Recognising team members' achievements and providing rewards for outstanding performance can help motivate and engage team members.

- Accountability
  Holding team members accountable for their performance and ensuring that they are empowered to take ownership of their work is key to effective performance management.

- Continuous improvement
  Encouraging a culture of continuous improvement helps team members identify areas for improvement and work together to implement changes that can enhance their performance.

Performance Review

Performance reviews are an essential aspect of performance management in organisations. They provide an opportunity for employees and their managers to assess performance, discuss strengths and weaknesses, set goals, and plan for future development.

There are several different approaches to performance reviews, including traditional annual reviews, ongoing feedback and coaching, and 360-degree feedback. Each

Copyrights 2023 Vocational Resources Australia. All Rights Reserved.

approach has its advantages and disadvantages, and the right approach will depend on the organisation's culture and goals.

Traditional performance reviews are the most common approach to performance reviews. They typically involve a structured meeting between the employee and their manager, during which the manager provides feedback on the employee's performance over the past year. The feedback may be based on specific goals and objectives set at the beginning of the year, or it may be more general in nature.

One advantage of traditional annual reviews is that they provide a formal opportunity for employees to receive feedback on their performance. This feedback can help employees understand how they are doing and identify areas for improvement. Additionally, annual reviews can help managers identify high-performing employees and provide them with opportunities for development and advancement.

However, one of the disadvantages of traditional annual reviews is that they can be time-consuming and difficult to schedule. Additionally, they often focus on past performance rather than future development, which can limit their effectiveness in driving performance improvement.

Another approach to performance reviews is ongoing feedback and coaching. With this approach, managers provide regular feedback and coaching to employees throughout the year. This can involve informal conversations, check-ins, and coaching sessions designed to help employees improve their performance.

Copyrights 2023 Vocational Resources Australia. All Rights Reserved.

One advantage of ongoing feedback and coaching is that it provides timely feedback to employees, which can help them improve their performance more quickly. Additionally, it allows for more frequent communication between managers and employees, which can help build stronger relationships and improve overall performance.

However, one of the challenges of ongoing feedback and coaching is that it can be time-consuming for managers. Additionally, it can be difficult to ensure that all employees receive regular feedback, which can create inconsistency and inequity.

A third approach to performance reviews is 360-degree feedback. With this approach, employees receive feedback from a variety of sources, including their manager, peers, subordinates, and customers or clients. This feedback can provide a more comprehensive view of an employee's performance and help them identify areas for improvement.

One advantage of 360-degree feedback is that it provides a more holistic view of an employee's performance. Additionally, it can help promote a culture of feedback and collaboration within an organisation.

However, one of the challenges of 360-degree feedback is that it can be difficult to implement effectively. It requires a significant amount of planning and coordination to ensure that feedback is collected and shared in a way that is fair and consistent.

In order to make performance reviews more effective:

Copyrights 2023 Vocational Resources Australia. All Rights Reserved.

- Set clear objectives
  Begin by setting clear objectives and expectations for the performance review. This will help the employee understand what the review process entails and what they are being evaluated on.

- Prepare feedback
  Prepare feedback in advance of the review. Think about the employee's strengths and weaknesses and how they can improve in areas where they need development.

- Be specific
  When providing feedback, be specific about what the employee did well and where they can improve. Avoid vague or general statements that may not be helpful to the employee.

- Encourage self-evaluation
  Encourage the employee to evaluate their own performance and provide feedback on what they think they did well and how they can improve.

- Set goals
  Set clear goals for the employee to work towards in the coming year. These goals should be specific, measurable, achievable, relevant, and time bound.

- Follow-up
  Follow-up on the review with the employee periodically to check on their progress and offer support as needed.

Copyrights 2023 Vocational Resources Australia. All Rights Reserved.

Making Performance Reviews More Effective

The following strategies can be applied to make performance reviews more effective.

- Reflect on the past but focus on the future.
  Traditional performance reviews tend to focus solely on past behaviour and performance, which is essential but insufficient for improving future performance. To drive continuous performance improvement, performance conversations must provide employees with opportunities to address and correct their performance in real-time and ensure their work aligns with organisational goals.

  Emphasising future-focused performance reviews also aligns with employees' expectations for more feedback and development opportunities. Employees desire timely feedback to improve their performance on an ongoing basis instead of solely relying on annual performance reviews. They also appreciate when managers demonstrate a genuine interest in their future, whether that involves continuing with the organisation or pursuing other opportunities.

- Ask the right performance review questions.
  Asking the right questions during a performance review is crucial for maintaining focus on topics that are essential to your employees' and organisation's success. Utilising a performance review template that prompts honest feedback and actionable improvement strategies can be an effective tool.

  Consider incorporating the following questions into your performance review:

Copyrights 2023 Vocational Resources Australia. All Rights Reserved.

- Which accomplishment(s) from the last quarter are you most proud of?
- What goals do you have for the upcoming quarter?
- What development goals would you like to set for the next six months?
- What obstacles do you face that impede your progress?
- What has been the impact of your performance on the team and the organisation?
- How can I improve as your manager?

Managers who approach performance conversations from an evaluation perspective may inadvertently make employees feel like they are being judged. Instead, use these questions to adopt a coaching mentality. Encourage employees to ask questions of their own, and work collaboratively to help them achieve their objectives.

- Choose your phrases carefully.
  When engaging in a performance conversation with your employees, it is important to be mindful of your choice of words as they can either inspire or demotivate your employees. To ensure that your words have a positive impact, you should take the time to prepare and be thoughtful in your approach.

  In choosing effective performance review phrases, you should:

Copyrights 2023 Vocational Resources Australia. All Rights Reserved.

    - Use specific language to provide clarity and context.

    - Use measurement-oriented language to quantify results and achievements.

    - Use powerful action words to convey impact and encourage action.

    - Stay positive and constructive to promote growth and development.
    - Focus on solving problems rather than just pointing them out.

    - Look for opportunities for growth and development.

    - Focus on the individual and avoid any biases or assumptions.

    - Treat good performance with respect and provide positive feedback where appropriate.

- Be an active listener.
  During performance conversations, it's important to engage in a meaningful dialogue and actively listen to your employees. This means asking follow-up questions and empathising with their emotions. You should aim to understand how they feel and regulate your own emotions as needed.

  Participating in the conversation doesn't always mean sharing your own point of view. Instead, after an employee shares their feedback, take a moment to

Copyrights 2023 Vocational Resources Australia. All Rights Reserved.

repeat back what you heard to ensure you understood them correctly. Remember that if you're busy preparing your response, you may not be fully listening to the other person.

- Wrap up the conversation with agreed upon next steps. Concluding a performance conversation doesn't mean it's the end of the road. Both managers and employees should review the notes taken during the meeting, agree on the next steps, and exchange feedback. Failing to do so can leave the conversation incomplete and ineffective. If you're looking to make a tangible impact on performance, crafting an action plan is essential.

- Following up after a performance review
  To ensure the success of the performance review process, it's crucial to follow up with employees after the meeting. This ongoing support and communication are vital for achieving the goals that were established together. Maintaining an open-door policy and keeping the conversation going can help employees feel supported and motivated to improve their performance.

- Keep the conversation going.
  Regular performance conversations are crucial for ongoing employee growth and development. As such, it is important to schedule the next performance review meeting at the end of the current one, or even schedule a series of meetings throughout the year. This regular cadence demonstrates your commitment to your employees' success and provides them with ongoing opportunities to receive feedback, ask questions, and set goals for themselves.

Copyrights 2023 Vocational Resources Australia. All Rights Reserved.

To foster a culture of continuous performance conversations, managers can adopt an open-door policy where employees feel comfortable discussing their performance throughout the year. This can be supplemented with regular 1-on-1 meetings and pulse checks at various points in the employee's lifecycle. Additionally, finding suitable performance review software can streamline the review process and make it more efficient.

Copyrights 2023 Vocational Resources Australia. All Rights Reserved.

Challenges of Performance Management

Performance management is not without its challenges. Some of the common challenges include:

- Poor goal setting
  Poorly set goals can lead to confusion and demotivation among employees. As mentioned in previous topics goals must comply with SMART principle.

- Biases
  Biases can affect the performance evaluation process. Employers should ensure that the performance evaluation process is fair and free from biases.

- Lack of feedback
  Lack of feedback can lead to demotivation and resentment among employees. Employers should provide regular feedback to employees to keep them motivated.

- Inadequate training
  Inadequate training can lead to poor performance among employees. Employers should provide employees with the necessary training and support to improve their skills.

- Resistance to change
  Employees may resist change, making it difficult to implement performance management systems. Employers should communicate the benefits of performance management and provide employees with the necessary support to embrace the change.

Copyrights 2023 Vocational Resources Australia. All Rights Reserved.

Under-Performance

Under-performance is referred to a situation when an employee consistently fails to meet the standards or expectations set for their role.

Under-performance can have a number of negative consequences for both the employee and the organisation. For the employee, it can lead to job insecurity, decreased opportunities for advancement, and lower pay. For the organisation, it can lead to decreased productivity, increased costs, and a negative impact on customer service.

Common Reasons of Under-Performance

Here are some of the most common factors that can contribute to a decline in employee performance:

- Lack of motivation
  If an employee is feeling demotivated or unengaged in their work, their performance is likely to suffer. This could be due to a variety of reasons such as lack of recognition, inadequate compensation, or feeling disconnected from the company's mission or values.

- Burnout
  Employees who are overworked or stressed may experience burnout, which can lead to a decline in productivity and quality of work. This can be caused by heavy workloads, tight deadlines, and a lack of work-life balance.

- Poor management
  Managers who don't provide clear expectations, feedback, or support can contribute to an employee's

Copyrights 2023 Vocational Resources Australia. All Rights Reserved.

underperformance. Employees need to feel valued, heard, and supported in order to perform to the best of their abilities.

- Lack of training or resources
  Employees who don't have the necessary tools or knowledge to do their job effectively can become frustrated and result in a decline in performance. Ongoing training and development are critical to keep employees engaged and up to date with the latest skills and technologies.

- Personal problems
  Personal problems such as illness, family issues, or financial stress can impact an employee's performance and productivity. It's important for managers to be understanding and supportive of employees who are going through difficult times.

- Poor metrics
  To effectively promote the desired performance, companies need to carefully select metrics that align with their goals and objectives. This often requires the use of a balanced scorecard that incorporates multiple metrics. When this is not done, problems can arise.

  For instance, some manufacturing plants set production targets for each shift individually, without considering the performance of all shifts throughout the day. As a result, workers are incentivised to prioritise their individual shift's performance rather than the overall daily production target.

Copyrights 2023 Vocational Resources Australia. All Rights Reserved.

To ensure that performance metrics promote desired outcomes, companies often use a balanced scorecard approach. However, some companies make the mistake of setting individual performance targets without considering how they fit into the larger picture.

For example, in manufacturing plants, each shift may have its own production targets, leading workers to focus on completing a single unit of work during their shift. If they are unable to complete it, they may slow down or stop altogether to avoid giving the next shift credit for their work.

As a result, productivity and output suffer. A better approach would be to set targets that align individual team goals with the plant's overall output, encouraging workers to support the next shift's success as well as their own.

- Poor targets
  Choosing the appropriate objectives involves both expertise and creativity. If the targets are too straightforward, they won't encourage the employees to enhance their performance. On the other hand, if the targets are impracticable, the staff won't even attempt to achieve them. The most effective objectives are realistic but require a certain level of effort to reach.

  However, to establish such goals, companies often have to overcome cultural obstacles. In certain Asian organisations, failing to meet targets is viewed as profoundly humiliating, so managers usually set them too low.

Copyrights 2023 Vocational Resources Australia. All Rights Reserved.

- Lack of transparency
  It is essential that employees perceive their targets as promoting significant accomplishments. However, often the connection between individual effort and company objectives is unclear, and as metrics and targets trickle down through the organisation, they can become diluted. Various levels of management may insert buffers into targets to boost their own standing or protect against underperformance elsewhere. Additionally, metrics at one level may have no logical link to those further up the cascade.

- Lack of relevance
  Selecting the appropriate metrics for a specific business segment relies on several factors, such as the company's size and location, the extent of its operations, the growth trends of its industry, and whether it is a fledgling or established business. To account for these variances, companies need to adopt a dual approach of top-down and bottom-up. One viable option is to use the Hoshin-Kanri (or policy-deployment) technique, where all employees are responsible for establishing the metrics and objectives for their respective parts of the organisation.

- Lack of dialogue
  For performance management to be effective, it requires regular, truthful, transparent, and productive communication. Metrics should not merely be viewed as a passive measure of progress but rather as an active component of the daily management of an organisation.

Copyrights 2023 Vocational Resources Australia. All Rights Reserved.

Regular activities such as daily shift huddles, toolbox talks, and after-action reviews are essential for engaging team members and sustaining focus on the most crucial tasks. Implementing the "plan-do-check-act" feedback loop, which is based on pioneering research by Charles Shewhart and W. Edwards Deming, enables teams to learn from their errors and identify useful concepts that can be applied elsewhere.

In many high-performing companies, supervisors act as coaches and mentors to their subordinates. One-on-one meetings between supervisors and employees show concern and reinforce good habits at every stage of career development.

- Lack of consequences
  Accountability is a crucial aspect of performance management, and weak accountability sends the message that minimal effort is acceptable. While most employees do not face the extreme "win or leave" pressure of professional sports, consequences must still exist for poor performance.

These are just a few examples of the many factors that can contribute to a decline in performance. In order to address these issues, it's important for employers to communicate with their employees, identify the root cause of the problem, and take appropriate action to support and motivate their staff.

Copyrights 2023 Vocational Resources Australia. All Rights Reserved.

Reviewing Performance Management Process

It is important to regularly review the performance management process to ensure that it is effective and aligned with the organisation's goals.

A performance management review should include the following steps:

- Assess the current process
  The first step is to assess the current performance management process. This includes identifying the strengths and weaknesses of the process, as well as the needs of employees and managers.

- Identify the desired outcomes
  The next step is to identify the desired outcomes of the performance management process. This includes what the organisation hopes to achieve through the process, such as improved employee performance, increased employee engagement, or reduced turnover.

- Develop a plan for improvement
  Once the current process has been assessed and the desired outcomes have been identified, a plan for improvement can be developed. This plan should include specific steps that can be taken to improve the process, such as providing more training for managers, developing new performance metrics, or creating a more supportive environment for feedback.

- Implement the plan
  Once the plan for improvement has been developed, it is important to implement the plan. This includes providing

Copyrights 2023 Vocational Resources Australia. All Rights Reserved.

training for managers, developing new performance metrics, or creating a more supportive environment for feedback.

- Evaluate the results
  Once the plan has been implemented, it is important to evaluate the results. This includes assessing whether the desired outcomes have been achieved and identifying any areas where further improvement is needed.

By following these steps, organisations can ensure that their performance management process is effective and aligned with their goals.

Here are some additional tips for reviewing the performance management process:

- Get input from employees and managers
  It is important to get input from employees and managers on the performance management process. This will help to ensure that the process is aligned with the needs of all stakeholders.

- Use data to drive improvement
  The performance management process should be data-driven. This means that the process should be based on objective data, such as performance metrics, rather than subjective opinions.

- Be transparent
  The performance management process should be transparent. This means that employees should

Copyrights 2023 Vocational Resources Australia. All Rights Reserved.

understand the process and how their performance will be evaluated.

- Be fair
  The performance management process should be fair. This means that all employees should be evaluated fairly, regardless of their race, gender, or other personal characteristics.

Training Managers in Performance Management and Review Process

Managers play a key role in performance management. They are responsible for setting clear expectations, providing regular feedback, and coaching employees to improve their performance.

However, many managers do not receive adequate training in performance management. This can lead to a number of problems, including:

- Ineffective performance reviews
  When managers do not know how to give effective feedback, performance reviews can be unproductive and demoralizing for employees.

- Unfair performance evaluations
  When managers do not have a clear understanding of the performance criteria, they may make unfair evaluations.

Copyrights 2023 Vocational Resources Australia. All Rights Reserved.

- Lack of employee development
  When managers do not provide regular feedback, employees may not have the opportunity to develop their skills and knowledge.

Training managers in performance management can help to address these problems and improve the effectiveness of the process.

The training should cover the following topics:

- The purpose of performance management
  Managers should understand the purpose of performance management and how it can be used to improve employee performance.

- The different components of performance management
  Managers should understand the different components of performance management, such as setting goals, providing feedback, and conducting performance reviews.

- How to give effective feedback
  Managers should learn how to give effective feedback that is specific, constructive, and actionable.

- How to conduct performance reviews
  Managers should learn how to conduct performance reviews that are fair, objective, and consistent.

By providing managers with training in performance management, organisations can improve the effectiveness of

Copyrights 2023 Vocational Resources Australia. All Rights Reserved.

the process and help to ensure that all employees are able to reach their full potential.

Here are some additional benefits of training managers in performance management:

- Increased employee engagement
  Employees are more likely to be engaged in their work when they feel that their performance is being managed effectively.

- Reduced turnover
  Employees are less likely to leave their jobs when they feel that they are being fairly evaluated and given opportunities for development.

- Improved morale
  Employees are more likely to have positive morale when they feel that their work is valued and that they are being given the opportunity to succeed.

Copyrights 2023 Vocational Resources Australia. All Rights Reserved.

Probation Period

A probation period is typically a trial period that an employee goes through at the beginning of their employment. During this time, the employer and employee have the opportunity to evaluate whether the job is a good fit for both parties. The length of the probation period can vary depending on the employer and can last from a few weeks to several months. At the end of the probation period, the employer will typically conduct a review to determine if the employee has met the job requirements and whether they should be offered a permanent position.

If either party decides that it's not working out, they can terminate the contract. Typically, the notice period required to terminate the contract during the probationary period is shorter than after the probationary period has ended.

For instance, terminating the contract may require only one week's notice during the probationary period, while it may require two weeks, one month, or even three months' notice after the probationary period. Employers may review employment contracts to determine the appropriate length of the probationary period or follow what's specified in the employment contract.

According to the Fair Work Act 2009 (Cth), there is no specific definition of what constitutes a probationary period. It is left to the discretion of the employer to specify the length of the probationary period in the employment contract, which the employee must agree to. Typically, probationary periods last between three to six months, although an employer may set any period as the probationary period. Getting an

Copyrights 2023 Vocational Resources Australia. All Rights Reserved.

employment contract review is a wise decision for this reason.

Setting Expectations

Probationary periods in employment contracts help set expectations for both employers and employees. During this testing period, both parties have the opportunity to assess whether the employment relationship is a good fit.

For employers, the probationary period allows them to evaluate whether the employee's skills and experience match what was expected during the interview process. For employees, it provides time to assess the work culture, duties, and expectations of the role, and whether they align with what was described during the interview. To ensure that this expectation-setting period is done correctly, it is recommended to conduct an employment contract review.

Copyrights 2023 Vocational Resources Australia. All Rights Reserved.

Recruitment

Recruitment is the process of identifying, attracting, and hiring the best-qualified candidate for a particular job opening. It is a critical function of human resource management as it helps to ensure that an organisation has the right talent to achieve its goals.

Recruitment Process

Here are the key steps involved in the recruitment process:

Job Analysis

The first step in the recruitment process is to conduct a job analysis. This involves identifying the duties, responsibilities, and qualifications required for a particular job. The job analysis may include a review of the job description, observation of the work, and interviews with current employees.

The output from job analysis is utilised by HR to create a job description and job specifications. The job description condenses and arranges the relevant information for use in the organisation's job-related operations. Typically, the job description and specifications are merged but kept separate to allow for independent updates when necessary.

Conducting Job Analysis

Some of the steps involved in conducting job analysis are:

1. Gather information about a position.
   To conduct a job analysis, you can observe and interview current employees in their roles. Encourage them to be specific when describing their responsibilities and how they perform their duties.

Copyrights 2023 Vocational Resources Australia. All Rights Reserved.

Additionally, review any manuals or documents related to the job. Compare the current job description with what employees are saying and doing, and document the results by department or individual position.

From the gathered information, create an inventory of all the tasks and skills required for the job. This will help you gain a comprehensive understanding of the job's requirements and identify any gaps in knowledge or skills necessary to perform the job effectively.

2. Evaluate the importance of each task and competency.
   Once you have identified the skills necessary to perform each task, you can evaluate the difficulty level of each task and skill. Determine the most critical skills required for each location and make note of which skills require entry-level and advanced expertise. It is possible that your perception of the job may differ from what you initially thought, and some tasks or skills may be more essential than originally assumed.

3. Research industry standards.
   Once you have identified the skills necessary to perform each task, you can evaluate the difficulty level of each task and skill. Determine the most critical skills required for each location and make note of which skills require entry-level and advanced expertise. It is possible that your perception of the job may differ from what you initially thought, and some

Copyrights 2023 Vocational Resources Australia. All Rights Reserved.

tasks or skills may be more essential than originally assumed.

4. Revise job descriptions and standards.
   After identifying the critical qualifications required for the job, create a comprehensive list of skills and requirements for each position. Use this list to update existing job descriptions or create new ones that accurately reflect your job analysis findings. Establish a set of criteria for each position that aligns with your employees' feedback and your own observations. Additionally, consider including expectations that you may not have previously considered but are based on industry best practices and research.

5. Use data to make changes.
   By examining the whole organisation, you can evaluate whether each task is appropriately assigned to the right position. If you discover that a task in one department is better suited for another team, consider transferring those responsibilities to the new job. Furthermore, by analysing job data, you may discover some departments have a heavier workload than others. Use this information to redistribute job responsibilities based on each job's capabilities.

Sourcing

Once the job analysis is complete, the organisation can begin to source candidates. This involves identifying potential candidates through various channels such as job boards, social media, employee referrals, and recruitment agencies.

Copyrights 2023 Vocational Resources Australia. All Rights Reserved.

Screening

Once candidates have been identified, they are screened to determine their suitability for the job. This may involve reviewing resumes, cover letters, and application forms to assess the candidate's qualifications, experience, and skills.

Selection

The next step is to shortlist the most qualified candidates for further consideration. This may involve conducting phone or video interviews, inviting candidates for in-person interviews, or administering skills tests. Other steps include:

1. Background Checks
   Before extending a job offer, the organisation may conduct background checks to verify the candidate's education, employment history, and criminal record.

2. Job Offer
   Once a candidate has been selected and their background check has been completed, the organisation can extend a job offer. The job offer should include details such as the job title, salary, benefits, and start date.

3. Onboarding
   The final step in the recruitment process is onboarding. This involves introducing the new employee to their job responsibilities, the organisation's culture, and its policies and procedures. It may include training, orientation, and introductions to key colleagues.

Copyrights 2023 Vocational Resources Australia. All Rights Reserved.

Advising Applicants

The following strategies are highly recommended:

- Be transparent
  Honesty is always the best policy. Provide applicants with clear and honest feedback about their application, even if they were not selected. This will help them understand why they may not have been selected and how they can improve for future applications.

- Be compassionate
  Being rejected from an opportunity can be difficult for applicants. Show empathy and understanding when delivering the news and offer support and guidance to help them move forward.

- Provide constructive feedback
  If an applicant was not selected, provide specific and constructive feedback on how they can improve their application for future opportunities. This will give them a better chance of success in the future.

- Offer alternative opportunities
  If there are other opportunities available that may be a better fit for the applicant, let them know about them. This will show that you value their interest and want to help them succeed.

Copyrights 2023 Vocational Resources Australia. All Rights Reserved.

Ensuring Compliance

To ensure that selection processes are compliant with legislative requirements, here are some steps you can take:

- Stay updated on relevant legislation
  It's important to be familiar with the most current legislation that applies to your industry and the selection processes used by your organisation.

- Develop clear policies and procedures
  Develop and implement policies and procedures that clearly outline the selection process to be followed. Ensure that these are communicated to all stakeholders involved in the selection process.

- Use objective criteria
  Use objective criteria that are directly related to the essential job requirements and that are not discriminatory on the basis of race, gender, ethnicity, or other protected categories.

- Maintain accurate documentation
  Keep a thorough record of all aspects of the selection process, including applications, resumes, interview notes, and other relevant materials. This information should be stored securely and kept confidential.

- Train your team
  Train your team on the importance of compliance with legislative requirements and how to follow the policies and procedures in place.

Copyrights 2023 Vocational Resources Australia. All Rights Reserved.

Improving the Recruitment Process

Some the strategies to improve the organisational recruitment process are:

- Refine your job description
  Ensure that your job descriptions are clear and concise, highlighting the skills required for the job.

- Leverage social media
  Use social media platforms to reach out to potential candidates and promote your company culture.

- Employee referrals
  Encourage your current employees to refer candidates who they think would be a good fit for the company.

- Streamline the application process
  Make the application process easy for candidates by using modern technology such as online applications or chatbots.

- Use data
  Use data analytics to track recruitment metrics and identify areas for improvement.

- Offer an attractive compensation package
  Offer competitive salary and benefits packages to attract top talent.

- Provide a positive candidate experience
  Ensure that candidates are treated with respect and care throughout the recruitment process to build a positive employer brand.

Copyrights 2023 Vocational Resources Australia. All Rights Reserved.

Recruitment Methods

There are quite a few recruitment methods to choose from, depending on your organisation's needs and resources. Some of them are discussed below:

- Job postings
  This is a classic recruitment method where you post job openings on job boards, company websites, and social media platforms. The advantage of this method is that it is easy to reach a large pool of potential candidates.

- Employee referrals
  This recruitment method involves asking your current employees to refer qualified candidates for job openings. This method can be cost-effective, and it has the added benefit of increasing employee engagement and retention.

- Campus recruitment
  This method involves visiting college campuses to recruit fresh graduates for entry-level positions. This is a great option if you are looking for candidates with little to no work experience but who have relevant qualifications.

- Headhunting
  This recruitment method involves researching and targeting specific individuals who would be a good fit for your organisation. This method can be time-consuming and expensive, but it can also yield high-quality hires.

- Social media recruitment
  This method involves using social media platforms like LinkedIn, Facebook, and Twitter to find and engage with

Copyrights 2023 Vocational Resources Australia. All Rights Reserved.

potential candidates. This method can be highly effective, particularly when you are targeting candidates with strong digital footprints.

- Job fairs
  This method involves participating in job fairs to connect with potential candidates and promote your organisation. This method can be particularly effective if you are looking to fill multiple positions quickly or if you want to build your employer brand.

Recruitment Types

There are several types of recruiting. Some of them are discussed below:

Internal Recruiting

Internal recruiting is the process of filling job openings with current employees from within the organisation.

Retained Recruiting

One way organisations hire a recruiting firm is through a method called retained recruiting. In this process, the organisation pays a fee upfront to the recruiting firm to fill a vacancy and the firm is responsible for finding suitable candidates until the position is filled. Additionally, the organisation agrees to exclusively work with the firm, meaning that they cannot hire multiple recruiting firms to fill the same position.

Contingency Recruiting

Contingency recruiting, like retained recruiting, involves an external firm. However, there is a key difference: there is no upfront fee with contingency recruiting. Instead, the

Copyrights 2023 Vocational Resources Australia. All Rights Reserved.

recruitment company is compensated only when a candidate they represent is hired by an organisation.

Staffing Recruiting

Staffing recruiters are employed by staffing agencies, which specialize in connecting qualified candidates with job openings. These agencies typically focus on filling short-term or temporary positions.

Outplacement Recruiting

Outplacement recruiting is a benefit sponsored by employers to aid former employees in transitioning to new jobs. Its purpose is to equip displaced employees with the resources they need to secure new positions or embark on new careers.

Reverse Recruiting

A process where an employee is encouraged to seek employment with a different organisation that is a better match for their skills and experience.

Psychometric Tests in Recruitment

Psychometric testing is a type of evaluation used in the hiring process to assess a candidate's cognitive abilities, personality traits, aptitudes, and other skills. Employers can use various types of tests, such as verbal reasoning, numerical reasoning, logical reasoning, and situational judgment tests, to measure a candidate's job suitability. Unlike traditional assessments that measure education or knowledge, psychometric tests provide a unique perspective on how a person demonstrates specific abilities or skills.

Copyrights 2023 Vocational Resources Australia. All Rights Reserved.

While educational background, achievements, and work experience are important criteria that employers consider during the application process, they don't always guarantee success in the workplace. Other factors, such as personality traits, work approach, and communication skills, are equally important in predicting a candidate's suitability for a job and organisational fit.

Psychometric testing is a valuable tool in recruitment as it offers a comprehensive understanding of a candidate's mental abilities, including their capacity for problem-solving, reasoning, and data analysis. Additionally, psychometric tests reveal personality traits and levels of integrity, which are crucial in determining how well a candidate will fit into an organisation's existing team.

Copyrights 2023 Vocational Resources Australia. All Rights Reserved.

Recruitment Plan

A recruitment plan is a strategy developed by an organisation to attract and hire the best-suited candidates for a job vacancy. It outlines the recruitment process, the timeline, the budget, and the resources required to attract a talented pool of candidates.

A recruitment plan lays out the specific tactics and channels to be used to attract potential candidates and outlines the screening and selection process. Recruitment plans can be short-term or long-term, depending on organisational needs.

A well-crafted recruitment plan can achieve the following benefits:

- Save time
- Optimise your recruitment budget
- Make better hiring decisions
- Ensure your recruitment goals are in line with the company's overall objectives
- Align your recruiters and hiring teams towards a common goal
- Focus your recruitment strategy on building the right talent pool
- Help you secure the necessary budget to meet your goals.

Copyrights 2023 Vocational Resources Australia. All Rights Reserved.

Developing a Recruitment Plan

Following are the steps to develop a recruitment plan:

1. Define your goals.
   To start creating a recruitment plan, it is crucial to define the recruitment goals clearly. This step focuses on high-level objectives, and the specific tactics will be addressed later. Although each organisation's objectives may vary, some common goals are observed among clients, such as increasing headcount, enhancing diversity, reducing the cost of hiring, decreasing the time taken to recruit, simplifying recruitment processes and minimising repetitive administrative work, enabling hiring managers to participate more actively in the recruitment process, improving employee retention, decreasing dependence on external recruiters, and developing a robust talent pipeline.

2. Forecast future hiring needs.
   Once you have established your recruitment goals, it's crucial to estimate the number of positions you will need to fill in the next year. This will allow you to proactively attract and cultivate suitable candidates, as well as budget and plan effectively. Although this projection will never be completely precise, the goal is to make a reasonable estimate.

3. Get your organisational chart up to date.
   To begin the headcount planning process, you should have an updated organisational chart on hand. If you don't already have one, you should consider start drafting one before proceeding to the other steps.

Copyrights 2023 Vocational Resources Australia. All Rights Reserved.

4. Identify likely promotions.
   Consider which employees in your current structure may be likely to move around, including any upcoming promotions that may create gaps. Use this information to update your org chart and identify any potential gaps in the team. Add any anticipated gaps to the headcount planning sheet in your hiring plan template.

5. Identify likely attrition and turnover.
   Consider factors such as retirement, resignation, redundancy, health issues, and performance to identify potential employee turnover within the next year. For larger organisations where individual data is not available, use historical trends as a starting point for planning. Keep in mind that turnover rates may fluctuate depending on the industry. Update your org chart to reflect these potential gaps and include them in your headcount planning sheet within your hiring plan template.

6. Growth.
   Once you have identified potential gaps in your existing workforce due to movement and promotions, it's time to consider growth opportunities. Determine if there are any teams or departments that require additional resources or if a big project is on the horizon. Consult with your managers to identify the roles they anticipate creating in the next 12 months. Ensure to add these roles to your org chart and incorporate them into your recruitment plan.

Copyrights 2023 Vocational Resources Australia. All Rights Reserved.

7. Skill gaps.
   Evaluate the skill sets of your teams. Do you notice any areas where additional skills are needed to enhance their performance? In some cases, larger organisations conduct a structured analysis of their skills gap. For smaller organisations, it may suffice to have an informal discussion with team leaders. Record these skill gaps in your recruitment plan. When creating job descriptions, advertising roles, and approving requisitions, keep in mind how you will attract qualified candidates to fill these gaps.

8. Get clear about the type of candidates you want to attract.
   Reflect on the traits and characteristics of your most successful team members and determine the values they share. Consider the type of individuals who have worked well in your company in the past and those who haven't. Are there common patterns or differences between different departments and locations? With this information in mind, use the Ideal Candidate Profile Template to create a profile for each type of candidate you want to attract.

9. Revisit your Employee Value Proposition (EVP).
   To attract the best candidates in a highly competitive job market, it's crucial for organisations to be clear about what sets them apart from their competitors and why someone would want to work for them. This is referred to as an EVP and is a key aspect of the employer brand. As an insider, you have a good understanding of the positive and negative aspects of

Copyrights 2023 Vocational Resources Australia. All Rights Reserved.

working for your organisation, such as the team dynamics, expectations, and ideal employee qualities.

However, as an applicant, these factors are not always obvious and may require effort on the employer's part to communicate effectively. Employers who make an effort to showcase their company culture, office environment, and team diversity are more likely to attract and retain top talent.

To avoid the disappointment and high turnover rate that come with a mismatch between the job and the candidate's expectations, it's crucial to clearly communicate what it's really like to work at your organisation. As a recruiter, it's your responsibility to attract the right people by providing an accurate picture of your business. When candidates have a clear understanding of what you offer, they are more likely to apply and new hires will not be in for a shock on their first day, reducing the risk of them leaving.

Therefore, take some time to review or create your employee value proposition (EVP) and ensure that it accurately reflects who you are as an organisation and what you offer to help you attract, hire, and retain the right candidates.

10. Develop your sourcing strategy.
    After crafting an EVP, it's important to create a strategy for attracting suitable candidates and assessing the effectiveness of your employer brand messaging in the market. Don't make the mistake of

Copyrights 2023 Vocational Resources Australia. All Rights Reserved.

assuming that you're already doing everything right because there is always room for improvement.

Use of Technology

One of the most important aspects of recruitment and selection is finding the right candidate for the job. With the help of technology, recruiters can now use job boards and search engines to find potential candidates. This has made the process much more efficient, as recruiters no longer have to rely on traditional methods of advertising jobs in newspapers or job fairs. Job boards and search engines allow recruiters to sort through thousands of resumes and applications in a matter of minutes.

Another way technology has helped with recruitment and selection is through the use of applicant tracking systems (ATS). ATS software can automatically review resumes and applications, This saves recruiters time and effort, as they no longer have to spend hours reviewing resumes manually. ATS can also help identify candidates who may not be an exact fit for the job, but who possess skills that may be valuable for future positions.

Interviews are another important part of the recruitment and selection process. Technology has revolutionised the way interviews are conducted. With the rise of video conferencing software such as Zoom and Skype, remote interviews have become much more convenient and cost-effective. This is especially important for companies that have locations in different parts of the world, as it allows them to interview candidates who may not be able to travel to the location of the job.

Copyrights 2023 Vocational Resources Australia. All Rights Reserved.

In addition to video conferencing, remote testing has also become increasingly popular. There are now a variety of online tests and assessments available that can help recruiters evaluate a candidate's skills and abilities. These tests can be customized to fit the requirements of the job and provide recruiters with valuable insights into a candidate's strengths and weaknesses.

Social media is another tool that has become increasingly important in the recruitment and selection process. Recruiters can use social media platforms such as LinkedIn, Facebook, and Twitter to connect with potential candidates and build relationships with them. Social media can also be used to promote job openings and attract candidates who may not have heard of the company otherwise.

Artificial intelligence (AI) is another technology that has the potential to revolutionize recruitment and selection. AI can be used to screen resumes, conduct initial phone screenings, and even analyse facial expressions during interviews. This can help identify candidates who may be a good fit for the job, based on their skills, experience, and personality traits.

Data analytics is another important technology that can assist with recruitment and selection. By analysing data from previous recruitment efforts, recruiters can identify patterns and trends that can help them improve their process. For example, if a company notices that they are not receiving enough applications from women, they may need to adjust their job descriptions or advertising methods to better target that demographic.

Copyrights 2023 Vocational Resources Australia. All Rights Reserved.

Risk Management

Risk management in HR is the process of identifying, assessing, and mitigating risks that could impact the organisation's workforce. These risks can include anything from employee safety to employee productivity.

HR risk management helps organisations to:

- Protect their employees
  By identifying and mitigating risks, organisations can help to protect their employees from harm.

- Reduce costs
  By preventing accidents, injuries, and illnesses, organisations can reduce the costs associated with employee health and safety.

- Improve productivity
  By reducing absenteeism, turnover, and low morale, organisations can improve employee productivity.

- Avoid legal liability
  By complying with employment laws, organisations can avoid legal liability.

There are many different types of HR risks, but some of the most common include:

- Employee safety
  This includes risks such as workplace injuries, violence, and harassment.

Copyrights 2023 Vocational Resources Australia. All Rights Reserved.

- Employee health
  This includes risks such as occupational diseases, mental health issues, and substance abuse.

- Employee productivity
  This includes risks such as absenteeism, turnover, and low morale.

- Employee compliance
  This includes risks such as discrimination, harassment, and wage and hour violations.

There are a number of different ways to manage HR risks. Some common methods include:

- Risk assessment
  This involves identifying and assessing the potential risks to the organisation's workforce.

- Risk mitigation
  This involves taking steps to reduce the likelihood or impact of risks.

- Risk monitoring
  This involves regularly reviewing and updating risk assessments to ensure that they are up to date.

By implementing a comprehensive HR risk management program, organisations can help to protect their employees, reduce costs, improve productivity, and avoid legal liability.

Copyrights 2023 Vocational Resources Australia. All Rights Reserved.

Here are some additional tips for managing HR risks:

- Create a culture of safety and compliance
  Employees are more likely to follow safety and compliance procedures if they believe that their employer is serious about these issues.

- Provide training
  Employees should be trained on safety, compliance, and other HR-related issues.

- Create a reporting system
  Employees should feel comfortable reporting safety and compliance concerns without fear of retaliation.

- Investigate concerns promptly
  When a safety or compliance concern is reported, it should be investigated promptly.

- Take corrective action
  When a safety or compliance concern is found, corrective action should be taken to address the issue.

Copyrights 2023 Vocational Resources Australia. All Rights Reserved.

Staff Development

Staff or Employee development refers to the process of training and developing employees to help them grow and improve in their roles within an organisation. It is a critical aspect of any successful business, as it can lead to increased productivity, employee satisfaction, and ultimately, business success.

There are many benefits to investing in employee development, including increased productivity, improved employee morale and retention, and enhanced organisational success.

Firstly, employee development can lead to increased productivity. By providing employees with the tools, skills, and knowledge they need to perform their jobs effectively, they are better equipped to meet the demands of their roles.

Secondly, employee development can improve employee morale and retention. When employees feel valued and invested in, they are more likely to be satisfied with their jobs and less likely to leave the organisation.

Finally, employee development can lead to enhanced organisational success. By developing employees and creating a culture of continuous learning, organisations can adapt to changing market conditions, stay ahead of the competition, and achieve long-term success.

Copyrights 2023 Vocational Resources Australia. All Rights Reserved.

Approaches to Employee Development

There are several different approaches to employee development, including on-the-job training, off-the-job training, coaching and mentoring, and job rotation.

On-the-Job Training

This involves providing employees with the opportunity to learn new skills and techniques while performing their regular job duties. This approach is often the most effective, as employees can immediately apply what they learn in a practical setting.

Off-the-Job Training

It involves providing employees with training and development opportunities outside of the workplace. This approach can include attending conferences, workshops, or other training programs that are relevant to their job.

Coaching and Mentoring

This involves pairing employees with experienced mentors who can provide guidance, support, and feedback as they learn and grow in their roles. This approach is particularly effective for developing leadership and management skills.

Job Rotation

It involves moving employees to different roles within the organisation to provide them with a broader range of skills and experiences. This approach is particularly effective for developing employees who are interested in advancing their careers within the organisation.

Copyrights 2023 Vocational Resources Australia. All Rights Reserved.

Best Practices

Implementing an effective employee development program requires careful planning and execution.

Here are some best practices to consider:

- Needs assessment
  Before implementing an employee development program, it is important to understand the specific needs of your organisation and its employees. Conduct a needs assessment to identify the skills and knowledge gaps that exist and to determine which development approaches are most appropriate.

- Set clear goals and objectives
  To ensure that your employee development program is effective, it is important to set clear goals and objectives. Outline what you hope to achieve through the program, and develop metrics to measure progress and success.

- Provide a variety of development opportunities
  To ensure that your employee development program meets the needs of all employees, provide a variety of development opportunities. This can include on-the-job training, off-the-job training, coaching and mentoring, and job rotation.

- Encourage participation and engagement
  Employee development programs are most effective when employees are engaged and motivated to participate. Encourage participation by communicating the benefits of the program, providing incentives for

Copyrights 2023 Vocational Resources Australia. All Rights Reserved.

completion, and fostering a culture of continuous learning.

- Measure and evaluate success
  To determine the effectiveness of your employee development program, it is important to measure and evaluate success. This can include tracking employee progress, gathering feedback from participants, and assessing the impact of the program on business outcomes.

Copyrights 2023 Vocational Resources Australia. All Rights Reserved.

Staffing Plan

A staffing plan, on the other hand, is a broader strategy that outlines the number of employees required for a specific time frame. It takes into consideration the organisation's objectives, workload, and budget to determine the optimal number of employees needed to fulfill business needs. A staffing plan identifies the roles and responsibilities required to achieve an organisation's goals and ensure that each role is filled with the right person, with the right skills, at the right time.

Staffing Plan - Goals

The primary goals of a staffing plan include:

- Ensuring adequate staffing levels
  The staffing plan ensures that the organisation has the right number of employees with the right skills and qualifications to meet its operational and business needs. This involves identifying the staffing needs and requirements of the different departments within the organisation.

- Recruiting and retaining top talent
  A staffing plan helps in attracting the best talent in the industry by outlining the necessary qualifications, skills, and experience required for each position. This includes developing recruitment strategies and compensation packages that attract and retain top talent.

- Cost-effective management of human resources
  A well-designed staffing plan helps in optimising the use of the workforce and minimising labour costs by identifying the right staff for each job, determining the

Copyrights 2023 Vocational Resources Australia. All Rights Reserved.

appropriate staffing levels, and managing staffing fluctuations.

- Enhancing organisational performance
  A staffing plan helps in enhancing the performance of the organisation by ensuring that the right people are in the right positions. This leads to increased productivity, improved quality of work, and a more efficient and effective workforce.

Determining Staffing Needs

Determining staffing needs involves identifying the number of employees required to effectively and efficiently run a business or organisation. It is a crucial part of a staffing plan, as it sets the foundation for the recruitment and retention process.

To determine staffing needs, an organisation needs to analyse its current workforce and identify any gaps in terms of skills, qualifications, and experience. It should also assess the workload and job requirements for each department to determine the number of employees needed to meet the demands of the organisation. Other factors that may influence staffing needs include the size of the organisation, the industry it operates in, and the level of competition. For instance, a growing business may require additional staff to manage new projects or expand to new markets.

Once staffing needs are identified, the organisation can begin to develop recruitment strategies and determine the appropriate compensation packages to attract and retain top talent. This will help ensure that the organisation has the

Copyrights 2023 Vocational Resources Australia. All Rights Reserved.

right people in the right positions to achieve its goals and objectives.

Methods for Determining Staffing Needs

Here are some methods that can be used to determine staffing needs:

Workload Analysis

One of the most commonly used methods for determining staffing needs is to analyse workload. This involves examining the volume of work, its complexity, and the time required to complete it. By assessing the workload, organisations can determine the number of staff required to complete the work in a timely manner and at the desired level of quality.

Ratio Analysis

This method involves determining the optimal ratio of staff to workload or to other factors such as sales volume or revenue. For example, a retail organisation may have a target ratio of one sales associate for every 100 customers per day. By establishing these ratios, organisations can ensure that they have the appropriate number of staff in proportion to the workload.

Trend Analysis

This method involves examining historical trends in staffing and workload to predict future needs. For example, an organisation might analyse its growth rate over the past few years to determine how many new staff members will be needed to support that growth in the future.

Copyrights 2023 Vocational Resources Australia. All Rights Reserved.

Benchmarking

This method involves comparing an organisation's staffing levels and practices to those of other similar organisations. By doing so, organisations can identify best practices and determine whether they are over- or understaffed in relation to their peers.

Skills Gap Analysis

This method involves identifying the skills and knowledge required for each job role within the organisation and assessing the current skills and knowledge of the existing workforce. By doing so, organisations can identify any skills gaps that need to be filled and determine whether additional staff are needed to fill those gaps.

Workforce Planning

This is a comprehensive approach that involves looking at the overall strategic goals of the organisation and determining the workforce required to achieve those goals. This involves analysing the workforce in terms of skills, knowledge, diversity, and demographics, as well as anticipating future trends and changes that may affect staffing needs.

Expert Opinion

This method involves seeking the opinions of experts within the organisation or industry to determine the appropriate staffing levels. For example, an HR manager may consult with department managers to determine whether they have enough staff to meet their needs.

Copyrights 2023 Vocational Resources Australia. All Rights Reserved.

Staff Retention

Staff retention is a crucial aspect of any organisation's success. Retaining employees with desirable skills and experience can significantly reduce turnover costs, improve productivity, and enhance workplace culture.

One of the primary factors that influence staff retention is workplace culture. Employee engagement and satisfaction depend heavily on the work environment, including the relationship between employees and management, the level of autonomy and support provided, and the overall atmosphere of the workplace. Therefore, it is essential to cultivate a positive and inclusive culture that prioritises employee well-being and recognises the value of their contributions.

Another significant factor that affects staff retention is career development opportunities. Employees who feel that they have opportunities to grow and develop within an organisation are more likely to remain committed to that organisation. Organisations that invest in employee development programs, mentoring, and coaching can provide employees with the necessary tools and skills to advance their careers and contribute more effectively to the organisation.

Compensation and benefits are also essential factors that influence staff retention. Employees need to feel that they are fairly compensated for their contributions and that their benefits package is competitive and supportive. Organisations need to conduct regular salary surveys and ensure that their compensation packages are consistent with industry standards. Additionally, providing benefits such as

Copyrights 2023 Vocational Resources Australia. All Rights Reserved.

health insurance, retirement plans, and paid time off can significantly improve employee retention.

Work-life balance is another critical factor that affects staff retention. Employees need to feel that they can balance their work and personal lives without undue stress or interference. Organisations that offer flexible work arrangements, such as telecommuting, flexible schedules, or part-time work, can significantly improve employee satisfaction and reduce turnover.

Recognition and appreciation are also crucial factors that influence staff retention. Employees need to feel valued and appreciated for their contributions to the organisation. Organisations that provide regular feedback, recognise achievements, and celebrate successes can significantly improve employee engagement and satisfaction.

Strategies to Improve Staff Retention

To retain staff, organisations can implement several strategies, such as:

- Developing a comprehensive onboarding program for new employees can help them acclimate to the organisation's culture and values.
- Providing ongoing training and development opportunities can help employees build new skills and advance in their careers.
- Offering competitive compensation and benefit packages can help attract and retain the most desirable employees.

Copyrights 2023 Vocational Resources Australia. All Rights Reserved.

- Creating a positive work environment that values diversity, equity, and inclusion can help build a strong workplace culture.
- Providing flexible work arrangements and recognising employee achievements and contributions can help build a positive and supportive work environment.

Copyrights 2023 Vocational Resources Australia. All Rights Reserved.

Succession Planning

Succession Planning is a process of identifying and developing potential successors for key positions in an organisation, with the aim of ensuring that the organisation is able to maintain continuity of operations and sustain or improve its performance in the long term. Succession Planning is a critical component of human resource management, as it helps organisations to retain top talent, reduce the risk of losing key employees, and build a stable and sustainable future.

There are several reasons why Succession Planning is important. Firstly, it helps organisations to identify and develop the skills and competencies required for future success. By identifying potential successors for key positions, organisations can ensure that they have the necessary talent and capabilities to continue to meet the changing needs of their customers and stakeholders. Secondly,

Succession Planning helps to reduce the risk of disruption to operations. By having a clear plan in place for the replacement of key employees, organisations can ensure that they can continue to deliver on their commitments, even if key personnel leave unexpectedly.

Thirdly, Succession Planning helps to retain top talent. By offering development opportunities and clear career paths, organisations can create a more engaged and motivated workforce, which is more likely to remain with the organisation in the long term.

Copyrights 2023 Vocational Resources Australia. All Rights Reserved.

Succession Planning - Steps

The Succession Planning process typically involves several steps. The crucial ones are discussed below:

1. Organisations need to identify the key positions that are critical to their success, and the competencies required for those positions. This might involve conducting a skills audit or using other tools to assess the current capabilities of the workforce.

2. Organisations need to identify potential successors for each key position. This might involve looking at the existing talent pool within the organisation, as well as external candidates who might be suitable for the role.

3. Organisations need to develop a plan to develop the skills and competencies of potential successors. This might involve providing training and development opportunities, mentoring, coaching, and other forms of support.

4. Organisations need to monitor the progress of potential successors, and provide feedback and guidance as required.

5. When a key employee leaves the organisation, organisations need to have a clear plan in place for the replacement of that employee.

Copyrights 2023 Vocational Resources Australia. All Rights Reserved.

Succession Planning - Challenges

Succession planning can be a complex process, and there are a number of challenges that organisations can face.

Here are a few examples:

- Identifying and developing internal talent
  One of the biggest challenges in succession planning is identifying and developing internal talent. This can be particularly difficult if an organisation has a limited talent pool or if certain key employees are difficult to replace.

- Ensuring diversity and inclusion
  Another challenge is ensuring that succession planning efforts are inclusive and diverse. It's important to ensure that all employees have equal opportunities to participate in development programs and leadership roles, regardless of factors like gender, ethnicity, or age.

- Balancing short-term and long-term goals
  Succession planning requires a delicate balance between short-term needs and long-term goals. It's important to identify and develop employees who can fill key leadership roles in the future, while also ensuring that the organisation has the necessary talent in the present to meet current business needs.

- Managing employee perceptions
  Succession planning can be challenging from a communications and employee engagement perspective. Employees may worry about their own job security or feel that they are being overlooked for development opportunities. It's important to communicate openly and

Copyrights 2023 Vocational Resources Australia. All Rights Reserved.

transparently about the reasons for succession planning and how it benefits both the organisation and its employees.

Copyrights 2023 Vocational Resources Australia. All Rights Reserved.

Termination

"Termination of employment is when an employee's employment with an employer ends. Employment can end for many different reasons. An employee may resign or can be dismissed (fired).

However it ends, it's important to follow the rules about dismissal, notice and final pay. There are also different rights and obligations when a job is made redundant or when a business is bankrupt.

Commonwealth workplace laws have rules about terminating employment. These rules establish whether the termination of the employment was unlawful or unfair, what entitlements an employee is owed at the end of their employment, and what must be done when an employee is dismissed because of redundancy.

The Fair Work Ombudsman and the Fair Work Commission regulate Commonwealth workplace laws about terminating employment." .... Source: Fair Work Ombudsman

Copyrights 2023 Vocational Resources Australia. All Rights Reserved.

Termination Process

The termination process can be complex and is dependent on various factors. However, in general the following steps are involved:

1. Identify the reason for termination
   The first step is to identify the reason for the termination. An employee can be terminated for a range of reasons, including poor performance, misconduct, redundancy, or serious breaches of company policy. For some of these reasons a separate set of processes may be involved.

2. Provide written notice of termination
   The employer must provide the employee with written notice of termination, including the date the termination will take effect, the reason for the termination, and any entitlements the employee may be entitled to, such as severance pay or notice period.

3. Pay out any accrued entitlements
   The employer must also pay out any accrued entitlements, such as unused annual leave or long service leave, as well as any outstanding wages or bonuses.

4. Follow any applicable employment laws
   The employer must ensure that they are following all applicable employment laws and regulations, including those related to unfair dismissal, discrimination, and workplace health and safety.

Copyrights 2023 Vocational Resources Australia. All Rights Reserved.

5. Offer support to the employee
   In some cases, the employer may offer support to the employee, such as career counselling or outplacement services, to help them transition to a new job.

Termination process can vary depending on the terms of the employee's contract and the reason for the termination. For example, redundancy may require additional steps, such as notifying the relevant government agency and offering redeployment opportunities to affected employees.

Unfair Dismissal

An unfair dismissal is when an employee is dismissed from their job in a harsh, unjust or unreasonable manner. Under the Fair Work Act 2009, an employee may be able to make an application to the Fair Work Commission if they have been unfairly dismissed.

The Fair Work Commission will consider the following factors when making a decision on whether or not an employee has been unfairly dismissed:

- The reason for the dismissal
  The Fair Work Commission will consider whether the reason for the dismissal was valid. A valid reason for dismissal is one that is related to the employee's performance, conduct, or capacity.

- The process followed by the employer
  The Fair Work Commission will consider whether the employer followed a fair process when dismissing the

Copyrights 2023 Vocational Resources Australia. All Rights Reserved.

employee. This includes considering whether the employee was given a warning or opportunity to improve their performance or conduct before being dismissed.

- The consequences of the dismissal
The Fair Work Commission will consider the impact of the dismissal on the employee, including their financial loss and emotional distress.

If the Fair Work Commission finds that an employee has been unfairly dismissed, they may order the employer to reinstate the employee, backpay the employee for any lost wages, or award the employee compensation.

Here are some examples of unfair dismissal:

- An employee is dismissed for taking sick leave.

- An employee is dismissed for refusing to do something that is illegal or unsafe.

- An employee is dismissed for making a complaint about discrimination or harassment.

- An employee is dismissed because of their race, gender, religion, or disability.

Copyrights 2023 Vocational Resources Australia. All Rights Reserved.

Training & Development

Training and development are essential for organisations to maintain a competitive edge in today's rapidly changing business environment. Investing in the development of employees is critical to the success of any organisation. It helps employees to acquire new skills, improve their performance, and become more efficient and effective in their roles.

Effective training and development programs can help organisations to:

- Attract and retain top talent
  Employees want to work for companies that invest in their growth and development. Organisations that offer training and development opportunities are more likely to attract and retain top talent.

- Improve employee performance
  Training and development programs can help employees to improve their performance by providing them with the knowledge and skills they need to do their job effectively.

- Increase job satisfaction
  Employees who receive training and development opportunities are more satisfied with their jobs. They feel valued by their employer and are more likely to stay with the organisation.

- Enhance productivity
  Well-trained employees are more productive and efficient in their roles. They are better equipped to handle new challenges and are more adaptable to change.

Copyrights 2023 Vocational Resources Australia. All Rights Reserved.

- Remain competitive
  In today's fast-paced business environment, it is essential for organisations to stay competitive. Training and development programs can help organisations to remain competitive by ensuring that employees have the skills and knowledge required to succeed.

Adult Learning

Adult learning refers to the education and training of individuals who are beyond the traditional age of compulsory education. This type of learning often takes place in post-secondary institutions, vocational training centres, and other learning environments that cater to the needs of adult learners.

Adult learners bring a wealth of experience and knowledge to the learning process, and as such, have unique learning needs and preferences. Some adult learners may prefer self-directed learning, while others may benefit from a more structured approach. Additionally, adult learners may have work and family commitments that need to be taken into account when designing educational programs and courses.

There are many different approaches to adult learning, including online learning, blended learning, and experiential learning. Whatever the approach, the goal of adult learning is to help individuals expand their knowledge, skills, and abilities, and to help them achieve their personal and professional goals.

Copyrights 2023 Vocational Resources Australia. All Rights Reserved.

Theory and Practice

First, let's talk about the theory. One of the most influential theories of adult learning is known as andragogy, which was developed by Malcolm Knowles. The andragogical approach emphasises the differences between adult and child learners, and as such, it suggests that adult learners need to be treated differently than children in terms of instruction and educational design. According to this theory, adult learners are more self-directed, have a wealth of prior experiences to draw from, and prefer to learn through problem-solving and application to real-world situations.

Another theory that is frequently referenced in adult learning is constructivism, which suggests that learning is an active process that occurs when learners actively engage in constructing their own knowledge and understanding. The idea here is that learners build upon their prior knowledge and experiences in order to create new knowledge and solve problems.

Now, let's talk about the practice of adult learning. In order to effectively facilitate adult learning, educational professionals need to ensure that instructional methods and activities are designed in a way that is meaningful and relevant to learners. This can involve using case studies, simulations, and other experiential learning methods that allow learners to apply new knowledge and skills to real-world challenges. It is also important to ensure that learners are motivated and engaged in the learning process, which can be accomplished through various means such as providing opportunities for self-reflection, encouraging learner autonomy and self-direction, and incorporating activities that are personally meaningful to learners.

Copyrights 2023 Vocational Resources Australia. All Rights Reserved.

Pedagogical Theory and Practice

Pedagogical theory refers to the study and understanding of how people learn, and the methods used to teach them. It includes examining the different learning styles and approaches, as well as the ways in which motivation and social interactions impact learning.

Pedagogical practice, on the other hand, refers to the implementation of those theories and methods in the classroom. This involves designing lessons and activities that align with the learning objectives and are tailored to meet the needs and preferences of the students.

There are several prominent pedagogical theories that inform teaching practices, including:

- Behaviourism
  Discussed below.

- Constructivism
  Emphasises the role of student-centred learning, where students actively construct their own understanding through real-world experiences and social interactions.

- Humanism
  Discussed below.

- Critical pedagogy.
  Emphasises the role of education in promoting social and political change and encourages critical thinking and dialogue to challenge social inequalities and injustices.

Copyrights 2023 Vocational Resources Australia. All Rights Reserved.

In practice, teachers may draw on a combination of these theories to create a classroom environment that fosters learning and growth. This may involve using a variety of instructional strategies and resources, including lectures, group discussions, hands-on activities, and technology-based tools.

Ultimately, the goal of pedagogical theory and practice is to help students develop the knowledge, skills, and attitudes needed to be successful in their academic, personal, and professional lives.

Behaviourism Learning Theory

Behaviourism is a learning theory that focuses on observable behaviour and the idea that behaviour can be shaped through positive and negative reinforcement. According to behaviourism, the environment plays a significant role in shaping behaviour, and learning is seen as a process of conditioning.

One of the key figures associated with behaviourism is B.F. Skinner, who developed the concept of operant conditioning. Operant conditioning is a type of learning that occurs through the consequences of behaviour. Positive reinforcement, such as praise or rewards, strengthens a behaviour, while negative reinforcement, such as punishment, weakens a behaviour.

Behaviourism also emphasises the importance of repetition and practice in learning. Through frequent exposure to a stimulus and the consequent reinforcement, the behaviour becomes more ingrained and automatic.

Copyrights 2023 Vocational Resources Australia. All Rights Reserved.

Critics of behaviourism argue that it ignores the role of mental processes in learning and that it oversimplifies complex human behaviour. However, behaviourism still has relevance today in areas such as animal training, behaviour management, and behaviour modification therapy.

Cognitive Learning Theory

The Cognitive Learning Theory is a psychological theory that explains how people learn new information, skills, and behaviours. According to this theory, learning occurs through a process of mental processing, including attention, perception, memory, and problem-solving.

The Cognitive Learning Theory was developed by psychologists such as Jean Piaget, Lev Vygotsky, and Jerome Bruner, among others. The theory suggests that learners actively construct their own understanding of the world based on their experiences and interactions with their environment.

One of the key concepts of the Cognitive Learning Theory is that learners must be actively engaged in the learning process in order to be successful. This means that learners must be motivated to learn, pay attention to relevant information, and actively participate in the learning process.

Another central idea of this theory is that learning is more effective when learners can connect new information to their existing knowledge. This is known as schema theory, and it suggests that learners have mental frameworks or "schemas" that organise their thoughts and help them make sense of new information.

Copyrights 2023 Vocational Resources Australia. All Rights Reserved.

In practical terms, the Cognitive Learning Theory has been used to develop educational interventions designed to help learners acquire new skills and knowledge more effectively. For example, instructional designers may use techniques such as scaffolding, which involves breaking down complex tasks into smaller, more manageable steps, to help learners build their understanding gradually.

Constructivism Learning Theory

The Constructivism Learning Theory is an educational theory that emphasises the active role of the learner in the learning process. According to this theory, learners construct their own understanding of the world based on their experiences and interactions with the environment.

The theory of Constructivism was developed by several psychologists and educational theorists, including Jean Piaget, Lev Vygotsky, and Seymour Papert. It suggests that learning is an active process of sense-making in which learners create their own mental representations of reality through interaction with their experiences and their environment.

One of the key ideas of Constructivism is that learners must be actively involved in the learning process in order to be successful. This means that learners must be motivated to learn, and that they should be given opportunities to explore, experiment, and solve problems on their own.

Another important concept of Constructivism is that learners must be allowed to build on their existing knowledge in order to construct new knowledge. This is achieved through the process of scaffolding, which involves providing learners with

Copyrights 2023 Vocational Resources Australia. All Rights Reserved.

support and guidance as they work towards building their understanding.

Constructivism also emphasises the importance of social interaction in the learning process. According to this theory, learners benefit from working together to solve problems, share ideas, and provide support to one another.

In practical terms, the Constructivism Learning Theory has been used to develop educational interventions that focus on student-centred learning. This includes techniques such as problem-based learning, which involves presenting learners with real-world problems and encouraging them to work together to find solutions, and inquiry-based learning, which involves learners exploring topics that interest them and developing their own questions to guide their learning.

Social Learning Theory

Social Learning Theory is a theory that explains human behaviour as a result of their interactions with their environment. It was developed by psychologist Albert Bandura in the 1960s and emphasises the importance of observational learning, imitation, and modelling in shaping behaviour.

According to this theory, people learn by observing the behaviour of others, and the consequences of that behaviour. Social Learning Theory suggests that people are more likely to imitate behaviour that they have seen rewarded, rather than punished. In other words, people learn what is considered acceptable or appropriate behaviour by observing the behaviours of others and the consequences of those behaviours.

Copyrights 2023 Vocational Resources Australia. All Rights Reserved.

Bandura also emphasized the concept of self-efficacy, which refers to an individual's belief in their ability to successfully perform a task or behaviour. This belief can be influenced by previous experiences or by observing others who are successful in a particular task or behaviour.

Social Learning Theory has many practical applications, particularly in the field of education. Teachers can use modelling and observation to teach students new behaviours and can reinforce positive behaviours through rewards and praise. This theory is also important in the field of psychology, as it helps to explain how behaviours are learned and how they can be modified through observation and reinforcement.

Humanistic Learning Theory

Humanistic Learning Theory is a psychological perspective that emphasises the importance of human potential, creativity, and self-actualization. It is based on the belief that all people have unique abilities and that these abilities can be developed and nurtured through learning. This theory focuses on the emotional and social aspects of learning, rather than just the cognitive aspects.

At the heart of humanistic learning theory is the idea that individuals have an inherent desire to grow and develop, and that this can be achieved through self-directed learning. This type of learning allows individuals to take control of their own learning process, identify their own strengths and weaknesses, and set their own goals. It is believed that this approach to learning can result in greater motivation and engagement, as well as better outcomes.

Copyrights 2023 Vocational Resources Australia. All Rights Reserved.

Humanistic learning theory is often associated with Abraham Maslow's hierarchy of needs, which suggests that individuals must have their basic needs met before they can focus on higher-level needs such as self-actualization. This means that teachers and educators must be attuned to the emotional and social needs of their students and create a safe and supportive learning environment that fosters growth and development.

One of the key tenets of humanistic learning theory is that learning should be focused on the whole person, rather than just the individual components of learning. This means that educators should take a holistic approach to teaching and learning, integrating cognitive, emotional, and social aspects of learning into their teaching practices.

Knowledge Transfer

Knowledge transfer is the process of sharing knowledge, skills, and information from one person or group to another. In a workplace, knowledge transfer is a critical element in ensuring the sustainability of an organisation. It ensures that the organisation's knowledge base is retained and passed on to new employees or team members.

Effective knowledge transfer involves identifying the essential skills and knowledge required for a specific job or role and ensuring that this information is shared with the relevant individuals. This can be done through a variety of methods, such as on-the-job training, formal training sessions, mentoring, job shadowing, and peer-to-peer learning.

Copyrights 2023 Vocational Resources Australia. All Rights Reserved.

Additionally, knowledge transfer can occur through the use of technology, such as a knowledge management system, where employees can access information and resources related to their job. This allows for continuous learning and development, ensuring that employees are always up to date with the latest information and best practices.

It's important to note that knowledge transfer is not a one-time event but an ongoing process. As the workplace evolves, the skills and knowledge required for employees to perform their jobs effectively change as well. Therefore, it's crucial to establish a culture of continuous learning and development, to ensure that knowledge transfer is an ongoing process.

Knowledge Transfer Methods

Here are a few methods that can be used to promote knowledge transfer in the workplace:

Mentorship programs

Pairing experienced employees with new hires or those seeking to learn a new skill can be an effective way to transfer knowledge. Mentors can provide guidance, answer questions, and offer feedback to help new employees develop the skills they need to be successful.

Training sessions

Offering regular training sessions can help employees learn new skills and stay up to date with changes in their field. These sessions can be conducted in-person or online, and can be customised to meet the needs of different departments or job roles.

Copyrights 2023 Vocational Resources Australia. All Rights Reserved.

Knowledge sharing platforms

Creating a platform where employees can share information, tips, and best practices can be a great way to promote knowledge transfer. This can be done through a company intranet, a shared drive, or even a social media group.

Job shadowing

Allowing employees to shadow those in more senior positions can be an effective way to transfer knowledge. Shadowing can provide an opportunity for employees to see first-hand how more experienced colleagues handle certain situations, and can help them develop new skills and perspectives.

Cross-functional teams

Creating cross-functional teams can help employees from different departments or job roles learn from one another. These teams can work on projects together, share their expertise, and learn new skills from their colleagues.

Learning & Assessment

Learning and assessment play a crucial role in employee development. By providing employees with the opportunity to learn and develop new skills, they are able to become more effective and efficient in their roles. This can lead to increased job satisfaction, motivation, and productivity.

Assessment is also important because it allows employers to measure the effectiveness of their training programs and identify areas where employees may need further development.

Copyrights 2023 Vocational Resources Australia. All Rights Reserved.

By regularly assessing employee performance, employers can ensure that their workforce is equipped with the skills and knowledge needed to succeed in their roles and contribute to the overall success of the organisation.

Learning & Assessment - Key Considerations

When it comes to learning and assessment of employees, there are a few key considerations to keep in mind.

First, it's important to identify the specific skills and knowledge that your employees need to perform their jobs effectively. This will help you develop targeted training and development programs that meet their needs.

Second, you should think about the best ways to deliver this training and assessment. This might involve a combination of in-person sessions, online courses, on-the-job training, and performance evaluations.

Finally, it's important to track and measure the effectiveness of your training and assessment programs. This will allow you to make adjustments and improvements over time, ensuring that your employees are always learning and growing in their roles.

Copyrights 2023 Vocational Resources Australia. All Rights Reserved.

Design & Management of Learning Objects and Content

Designing and managing learning objects and content involves planning and creating educational resources that are structured and organised to effectively facilitate learning.

Here are some tips to consider when designing and managing learning objects and content:

- Determine learning objectives.
  Before designing any learning content, it is important to establish clear learning objectives. This will help you determine what the learning object should cover and how it should be structured.

- Identify the target audience.
  It is important to identify who your target audience is, as this will affect the design and management of your learning object or content. Consider their age, educational background, and learning style.

- Plan and organise.
  Proper planning and organisation are essential for effective learning. Make sure to break down content into smaller, manageable chunks, and ensure that the flow of information is logical and easy to follow.

- Choose the right format.
  There are various formats for presenting learning content, such as multimedia, documents, and interactive presentations. Choose a format that best suits the subject matter and target audience.

Copyrights 2023 Vocational Resources Australia. All Rights Reserved.

- Use visuals and interactivity.
  A visual approach with interactive elements can significantly enhance the learning experience for the learner. Use graphics, animations, videos, and interactive quizzes to engage learners and help them retain information.

- Accessibility.
  Make sure the learning objects and content are accessible and compliant with standards such as ADA.

- Regular evaluation and updates.
  Evaluate your learning objects and content regularly to ensure that they are meeting the learning objectives and staying relevant. Revise and update the content as required to keep it fresh and engaging.

When designing and managing learning objects and content, it is important to keep the learner's needs and preferences in mind. By following the tips above, you can create effective and engaging learning content that motivates and supports learners in achieving their goals.

Strategies and Content Requirements

Vocational learning and assessment strategies refer to the methods and techniques used by vocational trainers to deliver training and assess the knowledge, skills, and competence of learners in a workplace setting. The main focus of vocational delivery and assessment strategies is to provide learners with the necessary skills to perform job-related tasks and responsibilities effectively. Below are the key contents and requirements of vocational delivery and assessment strategies:

Copyrights 2023 Vocational Resources Australia. All Rights Reserved.

- Quality and relevant resources
  The delivery and assessment strategies should be backed up by high-quality and relevant resources that support the learning process. These resources may include training manuals, workbooks, handouts, simulations, and e-learning platforms, among others.

- Flexible learning options
  The delivery and assessment strategies should provide learners with flexibility in learning options such as online learning, face-to-face training, workplace-based learning, and blended learning.

- Recognition of prior learning
  Learners should be given the chance to demonstrate their prior learning and experience through Recognition of Prior Learning (RPL) assessments.

- Collaborative learning
  The delivery and assessment strategies should encourage collaborative learning between learners and trainers, and also between learners themselves.

- Assessment methods
  There should be a clear assessment methodology that outlines the assessment process, the criteria for assessment, the mode of assessment, and the expected outcomes.

- Feedback and support
  There should be regular feedback and support to learners throughout the delivery and assessment process. This will enable learners to identify areas of

Copyrights 2023 Vocational Resources Australia. All Rights Reserved.

learning that need improvement and receive guidance on how to improve.

- Continuous improvement
  The vocational delivery and assessment strategies should be continuously reviewed and refined to ensure that they meet the changing needs of the learners, the industry, and the workplace.

Developing Learning Resources

When developing learning resources and materials, it is important to take into account the following key considerations:

- Learning objectives
  Materials and resources should be aligned with the specific learning objectives for the lesson or course.

- Learning styles
  Consider the different learning styles of learners and provide resources that are well-suited for each style, such as visual aids, interactive activities, or written materials.

- Accessibility
  Materials should be designed to be accessible to all learners, including those with disabilities or who use assistive technology.

- Clarity
  Resources should be clear and easy to understand, with simple language and diagrams where appropriate.

Copyrights 2023 Vocational Resources Australia. All Rights Reserved.

- Relevance
  Materials should be relevant and engaging, providing real-world examples and scenarios that learners can relate to.

- Appropriateness
  Materials and resources should be age and culturally appropriate for the target audience.

- Feedback and assessment
  Resources should provide learners with opportunities to receive feedback on their progress and assess their understanding of the materials.

- Technology
  Consider the use of technology in learning resources, such as online simulations or interactive tools, to enhance the learning experience.

Developing Compliant Assessments

When it comes to developing compliant assessments for workplace training, there are a few key considerations to keep in mind.

- Ensure that the assessment aligns with the learning objectives.
  The assessment should test the knowledge and skills that were taught during the training. Make sure that the questions are relevant to the material covered.

Copyrights 2023 Vocational Resources Australia. All Rights Reserved.

- Keep the questions clear and concise.
  Use simple language and avoid using technical jargon or overly complex sentence structures. This will help ensure that the questions are easy to understand and interpret.

- Avoid bias.
  The assessment questions should not be written in a way that favours one particular group over another. This includes avoiding questions that may be culturally insensitive or discriminatory.

- Use a variety of question types.
  Different people learn in different ways, so it's a good idea to include a variety of question types, such as multiple-choice, true/false, and short answer questions.

- Use technology to your advantage.
  There are many online tools and platforms available that can help you create engaging and interactive assessments. Consider using tools like quizzes, interactive video, or gamification to make the assessment more enjoyable and effective.

Copyrights 2023 Vocational Resources Australia. All Rights Reserved.

Learning & Instructional Design Principles

Learning principles are theoretical concepts that explain how people learn, while instructional design principles are practical guidelines for designing effective instruction that align with these learning principles.

Learning principles are based on research in fields such as cognitive psychology and neuroscience and describe how people acquire new knowledge, skills, and attitudes. Examples of learning principles include the importance of activating prior knowledge, the role of feedback in learning, or the impact of motivation on performance.

Instructional design principles, on the other hand, provide guidance for applying these learning principles to create effective instruction. They describe how to organise information, design activities, and use multimedia to create a learning experience that aligns with the needs of the learners. Examples of instructional design principles include the use of clear learning objectives, the alignment of assessment with objectives, or the importance of providing opportunities for practice and feedback.

Learning Principles

Workplace learning refers to any learning that occurs in an organisational setting. This type of learning takes place in the context of employees' work roles and is designed to improve their job performance or prepare them for future job responsibilities. In essence, workplace learning is the process of continuous education that employees undergo in order to maintain or improve their skills, knowledge, and competencies in their jobs. Organisations invest in workplace learning programs as a way to increase their

Copyrights 2023 Vocational Resources Australia. All Rights Reserved.

employees' skills, productivity, and engagement while also maintaining a competitive edge against other companies in the industry.

Workplace learning can take many different forms, including on-the-job training, coaching, mentoring, interactive workshops, e-learning, and self-directed learning. Regardless of how workplace learning is structured or delivered, there are certain principles that must be followed for it to be effective. In this paper, we will discuss five key principles that underpin effective workplace learning.

- Alignment
  The first principle of workplace learning is that it must be aligned with organisational goals. In order for workplace learning to be successful, it must be directed towards meeting the specific goals of the organisation. For example, if the organisation's goal is to increase sales, workplace learning programs should be focused on improving sales skills, such as effective communication, product knowledge, and customer service. This alignment ensures that workplace learning is directly contributing to the success of the organisation and that employees are learning skills that are relevant to their work.

- Flexibility & Adaptability
  The second principle of workplace learning is that it should be flexible and adaptable. Workplace learning programs must be flexible enough to meet the changing needs of the organisation and the evolving roles of employees. This principle recognises that workplace learning is not a one-time activity, but rather an ongoing process that should be tailored to the needs of the

Copyrights 2023 Vocational Resources Australia. All Rights Reserved.

organisation and its employees. This flexibility ensures that workplace learning programs remain relevant, effective, and engaging.

- Learner-Centred
  The third principle of effective workplace learning is that it must be learner-centred. This means that the learning experience should be designed with the learner in mind. Employees should be given the opportunity to participate in the design, development and delivery of workplace learning programs. This involvement helps to ensure that the learning experience is meaningful, engaging, and relevant to the needs of the learner. Learner-centred workplace learning programs are more effective because they take into account the different learning styles and preferences of individual learners.

- Inclusive
  The fourth principle of workplace learning is that it must be inclusive. Inclusive workplace learning recognises and respects the diversity and uniqueness of individuals. All employees should have equal access to workplace learning programs, regardless of their background, education, or experience. Inclusive workplace learning requires that organisations create an environment that is welcoming and supportive for all employees. This principle recognises that diversity is a source of strength and that inclusive workplaces are more innovative, productive, and successful.

- Outcome-Focused
  The fifth and final principle of effective workplace learning is that it should be outcomes-focused. The ultimate goal

Copyrights 2023 Vocational Resources Australia. All Rights Reserved.

of workplace learning is to achieve specific outcomes, such as improved job performance, increased productivity, and higher employee engagement. Workplace learning programs must be designed with these outcomes in mind, and organisations should track and measure the impact of their workplace learning initiatives. This ensures that workplace learning is effective and that it is contributing to the success of the organisation.

Instructional Design Principles

There are several instructional design principles. Some of them are discussed below:

- Goal orientation
  Instructional design should be goal-oriented. This means that the learning objectives should be clear and specific, and the instructional process should be designed to help learners achieve those goals.

- Feedback
  Feedback is a key component of effective instruction. Learners should receive feedback on their progress throughout the instructional process, so that they can adjust their learning strategies as needed.

- Active learning
  Active learning involves engaging learners in the instructional process through activities that require them to process information and apply it in real-world situations. This can include activities such as simulations, case studies, and problem-solving exercises.

Copyrights 2023 Vocational Resources Australia. All Rights Reserved.

- Multimedia
  Using multimedia, such as videos, graphics, and animations, can enhance the learning experience and make it more engaging for learners.

- Collaboration
  Collaboration is a valuable instructional design principle. Group work and collaboration can help learners develop critical thinking and problem-solving skills, as well as communication and interpersonal skills.

- Adaptation
  Instructional design should be adaptable to the needs of different learners. This means that instructional designers should take into account factors such as learning styles, prior knowledge, and cultural backgrounds when designing instructional materials.

- Assessment
  Assessment is an important part of the instructional process. It allows instructors to evaluate learners' progress and identify areas where they may need additional support.

Copyrights 2023 Vocational Resources Australia. All Rights Reserved.

Learning Styles

Learning is an important aspect of human life, and people learn in different ways. Everyone has a unique preferred method of learning, and this is influenced by factors such as personal experiences, cognitive abilities, interests, and even social and cultural background. Psychologists have conducted extensive research to identify and categorise different learning styles. These learning styles can be defined as the preferred method of acquiring, processing, and retaining information. Some of the styles are discussed below:

- Auditory learning style.
  Auditory learners prefer learning through hearing and listening. They process information by listening to lectures, group discussions, and podcasts. They enjoy hearing stories, music, and rhythmic patterns. Auditory learners may use mnemonic devices and rhymes to remember things. Teachers can use speech or sounds to help auditory learners understand and remember important information.

- Kinaesthetic learning style.
  Kinaesthetic learners prefer to learn through physical activities, movement, and touch. They enjoy hands-on activities and prefer to learn by doing. Kinaesthetic learners often use gestures and body movements when they talk, and they are more likely to remember things when they are physically involved in the learning process. Teachers can use experiments, role-playing, and field trips to help kinaesthetic learners understand and remember complex topics.

Copyrights 2023 Vocational Resources Australia. All Rights Reserved.

- Reading/Writing learning style.
  Reading/writing learners prefer to learn through reading and writing. They enjoy reading books, taking notes, and writing summaries of lectures. They like to express themselves through writing and often create outlines and lists to organise their thoughts. Reading/writing learners may also use flashcards and other memory aids to help them remember important information. Teachers can use textbooks, handouts, and written materials to help reading/writing learners understand and remember information.

- Social learning style.
  Social learners prefer to learn in groups and enjoy learning through interactions with others. They enjoy discussing and debating ideas and collaborating with peers. Social learners often work well in group projects, and they prefer learning environments that are cooperative rather than competitive. Teachers can create opportunities for social learners to collaborate and work in groups to help them understand and remember information.

- Visual learning style.
  Visual learners prefer to use pictures, diagrams, and visual aids to understand and remember information. They enjoy learning through images, videos, and other graphical representations of information. For example, they may respond well to flowcharts, mind maps, and infographics. Visual learners are more likely to remember things they have seen as compared to things they have heard. Teachers can use PowerPoint presentations,

Copyrights 2023 Vocational Resources Australia. All Rights Reserved.

videos, or visual aids to help visual learners understand complex topics.

Learner Types

- Activist learners

  Activist learners are individuals who learn best through hands-on experiences and direct involvement in tasks. They are often characterised as being curious and enthusiastic about learning, as well as being highly engaged in the learning process.

  Activist learners tend to enjoy activities such as role-playing, simulations, and other interactive learning experiences. They are often highly motivated to learn and are always seeking new challenges and opportunities to grow and develop their skills.

  One of the advantages of being an activist learner is that it allows individuals to experience things in a more immersive and meaningful way. This can help them to retain information more effectively, and to apply that knowledge to real-world situations.

- Audio learners

  They tend to retain and process information better when it's presented to them through sound, such as lectures, podcasts, audiobooks, and music.

  Audio learners often have strong listening and verbal skills, and they may struggle with visual aids or reading comprehension. However, they can also benefit from

Copyrights 2023 Vocational Resources Australia. All Rights Reserved.

visual aids that complement the auditory information, such as diagrams, images, or transcripts.

- Auditory learners
  These students learn best through listening and speaking. They often enjoy group discussions and debates, and benefit from hearing information presented in a clear and organised manner. Auditory learners may struggle with written materials or long periods of silence, and often benefit from recording lectures or taking notes while listening.

- Kinaesthetic learners
  Kinaesthetic learners are individuals who prefer to learn through physical activities that involve movement and hands-on experiences. They tend to learn best when they can engage their sense of touch and interact with the material they are trying to learn.

  Kinaesthetic learners often enjoy activities such as sports, dance, or other physical activities that allow them to be active and engage their bodies. They may also enjoy taking things apart and putting them back together, as this can help them understand how things work.

- Left and Right brain learners
  Left-brain learners are often considered to be more analytical, logical and detail-oriented. They tend to excel in subjects like mathematics, science and programming. They also tend to be more methodical and organised in their approach to learning.

Copyrights 2023 Vocational Resources Australia. All Rights Reserved.

On the other hand, right-brain learners are often considered to be more creative, intuitive and holistic in their thinking. They tend to excel in fields like art, music, and literature. They may have a more fluid and improvisational approach to learning, and they may be more comfortable with ambiguity and uncertainty.

It's important to note that most people don't fit neatly into one category or the other. We all use both sides of our brain to some extent, and many people have strengths in both analytical and creative activities.

- Pragmatic learners
  Pragmatic learners are individuals who learn best by applying concepts and theories to practical situations. They are often hands-on learners and prefer to engage in activities that allow them to experiment and explore new ideas. These learners tend to be practical, action-oriented, and results-focused. They are more interested in learning things that they can use in the real world, rather than just accumulating knowledge for its own sake.

  Pragmatic learners often thrive in environments that allow them to work independently or in small groups. They prefer to learn by doing, rather than by listening or reading. They also tend to benefit from feedback, so they can adjust their approach and improve their performance.

- Reflective learners
  Reflective learners are individuals who prefer to think deeply about what they have learned and experienced. They tend to take their time to analyse their thoughts and feelings, and they often use various strategies to help

Copyrights 2023 Vocational Resources Australia. All Rights Reserved.

them process and understand the information they have acquired.

Reflective learners often enjoy writing in a journal or creating mind maps as a way to organise their thoughts. They also like to discuss their ideas with others, as this can often help them gain new insights and perspectives.

- Tactile learners
  These students learn best by doing. They prefer hands-on activities, such as building or creating something, and enjoy taking things apart and putting them back together. Tactile learners may struggle with lectures or written materials, and often need to physically engage with the material in order to truly understand it.

- Theoretical learners
  Theoretical learners are individuals who prefer to understand the underlying principles and concepts of a topic before diving into the practical applications. They often enjoy analysing and reasoning through complex ideas, and they tend to appreciate structured, logical approaches to learning.

  Theoretical learners are often drawn to fields such as science, mathematics, and philosophy, as these subjects provide ample opportunities for delving into theoretical concepts. They may struggle with subjects that require rote memorization or a focus on practical skills without first understanding the underlying principles.

- Visual learners

Copyrights 2023 Vocational Resources Australia. All Rights Reserved.

These students learn best through seeing and observing. They often enjoy diagrams, charts, and videos, and benefit from having information presented in a visual and organised manner. Visual learners may struggle with lectures or lengthy written materials and may benefit from having information broken down into smaller, more manageable pieces.

Vocational Learning & Assessment

Vocational learning and assessment is a type of education that focuses on developing practical skills and knowledge related to specific industries and occupations. It is typically provided through vocational schools, training centres, apprenticeships, or on-the-job training programs.

Vocational assessment, on the other hand, is the process of evaluating a person's skills and abilities to determine their suitability for a particular occupation or vocational training program. The goal of vocational learning and assessment is to prepare individuals for successful careers in their chosen fields and to help them maximise their potential.

Advances in Vocational Learning Practices

Advances in vocational learning practices have been numerous in recent years, spurred on by new technologies and changes in the global economy. In this essay, we will discuss some of the most significant innovations in vocational learning practices in the past decade.

One of the most evident advances in vocational learning practices has been the increasing use of technology in education. This transformation has been largely driven by the widespread availability of digital devices and the internet.

Copyrights 2023 Vocational Resources Australia. All Rights Reserved.

The use of digital technology has allowed educators to create new and more engaging ways to present information and teach skills. Students can now access course materials from anywhere at any time, allowing for more flexible learning schedules that can be adapted to their needs and learning styles.

Online learning platforms have also evolved significantly in recent years. They have become more user-friendly and interactive, making it easier for students to participate in discussions, ask questions, and collaborate with their peers. With many vocational courses now available online, students can gain new skills and knowledge without leaving their homes or taking time off work.

Another aspect of vocational learning that has seen significant advances is blended learning. This is an approach that combines traditional face-to-face instruction with online learning. Blended learning has allowed educators to optimise classroom time by using online materials to supplement in-person learning. This approach also allows students to work at their own pace and review course materials as many times as they need to before moving on. Blended learning has also made it possible for students to seek additional support from instructors and peers even after they leave the classroom.

The use of simulations and virtual reality in vocational learning is another breakthrough in recent years. These technologies allow students to learn and experience various scenarios without having to be physically present. For example, medical students can practice surgical procedures without having to perform them on live patients. Similarly,

Copyrights 2023 Vocational Resources Australia. All Rights Reserved.

pilots can train for flying without ever leaving the ground. This has made vocational training both safer and more cost-effective.

Gamification is another innovation that has been used in vocational learning. Gamification involves incorporating game-like elements such as points, badges, leader boards, and challenges into the learning process. This approach can significantly increase student engagement and motivation as they are encouraged to compete with one another and earn rewards for their efforts. Gamification can be particularly effective in teaching soft skills such as teamwork, communication, and problem-solving.

An essential aspect of vocational learning is work-based training, which involves providing students with practical experience in a real-world work environment. Many training programs have now adopted an apprenticeship model, where students work alongside experienced professionals to hone their skills. This approach has proven successful in many sectors, including construction, manufacturing, and healthcare. Apprenticeships allow students to learn the necessary skills and gain practical experience in a safe and supportive environment, which is crucial for building confidence and competence.

Advances in artificial intelligence and data analytics have enabled educators to personalise learning for each student's needs. Adaptive learning technologies use AI algorithms to analyse student performance data and provide personalised feedback and recommendations. This approach ensures that students receive timely and relevant support, allowing them to fill knowledge gaps and progress quicker.

Copyrights 2023 Vocational Resources Australia. All Rights Reserved.

Approaches/ Strategies/ Techniques

There are several approaches/ strategies to vocational learning and assessment that can be used in different settings, such as:

- Apprenticeships
  This approach combines work-based learning with classroom instruction. It involves a structured, long-term training program that leads to a recognised qualification and on-the-job experience.

- Classroom training
  Classroom training involves employees attending a structured training program in a traditional classroom setting. This technique is effective in providing employees with in-depth knowledge and understanding of a particular subject.

- Coaching
  Coaching involves providing employees with one-on-one guidance and support to help them improve their skills and performance.

- Collaborative learning
  Collaborative learning involves participants working together in groups to solve problems and complete tasks. Collaborative learning can help build teamwork skills and enhance communication and decision-making.

- Competency-based learning & assessment
  This approach focuses on learning specific skills and knowledge that are required for a particular job or

Copyrights 2023 Vocational Resources Australia. All Rights Reserved.

occupation. Competencies are defined in advance, and learning and assessment are structured around them.

- Demonstration
  Demonstrations play an important role in adult learning as they allow learners to see concepts in action and gain a better understanding of how they work. Demonstrations provide practical examples that help learners to visualise and better comprehend complex ideas.

  By showing learners how to apply theoretical knowledge in real-world scenarios, demonstrations help to reinforce learning and make it more memorable.

  In addition, demonstrations can also be used to enhance learner engagement and motivation. By offering opportunities to participate in hands-on activities, learners are able to build their confidence, practice new skills, and gain a deeper appreciation for the subject matter.

- E-learning
  E-learning involves employees completing training courses online. This technique is popular as it allows employees to complete the training at their own pace and convenience.

- Gamification
  Gamification involves adding game-like elements, such as points, badges, and leader boards, to training programs. Gamification has been shown to increase engagement, motivation, and knowledge retention.

Copyrights 2023 Vocational Resources Australia. All Rights Reserved.

- Group, pair and team activities
  Group, pair, and team activities play an important role in adult learning as they encourage collaboration and social interaction, which can enhance the learning experience.

  Group activities, such as classroom discussions or peer reviews, allow adult learners to share their experiences and perspectives with others. This can help them to gain new insights and ideas, as well as build relationships with their classmates.

  Pair activities, such as role-playing or problem-solving exercises, can help adult learners to develop their communication skills and build trust with a partner. This can be particularly useful in workplace training, where collaboration and teamwork are essential.

  Team activities, such as group projects or case studies, allow adult learners to work together to solve complex problems and achieve common goals. This can help to foster a sense of community and accountability, as well as develop leadership and project management skills.

- Hands-on training and practical experience
  This can involve shadowing experienced professionals, undertaking work placements, or participating in apprenticeships.

- Individual activities
  The role of individual activities in adult learning is crucial as they offer learners the chance to take control of their own learning and tailor it to their personal learning preferences and needs. These activities can be self-

Copyrights 2023 Vocational Resources Australia. All Rights Reserved.

directed or guided, and could include things like reading, watching educational videos or podcasts, practicing exercises or reflections on what they've learned.

Individual activities allow adult learners to engage with the material in a way that is most effective for them, based on their learning style and unique needs. These activities can help learners deepen their understanding, develop critical thinking skills, and apply the information to real-life situations.

Moreover, individual activities can provide a level of flexibility in adult learning, as learners can set their own pace and schedule. This is particularly useful for adult learners who have other responsibilities, such as work or family commitments.

- Instruction and explanation
  Instruction and explanation are critical in adult learning for several reasons. Firstly, adults need to understand the rationale behind what they are learning in order to be engaged. They want to know why they are learning something and how it will benefit them. This helps to motivate them to learn and stay engaged in the learning process.

  Secondly, adults have a wealth of knowledge and experience, which can be leveraged to enhance their learning. Instruction and explanation should be tailored to the adult learners' prior knowledge and experience to help them make connections with what they already know. This will help them to better understand new concepts and apply them in practical situations.

Copyrights 2023 Vocational Resources Australia. All Rights Reserved.

Thirdly, adults have different learning styles and preferences. Some prefer visual aids, while others prefer hands-on learning or group activities. Instruction and explanation should cater to different learning styles to ensure that all learners are engaged and can learn effectively.

Lastly, instruction and explanation should be clear, concise, and easy to understand. Adult learners may have limited time available for learning, so it is important to make the most of the time available and ensure that the learning is effective.

- Interactive training
  Interactive training involves hands-on exercises, simulations, and games. This technique allows participants to practice skills and apply knowledge in a real-world setting.

- Job-specific simulations
  Using virtual or physical simulations to mimic real-life job situations allows learners to practice and gain confidence in the skills required for their chosen vocation.

- Mentoring
  Mentoring involves pairing employees with more experienced colleagues who can guide and support them in their career development.

- Microlearning
  Microlearning involves delivering short, focused bursts of content in a variety of formats, such as videos, podcasts,

Copyrights 2023 Vocational Resources Australia. All Rights Reserved.

and infographics. Microlearning is an effective way to support just-in-time learning and reinforce key concepts.

- On-the-job training
  On-the-job training involves learning while performing the job itself. It is a popular training technique as it allows employees to learn new skills and techniques while actually doing their job.

- Practice
  Practice is essential for adult learning as it helps to reinforce newly acquired skills and knowledge, making them more likely to be retained and used in the future. Adults often have busy lives and limited time for learning, so practice is even more critical to ensure that they can apply what they have learned effectively.

  Practice also allows adults to identify areas where they may need further development, enabling them to focus on specific skills or knowledge gaps. By practicing, adults can build confidence in their abilities and feel more comfortable using what they have learned in real-world situations.

- Personalised and adaptive learning
  Personalised learning involves tailoring the training experience to the individual needs and preferences of each participant. Personalised learning can be achieved through adaptive learning technologies or through more conventional means such as coaching and mentoring.

Copyrights 2023 Vocational Resources Australia. All Rights Reserved.

- Project-based learning
  This approach involves learners working on a specific project that requires them to apply their skills and knowledge in a real-world situation. Assessment is based on the quality of the final product or outcome.

- Questioning
  Questioning is an essential element in adult learning. Asking questions can help stimulate critical thinking, encourage reflection, and promote a deeper understanding of the subject matter.

  When learners are encouraged to ask questions, it allows them to take an active role in their learning process. It helps to build their confidence, fosters curiosity, and leads to a more dynamic and interactive learning experience.

  Questioning also plays an important role in problem-solving. By asking the right questions, learners can identify and define problems, explore possible solutions, and evaluate the effectiveness of their actions.

- Role-playing
  Role-playing involves participants taking on different roles to practice communication and problem-solving skills. Role-playing can be particularly effective for teaching leadership, negotiation, and conflict resolution skills.

- Storytelling
  Storytelling involves sharing stories and anecdotes that illustrate key concepts and theories. Storytelling is an

Copyrights 2023 Vocational Resources Australia. All Rights Reserved.

effective way to engage learners emotionally and enhance their recall of important information.

- Use of multimedia
  Using various forms of multimedia such as videos, podcasts or interactive diagrams, to represent and present information in a more engaging and interactive format can be more effective for vocational learners.

- Work-based learning
  This approach emphasises learning through practical experience in a workplace or simulated work environment. Learning is contextual, and assessment is based on the ability to perform job-specific tasks.

- Written information
  Written information plays a crucial role in adult learning as it provides a permanent record of the knowledge and skills that have been learned. Written materials can include textbooks, manuals, handouts, and other resources, and they are often used as reference materials for future use. Adults are often more independent learners, and written information allows them to learn at their own pace, to review material repeatedly and to refer back to it as needed.

  Additionally, written materials can help to reinforce learning by presenting information in a structured and organised way. They can also be used to communicate complex concepts and ideas that may be difficult to convey verbally. Furthermore, written material can be easily shared and distributed, making it a cost-effective method of providing learning resources.

Copyrights 2023 Vocational Resources Australia. All Rights Reserved.

Regardless of the approach used, effective vocational learning and assessment should be aligned with industry standards, be relevant to the needs of employers and learners, and provide opportunities for feedback and continuous improvement.

Aligning Learning Practice with the Nominated Qualification Requirements

To ensure that learning practice reflects the qualification requirements for the nominated qualification, you can follow these steps:

1. Review the qualification requirements
   Start by reviewing the qualification requirements to understand the skills, knowledge, and competencies that learners need to acquire to meet the qualification requirements.

2. Develop learning outcomes
   Based on the qualification requirements, develop clear learning outcomes that describe what learners will achieve after completing the learning program.

3. Create learning activities
   Design a range of learning activities that will help learners achieve the learning outcomes. These activities should be relevant to the qualification requirements and should provide learners with opportunities to apply their knowledge and skills.

Copyrights 2023 Vocational Resources Australia. All Rights Reserved.

4. Use assessment tools
   Develop assessment tools that align with the learning outcomes and qualification requirements. These tools should measure the learners' knowledge and skills and provide evidence that they have met the qualification requirements.

5. Review and evaluate
   Regularly review and evaluate the learning materials, activities, and assessment tools to ensure that they continue to align with the qualification requirements and meet the learners' needs.

Catering Individual Learner's Needs

Analysing interests, abilities, relationships, and contextual needs is a critical step towards promoting improved learning practices among employees.

Here's a breakdown of each element:

- Interests
  Employees are more likely to be engaged in learning activities if they find them interesting and relevant to their career goals. Analysing their interests can help identify topics and formats that would be most effective for their development.

- Abilities
  Employees have varying levels of knowledge, skills, and competencies. Analysing their abilities can help identify areas where they need improvement and tailor learning interventions accordingly.

Copyrights 2023 Vocational Resources Australia. All Rights Reserved.

- Relationships
  Learning is often social, and employees can benefit from interacting and collaborating with peers and mentors. Analysing their relationships can help identify opportunities for peer-to-peer learning, coaching, and mentoring.

- Contextual needs
  The work environment, organisational culture, and other contextual factors can influence the effectiveness of learning interventions. Analysing contextual needs can help identify barriers and enablers of learning and ensure that interventions are aligned with the organisation's goals and values.

Effective Implementation of Training & Development Programs

To ensure the effective implementation of training and development programs, organisations need to follow certain guidelines. These guidelines include:

- Developing clear goals and objectives
  Organisations need to develop clear goals and objectives for their training and development programs. This will help to ensure that the training is relevant and effective.

- Customising training programs
  Organisations need to customize their training programs to meet the specific needs of their employees. This will help to ensure that the training is relevant and engaging.

Copyrights 2023 Vocational Resources Australia. All Rights Reserved.

- Providing ongoing support
  Organisations need to provide ongoing support to employees after the training has been completed. This will help to reinforce the learning and ensure that the training is effective.

- Evaluating the effectiveness of training programs
  Organisations need to evaluate the effectiveness of their training programs to ensure that they are meeting their goals and objectives.

Role of Technology

Today, technology has become an integral part of daily life. It has transformed the education industry, making it easier for learners to access and gain knowledge. It has provided limitless opportunities for improving student achievements and instructional approaches, including education and communication technology.

The application of Information and Communications Technology (ICT) to learning and teaching has the potential to significantly enhance education systems' effectiveness, efficiency, and equity. This essay will discuss the imperative application of ICT to learning and teaching.

- ICT and learning
  ICT has transformed the learning process- enabling knowledge to be available at the click of a button. Multimedia has enabled learners to access vast resources and knowledge, from any place across the globe- thanks to the internet. Virtual platforms such as online libraries, discussion forums, blogs, and online courses have become the norm, offering learners

Copyrights 2023 Vocational Resources Australia. All Rights Reserved.

flexibility and convenience in accessing educational content.

The availability of interactive computer software programs, including simulations, games, and other multimedia tools, has enhanced comprehension and retention of knowledge. In addition, the availability of mobile devices such as smartphones, tablets, and laptops has made it easier for learners to access educational data on the go.

- ICT and teaching
  ICT has also brought about significant benefits to teaching. Teachers can use various multimedia to present instructional materials in diverse formats, from text to video and audio media. The use of multimedia, such as visual aids, slideshows, videos, and interactive whiteboards, has made teaching more interactive, engaging, and fun. It has also enhanced the presentation of abstract concepts and theories, making them easier to comprehend.

  Additionally, ICT has made it easier for teachers to prepare instructional materials and assessments through the use of computer software such as Microsoft Office Suite and learning management systems (LMS).

- ICT and classroom management
  ICT has revolutionised classroom management. The use of centralised platforms such as LMS and educational software enables the efficient organisation of instructional materials, assessment results, and feedback for individual learners.

Copyrights 2023 Vocational Resources Australia. All Rights Reserved.

Furthermore, LMS provides students with self-paced learning opportunities and instant feedback, reducing the need for manual grading of exams and other assessments. Teachers can also use LMS to track and assess student progress in real-time. This data can offer insightful feedback and guide the teacher in the development of individualized instruction and support.

- ICT and equity in education
  ICT has the potential to reduce the traditional education system's inequalities. The internet has enabled access to educational resources for students living in remote locations and those who lack the necessary infrastructure to access education.

  Online courses have also made higher education accessible to students who cannot afford the cost of a conventional college.

  Additionally, the use of LMS and other educational software can provide learners with access to digital libraries, online tutors, and other support services that would otherwise be unavailable.

Copyrights 2023 Vocational Resources Australia. All Rights Reserved.

Developing Vocational Training Practices

- Collaboration between industry and educational institutions.
  Encouraging partnerships between educational institutions and relevant industries can create better vocational training programs that meet the needs of employers and provides learners with the skills necessary to succeed in the workforce.

- Regular evaluation and updating of programs.
  A regular evaluation of vocational training programs can help educators in identifying areas of weakness and strengths that need improving.

- Increasing the use of technology.
  Incorporating digital and virtual reality tools in vocational training programs is an excellent way to provide students with practical experience in their fields.

- Providing career guidance and mentorship.
  Mentorship programs can be an excellent way of ensuring that students learn from skilled professionals in their field; it provides practical insights, strengthens communication, and networks.

- Personalised learning.
  Tailoring vocational training programs to meet individual learning needs can enhance student engagement, leading to better performance.

Copyrights 2023 Vocational Resources Australia. All Rights Reserved.

- Measuring outcomes.
  Collecting data on learners' outcomes and making necessary decisions that ensure that students graduate equipped with the relevant knowledge and skills.

- Continuous learning.
  Making continuous learning a part of the students and employees' training structure can result in the frequent reskilling and upskilling necessary to adapt to changing trends and work environments.

- Continuous evaluation.
  Evaluate the effectiveness of vocational training programs regularly to identify areas that require improvement and modify training practices as needed. Stay informed about emerging trends in training and adjust accordingly.

- Advocate for financial support.
  Advocate for the government and other funding organisations to invest in more vocational training initiatives and increase support for disadvantaged populations who lack access to high-quality vocational learning opportunities.

Copyrights 2023 Vocational Resources Australia. All Rights Reserved.

Advocating Improved Vocational Training Practices

- Conduct research
  Research to gather information about the current vocational training practices and identify the areas where improvements are needed.

- Collaborate with industry experts
  Collaborate with experts from the respective industries to identify the skills and knowledge that are required to excel in these fields. This will help in designing more effective training programs.

- Build effective partnerships
  Build partnerships with employers and industry associations to help ensure that the training provided is aligned with the current industry demands and can prepare graduates for the workforce.

- Develop customized training programs
  Develop customized training programs that are tailored to meet the specific needs of the student and the industry. This can help individuals acquire the exact skills they need to thrive in their preferred fields.

- Use modern tools and technologies
  Encourage the use of modern tools and technologies to enhance the vocational training programs. This can include the use of virtual reality to simulate real-world work environments, online learning platforms to enable remote learning, and various other tools to help students get hands-on experiences.

Copyrights 2023 Vocational Resources Australia. All Rights Reserved.

Reviewing existing Learning Practices

Reviewing and challenging existing learning practices in the workplace can be a valuable exercise to ensure that the organisation is making the most of its training efforts and that employees are able to learn and apply new skills and knowledge effectively.

Here are some steps that you can take to review and challenge existing learning practices in the workplace:

1. Analyse your current learning practices
   Start by looking at the current learning practices in your organisation. Examine the types of training that are being offered, the methods used to deliver the training, and the outcomes that are being achieved. This can help you identify any areas where you need to improve or make changes.

2. Gather feedback from employees
   It's important to get feedback from employees in order to understand their perspective on the existing learning practices. You can do this through surveys, focus groups, or one-on-one interviews. This feedback can help you identify areas where employees feel that the current practices are not effective or could be improved.

3. Identify gaps and areas for improvement
   Based on the analysis and feedback, identify any gaps or areas for improvement in your current learning practices. This might include updating or revising training materials, changing the delivery method, or incorporating new technologies.

Copyrights 2023 Vocational Resources Australia. All Rights Reserved.

4. Develop a plan for improvement
   Once you have identified areas for improvement, develop a plan to address them. This might involve creating new training materials, investing in new technologies, or providing additional support to employees.

5. Monitor and evaluate the results
   It's important to monitor and evaluate the results of any changes that you make to your learning practices. This can help you determine whether the changes that you have made have been effective or whether further improvements need to be made.

Design and Test Improved Learning Practice

Key steps involved in designing and testing the improved learning practice are outlined below:

1. Identify the problem
   First, you need to figure out what the problem is that you're trying to solve. This could be a lack of engagement in the learning process, poor academic performance, or something else.

2. Research
   Next, do some research to find out what other experts in the field have done to address similar problems. This can help you generate ideas and inspire your own approach.

Copyrights 2023 Vocational Resources Australia. All Rights Reserved.

3. Develop a plan
   Once you have a sense of what you want to accomplish, create a plan for how you're going to do it. This plan should include a clear set of goals, a timeline, and a budget.

4. Implement your plan
   Once your plan is in place, start implementing it. Make sure to track your progress and adjust your plan as needed.

5. Evaluate your results
   Finally, evaluate your results to see if your approach is working. This might involve conducting surveys or focus groups to gather feedback from learners or analysing quantitative data like test scores.

Workplace Training

Workplace training is a process of providing employees with the knowledge, skills, and abilities they need to perform their jobs effectively. It can be delivered in a variety of ways, including formal classroom instruction, on-the-job training, and e-learning.

There are many benefits to workplace training. It can help employees:

- Increase their productivity and efficiency
- Improve their job performance
- Stay up to date on new technologies and procedures
- Develop new skills and competencies
- Be more engaged and motivated in their work
- Reduce the risk of accidents and injuries

Copyrights 2023 Vocational Resources Australia. All Rights Reserved.

- Improve the company's bottom line

The best way to deliver workplace training depends on the specific needs of the company and the employees. For example, if the training is complex or technical, classroom instruction may be the best option. If the training is less complex or technical, on-the-job training or e-learning may be more effective.

Workplace training is an important investment for businesses of all sizes. It can help employees improve their job performance, stay up to date on new technologies and procedures, develop new skills and competencies, and be more engaged and motivated in their work. All of these factors can lead to increased productivity, improved safety, and a stronger bottom line.

The following should be considered for an effective workplace training program:

- Make sure the training is aligned with the company's goals and objectives.
- Tailor the training to the specific needs of the employees.
- Use a variety of training methods to keep employees engaged.
- Provide opportunities for employees to practice what they've learned.
- Evaluate the effectiveness of the training program and make improvements as needed.

Copyrights 2023 Vocational Resources Australia. All Rights Reserved.

Competency Based Training

Competency-based training (CBT) is a training method that focuses on the learner's ability to perform specific tasks or roles, rather than on the amount of time spent in training. CBT is often used in the workplace, but it can also be used in other settings, such as schools and healthcare organisations.

CBT is based on the idea that learning should be focused on the skills and knowledge that are needed to perform a specific task or role. This approach to training is different from traditional training methods, which often focus on teaching general knowledge or concepts.

CBT is designed to be learner-centred, which means that it is tailored to the individual learner's needs and abilities. This is done by identifying the learner's current skills and knowledge, and then developing a training plan that will help them to reach their desired level of competency.

CBT is also designed to be performance-based, which means that the learner's progress is assessed based on their ability to perform specific tasks or roles. This is done through a variety of methods, such as demonstrations, simulations, and assessments.

CBT has a number of benefits, including:

- It is learner-centred and performance-based, which can lead to better learning outcomes.
- It is flexible and can be tailored to the individual learner's needs.

Copyrights 2023 Vocational Resources Australia. All Rights Reserved.

- It can be delivered in a variety of formats, including online, in-person, and blended learning.
- It can be more cost-effective than traditional training methods.

CBT is not without its challenges, however. One challenge is that it can be more time-consuming to develop CBT programs than traditional training programs. Another challenge is that CBT requires a high level of learner engagement and motivation.

Despite these challenges, CBT is a valuable training method that can be used to improve the skills and knowledge of learners in a variety of settings.

Here are some of the key features of competency-based training:

- Focus on performance: CBT focuses on the learner's ability to perform specific tasks or roles, rather than on the amount of time spent in training.
- Learner-centred: CBT is tailored to the individual learner's needs and abilities.
- Performance-based: The learner's progress is assessed based on their ability to perform specific tasks or roles.
- Flexible: CBT can be delivered in a variety of formats, including online, in-person, and blended learning.

Copyrights 2023 Vocational Resources Australia. All Rights Reserved.

- Cost-effective: CBT can be more cost-effective than traditional training methods.

If you are considering using CBT in your organisation, there are a few things you should keep in mind:

- Identify your training needs
  The first step is to identify the skills and knowledge that your employees need to be successful in their roles.

- Develop competency-based training programs
  Once you have identified your training needs, you can develop competency-based training programs to address those needs.

- Provide ongoing support
  It is important to provide ongoing support to employees who are participating in CBT programs. This support can include coaching, mentoring, and feedback.

Compliance Requirements

Compliance requirements in the context of workplace training refer to the set of legal, ethical, and regulatory standards that a company or organisation needs to meet in order to ensure that its employees are working within the bounds of the law. These compliance requirements can vary depending on the industry and the nature of the work being carried out, but they generally include things like health and safety regulations, data privacy laws, anti-discrimination policies, and financial reporting requirements.

When it comes to workplace training, compliance requirements are an important consideration because they

Copyrights 2023 Vocational Resources Australia. All Rights Reserved.

help to ensure that employees are aware of their legal and ethical obligations and are equipped with the knowledge and skills they need to meet these requirements. This can be achieved through a variety of training methods, including online courses, in-person seminars, and on-the-job training.

The key requirements are:
- Clear and transparent communication
- Training needs analysis
- Equity and opportunity
- Training sufficiency
- Recordkeeping
- Feedback
- Monitoring
- Review.

Consultation & Communication
Consultation plays an important role in ensuring that the training aligns with the needs and goals of the organisation. Before designing and implementing any training program, it's crucial to consult with stakeholders such as employees, managers, and subject matter experts to determine what skills and knowledge are needed and how best to deliver them.

By involving key stakeholders in the planning process, you can ensure that the training meets the needs of the organisation and is more likely to be effective.

In addition to consultation, communication is also essential for effective workplace training. Clear communication helps to ensure that employees understand what they need to learn, why it's important, and how they will be evaluated on

Copyrights 2023 Vocational Resources Australia. All Rights Reserved.

their performance. Effective communication can also help to motivate employees to participate in the training and take it seriously. This is especially important when training is mandatory or when employees may not see the immediate benefits of the training.

Developing Procedures to Liaise with Stakeholders

The following should be considered while developing organisational procedures to liaise with educators, learners, and others:

- Define your communication goals
  Start by determining what you hope to achieve with your communication efforts. For example, are you seeking to improve engagement with learners or build relationships with educators? Having clear goals in mind will help you develop procedures that are effective and efficient.

- Identify your target audience
  Once you know what you want to accomplish, it's time to identify the people you'll be communicating with. This may include learners, educators, administrators, and other stakeholders.

- Determine the best communication channels
  Depending on your target audience, some communication channels may be more effective than others. For example, email might work best for communicating with educators, while social media might be more effective for engaging with learners.

Copyrights 2023 Vocational Resources Australia. All Rights Reserved.

- Outline the procedures
  Once you have a clear understanding of your goals, target audience, and communication channels, it's time to outline the procedures you'll follow. This might include creating communication templates, determining frequency of communication, and establishing a process for tracking responses.

The procedures should entail:

- Clear communication guidelines
  Your procedures should outline clear guidelines for how communication should be conducted. This might include tone of voice, language to use, and expectations for response time.

- Regular check-ins
  Consistent communication is key to building strong relationships. Consider scheduling regular check-ins with your various stakeholders to stay on top of their needs and concerns.

- Transparency
  Be open and honest in your communication. Transparency builds trust and fosters strong relationships.

- Flexibility
  Recognise that different situations may require different communication approaches. Be flexible and willing to adapt your procedures as needed.

Copyrights 2023 Vocational Resources Australia. All Rights Reserved.

Learning Plan

A learning plan is a document that outlines the goals, objectives, and activities of a training program. It is a valuable tool for both trainers and learners, as it helps to ensure that the training is effective and meets the needs of the learner.

Here are some reasons why a learning plan is required for workplace training:

- To ensure that the training is effective
  A learning plan can help to ensure that the training is effective by ensuring that it is aligned with the organisation's goals, objectives, and needs. It can also help to ensure that the training is relevant to the learner's job role and responsibilities.

- To save time and money
  A learning plan can help to save time and money by ensuring that the training is well-organised and efficient. It can also help to avoid the need for unplanned or unnecessary training.

- To improve employee performance
  A learning plan can help to improve employee performance by providing them with the knowledge and skills they need to do their jobs effectively. It can also help to motivate employees and encourage them to take on new challenges.

- To comply with regulatory requirements
  In some cases, organisations may be required to provide training to their employees in order to comply with

Copyrights 2023 Vocational Resources Australia. All Rights Reserved.

regulatory requirements. A learning plan can help to ensure that the organisation is meeting these requirements.

A learning plan should include the following elements:

- Goals and objectives
  The goals and objectives of the training program should be clearly defined. Goals are broad statements of what the learner should be able to do after completing the training, while objectives are specific, measurable statements that describe how the learner will achieve the goal.

- Audience
  The audience for the training program should be clearly defined. This will help the trainer to select the appropriate content and delivery methods.

- Content
  The content of the training program should be relevant to the goals and objectives of the program. It should also be accurate, up to date, and presented in a way that is easy for the learner to understand.

- Delivery methods
  The delivery methods used for the training program should be appropriate for the audience and the content. Some common delivery methods include lectures, workshops, simulations, and e-learning.

Copyrights 2023 Vocational Resources Australia. All Rights Reserved.

- Assessment
  The learning plan should include a plan for assessing the learner's progress. This may involve tests, quizzes, or performance assessments.

Implementation

There are a number of ways to implement a learning plan in the workplace. One common approach is to use a blended learning approach, which combines traditional classroom instruction with online and self-paced learning. This approach can be effective for a variety of reasons, including:

- It can be more cost-effective than traditional classroom instruction.

- It can be more flexible, allowing employees to learn at their own pace and in their own time.

- It can be more engaging, as employees can choose learning activities that are relevant to their interests and needs.

Another approach to implementing a learning plan is to use a mobile learning platform. Mobile learning platforms allow employees to access learning content and activities on their smartphones or tablets. This can be a convenient and effective way for employees to learn new skills and knowledge, even when they are on the go.

No matter which approach is used, it is important to ensure that the learning plan is aligned with the organisation's goals and objectives. This will help to ensure that the learning is

Copyrights 2023 Vocational Resources Australia. All Rights Reserved.

relevant and that employees are able to apply what they learn to their work.

The following strategies should be adopted in implementation of the learning plans:

- Start with a needs assessment
  The first step in implementing a learning plan is to assess the needs of the employees. This will help you to determine what skills and knowledge they need to develop in order to be successful in their roles.

- Set clear goals and objectives
  Once you have identified the needs of the employees, you need to set clear goals and objectives for the learning plan. This will help to ensure that the learning is focused and that employees are able to track their progress.

- Choose the right learning methods
  There are a variety of learning methods available, so it is important to choose the right ones for your employees. Some common methods include classroom instruction, online learning, and mobile learning.

- Provide opportunities for feedback
  It is important to provide opportunities for employees to provide feedback on the learning plan. This will help you to identify any areas that need improvement and to make sure that the learning is meeting the needs of the employees.

Copyrights 2023 Vocational Resources Australia. All Rights Reserved.

- Track progress and measure results
  It is important to track the progress of the learning plan and measure the results. This will help you to determine whether the learning is effective and to make adjustments as needed.

Developing Procedures for Resource Allocation

Developing processes and procedures for allocating and managing resources, to implement an organisational learning strategy can be broken down into the following steps:

1. Identify the organisation's learning goals and objectives.
   This will help you determine what resources are needed to achieve these goals.

2. Conduct a resource assessment.
   This step involves identifying what resources, such as personnel, equipment, and funds, are currently available and what additional resources may be needed.

3. Develop a resource allocation plan.
   Based on the resource assessment, you can develop a plan that outlines how resources will be allocated to achieve learning goals and objectives.

4. Establish procedures for managing resources.
   This includes developing processes for requesting and approving resources, tracking resource usage, and evaluating resource effectiveness.

Copyrights 2023 Vocational Resources Australia. All Rights Reserved.

5. Monitor and evaluate resource allocation.
   This step involves regularly reviewing the resource allocation plan to ensure it is still aligned with the organisation's learning goals and making any necessary adjustments.

It is important to involve key stakeholders in the process of developing processes and procedures for allocating and managing resources required to implement an organisational learning strategy. This ensures that everyone is aligned and understands the plan, which increases the likelihood of success for implementing the learning strategy.

Identifying Required Resources

The following steps can be adopted to identify the resources & time required in implementing the learning plan:

1. Start by identifying the learning goals and objectives. What do you want employees to learn? What skills do you want them to develop? Once you know what you want to achieve, you can start to identify the resources and time that will be needed.

2. Identify the training methods that will be used.
   Will you use traditional classroom training, e-learning, or a combination of both? The training method you choose will have a big impact on the resources and time required.

3. Identify the trainers or facilitators who will be involved. If you are using traditional classroom training, you will need to identify trainers who are qualified to deliver the training. If you are using e-learning, you may need

Copyrights 2023 Vocational Resources Australia. All Rights Reserved.

to identify facilitators who can help employees with the training.

4. Identify the materials that will be used.
   If you are using traditional classroom training, you will need to identify the materials that will be used, such as training manuals, handouts, and PowerPoint presentations. If you are using e-learning, you will need to identify the materials that will be used, such as online courses, videos, and simulations.

5. Identify the time that will be needed for training.
   How long will it take employees to complete the training? The amount of time required will depend on the training method, the content of the training, and the level of experience of the employees.

6. Identify the costs associated with training.
   What will it cost to implement the training plan? The costs associated with training will vary depending on the training method, the materials used, and the trainers or facilitators involved.

7. Talk to other organisations that have implemented similar learning plans. They may be able to share insights and resources that can help you.

8. Consider using a learning management system (LMS).
   An LMS can help you track progress, manage resources, and communicate with employees.

Copyrights 2023 Vocational Resources Australia. All Rights Reserved.

9. Be flexible and willing to make adjustments as needed.
   Things don't always go according to plan, so it's important to be prepared to make changes as needed.

Once you have identified the resources and time required, you can develop a budget and timeline for the implementation of the employee learning plan. By carefully planning and budgeting for training, you can ensure that it is effective and that it does not overextend your resources.

Monitoring

The following strategies can be adopted to monitor the implementation of learning plans:

- Set up a system for collecting data. This could include surveys, interviews, or focus groups.
- Analyse the data to identify areas where improvement is needed.
- Collect feedback. It allows learners to identify their strengths and weaknesses, track their progress, and make adjustments as needed. Feedback can also help learners stay motivated and engaged in the learning process.
- Take action to address any issues that are identified.
- Communicate with employees about the progress of the learning plan.
- Celebrate successes along the way.

Copyrights 2023 Vocational Resources Australia. All Rights Reserved.

Learning Strategy

Workplace learning strategy is a systematic and organised approach to developing and enhancing the knowledge, skills, and abilities of employees in an organisation.

The purpose of this strategy is to improve employee performance and productivity while also creating a learning culture within the organisation.

Key steps in developing & implementing a workplace learning strategy are:

1. Identify the business objectives
   The first step in developing a workplace learning strategy is to identify the business objectives and goals of the organisation. This will help to ensure that the learning strategy is in alignment with the overall mission and vision of the company.

2. Analyse training needs
   Once the business objectives have been identified, the next step is to analyse the training needs of employees.

   This can be done through surveys, interviews, or assessments to determine the skills and knowledge gaps that need to be addressed.

3. Select appropriate training methods
   Based on the training needs analysis, appropriate training methods should be selected. These can include classroom training, e-learning, on-the-job training, coaching, mentoring, and job shadowing.

Copyrights 2023 Vocational Resources Australia. All Rights Reserved.

4. Develop training content
   Once the training methods have been selected, the training content should be developed. This should be based on the specific needs of the employees and should be designed to meet the learning objectives.

5. Deliver the training
   After the training content has been developed, it should be delivered to employees in a way that is engaging and effective. This may involve the use of technology, such as e-learning modules or virtual training sessions, or in-person training sessions.

6. Measure the effectiveness of the training
   It is important to measure the effectiveness of the training. This can be done through assessments, surveys, or performance evaluations to determine if the training has improved employee performance and productivity.

Aligning Learning Strategy

Aligning learning strategy with human resources and organisational learning requirements is an important step in promoting employee development and growth within the company.

Key steps involved are:

1. Identify organisational goals
   Start by identifying the organisational goals and objectives that the learning strategy should support. This may include improving productivity, reducing

Copyrights 2023 Vocational Resources Australia. All Rights Reserved.

costs, enhancing customer service, and increasing sales, for example.

2. Assess learning needs
   Conduct a comprehensive assessment of learning needs across the organisation. This can help identify the skills and knowledge employees need to support the organisational goals.

3. Choose appropriate learning methods
   Choose appropriate learning methods that align with the organisation's goals. This may include traditional classroom training, online learning, coaching, mentoring, or on-the-job training.

4. Develop learning programs
   Develop learning programs that are designed to meet the specific needs of the organisation. This may involve developing new training materials or modifying existing ones to better align with the organisational requirements.

5. Measure learning outcomes
   Implement metrics to measure the effectiveness of the learning programs in meeting the organisational requirements. This can help identify areas where improvements can be made and ensure that the learning strategy is effectively aligned with the organisational goals.

6. Continuously review and improve
   Continuously review and improve the learning strategy to ensure that it stays aligned with the

Copyrights 2023 Vocational Resources Australia. All Rights Reserved.

organisational requirements. This may involve making adjustments to the learning programs or identifying new training needs as the organisation's goals change over time.

Analysing Organisational Requirements

When it comes to developing a learning strategy, it's important to first understand the specific requirements and needs of the organisation. This is where analysing organisational requirements comes into play.

To start, you'll want to identify the goals and objectives of the organisation, as well as any challenges or areas in need of improvement. This can be done through a variety of methods, such as conducting surveys, analysing performance data, and consulting with key stakeholders.

Once you have a clear understanding of the organisational requirements, you can start developing a learning strategy that is tailored to meet those specific needs. This might involve identifying skills gaps and designing training programs to address them, or creating resources that support ongoing learning and development within the organisation.

It's also important to consider the broader context in which the organisation operates, such as industry trends and regulatory requirements, to ensure that the learning strategy is aligned with those factors as well.

Copyrights 2023 Vocational Resources Australia. All Rights Reserved.

Common Approaches to Learning Strategy Design

There are several approaches to consider when designing a learning strategy. Some of them are discussed below:

- Needs assessment
  Start by identifying the learning needs and gaps in your organisation. Conduct surveys, focus groups, and interviews to understand what skills and knowledge your employees need to perform their jobs effectively.

- Goals and objectives
  Set clear goals and objectives for the learning strategy that are aligned with the organisational goals. This will ensure that the learning program supports the overall mission and vision of the company.

- Learning methods
  Consider the different learning methods available such as e-learning, in-person training, and on-the-job training. Select the methods that are most appropriate for the learners and the content.

- Learning content
  Develop relevant and engaging learning content that is tailored to the learners' needs. Use a variety of formats such as videos, interactive activities, and case studies to keep learners engaged.

- Evaluation
  Evaluate the effectiveness of the learning program regularly. Use metrics such as learner feedback, performance data, and business outcomes to measure the impact of the learning program.

Copyrights 2023 Vocational Resources Australia. All Rights Reserved.

Continuous Improvement

Some of the strategies to incorporate continuous improvement in workplace learning strategy are outlined below:

- Gather feedback
  Collect feedback from employees, trainers, and managers on the effectiveness of the current learning strategy. This feedback can be used to identify areas for improvement and to tailor learning to meet specific needs.

- Use data to inform decisions
  Use data to track the effectiveness of training programs and identify areas where improvement is needed. For example, you can track employee performance before and after training to see if the training has had a positive impact.

- Encourage ongoing learning
  Encourage employees to continuously learn and develop new skills by providing opportunities for ongoing training and development.

- Create a culture of learning
  Foster a culture of learning by creating opportunities for knowledge sharing, providing resources for learning, and recognising employees who participate in learning activities.

Copyrights 2023 Vocational Resources Australia. All Rights Reserved.

- Implement new technologies
  Incorporate new technologies that can support learning and development, such as learning management systems, virtual reality training, and gamification.

Evaluation

Evaluating the implementation of workplace learning strategy can be a complex process, but it's necessary to ensure that the strategy is effective and producing results.

Key steps to evaluate the implementation of workplace learning strategy are outlined below:

- Determine the goals and objectives of the learning strategy.
  Before you evaluate the implementation of your workplace learning strategy, it's important to have clear goals and objectives in mind. What do you hope to achieve with this strategy? What skills or knowledge do you want your employees to gain? By having a clear understanding of your goals, you can better evaluate the success of your strategy.

- Measure the effectiveness of the training.
  One way to evaluate the implementation of workplace learning strategy is to measure the effectiveness of the training. This can be done through assessments, surveys, or other metrics. For example, you can assess employees' knowledge before and after the training to determine how much they have learned. You can also ask employees to rate the quality of the training or provide feedback on how it can be improved.

Copyrights 2023 Vocational Resources Australia. All Rights Reserved.

- Evaluate the impact on employee performance.
  Another way to evaluate the implementation of workplace learning strategy is to evaluate the impact on employee performance. This can include measuring changes in productivity, job satisfaction, or other key performance indicators. By comparing the performance of employees who have received the training to those who have not, you can determine whether the training has had a positive impact.

- Analyse the return on investment.
  Evaluating the implementation of workplace learning strategy also involves analysing the return on investment. This means looking at the cost of the training compared to the benefits it has produced. For example, if the training has led to increased productivity, you can calculate the value of that increased productivity compared to the cost of the training.

- Adjust the strategy as needed.
  Evaluating the implementation of workplace learning strategy may require making adjustments to the strategy itself. Based on the results of your evaluation, you may need to modify the training program, adjust the goals and objectives, or make other changes to improve its effectiveness.

Copyrights 2023 Vocational Resources Australia. All Rights Reserved.

Incorporating Flexible Learning Approaches

When incorporating flexible learning into an organisational learning strategy, there are a few key considerations to keep in mind. Some of them are discussed below:

- Define your learning goals
  Before introducing flexible learning, it's important to understand what you want to achieve from your learning programs. Are you looking to upskill your employees, prepare them for new roles, or improve overall performance? Once you have your objectives clearly defined, you can tailor your flexible learning approach accordingly.

- Assess your learners
  It's essential to understand your learners' preferences and needs when designing flexible learning programs. Are they comfortable with digital learning platforms? Do they prefer a self-paced or structured learning approach? Knowing this information can help you create a more effective learning experience.

- Choose the right technology
  There are a variety of tools and technologies available for delivering flexible learning. From learning management systems (LMS) to virtual classrooms, it's important to select the technology that best suits your organisation's needs and budget.

- Measure success
  Just like any other learning program, you need to measure the effectiveness of your flexible learning strategy. Determine what metrics you will use to evaluate

Copyrights 2023 Vocational Resources Australia. All Rights Reserved.

the program's success, such as engagement rates, completion rates, or feedback from learners.

Quality Management Requirements

Quality management is a crucial aspect of workplace training, as it ensures that the training provided is effective and meets the needs of both the organisation and its employees.

In order to achieve this, there are a number of quality management requirements that should be taken into consideration. Some of them are discussed below:

- It's important to have clear learning objectives for the training. This means that the goals of the training should be clearly defined, and the content of the training should be designed to meet these objectives. This helps to ensure that the training is relevant and that employees are able to apply what they have learned in their work.

- The training should be delivered in a way that is engaging and interactive. This means that the training should use a variety of methods, such as videos, games, and group activities, to keep employees engaged and interested.

- The training should be evaluated to ensure that it is effective. This means that feedback should be gathered from employees to assess their understanding of the material, and the training should be modified based on this feedback to make it more effective.

Copyrights 2023 Vocational Resources Australia. All Rights Reserved.

- It's important to ensure that the training is delivered consistently across the organisation. This means that the same training should be provided to all employees, and that the training should be updated regularly to ensure that it remains relevant.

Recordkeeping

Recordkeeping is essential for compliance, monitoring, and ongoing implementation purposes.

The specific records that need to be kept will vary depending on the type of training and the industry in which the business operates. However, some common types of records that may need to be kept include:

- Attendance records
  This should include the date, time, and location of the training, as well as the names of the employees who attended.

- Training materials
  This could include any handouts, PowerPoint presentations, or other materials that were used during the training.

- Instructor qualifications
  This should include the instructor's name, title, and qualifications.

- Evaluations
  This should include the employees' feedback on the training.

Copyrights 2023 Vocational Resources Australia. All Rights Reserved.

A couple of other points to consider are:

- Duration
  The length of time that records need to be kept will also vary depending on the type of training and the industry in which the business operates. However, in general, records should be kept for at least three years.

- Storage & Access
  Records should be kept in a safe and secure location where they can be easily accessed by authorised personnel.

  Access to records should be limited to authorised personnel, such as the human resources department, safety manager, or training manager.

  Records should be maintained in a consistent and organised manner. This will make it easier to find and access the records when needed.

Copyrights 2023 Vocational Resources Australia. All Rights Reserved.

Relevant Policies & Procedures

Some common organisational policies/ procedures that may be relevant to workplace training:

- Training and Development Policy
  This policy outlines the organisation's commitment to providing training and development opportunities to its employees.

- Learning and Development Policy
  This policy covers the various types of learning and development programs available to employees and how they can access them.

- Employee Development Plan Procedures
  The procedures outline the process for creating individual employee development plans, which include training and development goals.

- Training Reimbursement Procedures
  The procedures cover the reimbursement of expenses related to training and development programs.

- Time Off for Training Procedures
  The procedures outline the policy & process on granting time off to employees for training and development purposes.

- Training Evaluation Procedures
  The procedures cover the evaluation of training and development programs to ensure they are effective and meet the needs of the organisation and its employees.

Copyrights 2023 Vocational Resources Australia. All Rights Reserved.

Role of Training & Development Policy

The role of training and development policy in the workplace is multifaceted.

Firstly, it helps to promote employee growth and development, which in turn improves their skills and knowledge. This leads to better job performance, higher employee morale, and increased job satisfaction.

Secondly, a well-designed training and development policy can help organisations to attract and retain top talent. This is because employees are more likely to stay with a company that invests in their professional development.

Moreover, training and development can help address skill gaps and improve job performance, which can lead to increased productivity, efficiency, and profitability for the organisation.

Copyrights 2023 Vocational Resources Australia. All Rights Reserved.

Key Features of Training & Development Policy

The key features of a training & development policy may include:

- Purpose and objectives
  The policy should clearly state the purpose and objectives of training and development initiatives.

- Eligibility criteria
  The policy should specify the eligibility criteria for employees to participate in training and development programs.

- Training methods
  The policy should outline the various methods of training and development that may be used, such as classroom training, online courses, workshops, mentoring, and coaching.

- Budget and funding
  The policy should provide clarity on the budget and funding available to support training and development initiatives.

- Performance evaluation
  The policy should outline the procedures for evaluating the effectiveness of training and development programs.

- Career development
  The policy should include provisions for career development and advancement opportunities for employees.

Copyrights 2023 Vocational Resources Australia. All Rights Reserved.

- Roles and responsibilities
  The policy should clearly define the roles and responsibilities of employees, managers, and the organisation in regard to training and development.

- Compliance requirements
  The policy should ensure compliance with legal and regulatory requirements related to training and development.

System Requirements

An effective organisational system for workplace training and development should include several key elements, such as:

- Goals
  It should have a clear and well-defined set of goals and objectives that align with the overall vision and mission of the organisation. This will help ensure that training and development efforts are focused and targeted towards achieving specific outcomes that are relevant to the organisation.

- Structured approach
  The system should have a structured approach to identifying training needs and requirements. This could involve conducting needs assessments, analysing performance data, or soliciting feedback from employees and managers.

- Variety
  The system should provide a variety of training and development opportunities that cater to different learning styles and preferences. This could include online

Copyrights 2023 Vocational Resources Australia. All Rights Reserved.

courses, classroom training, job shadowing, mentoring, coaching, and more.

- Monitoring
  It should have a mechanism for measuring the effectiveness of training and development initiatives. This could involve collecting feedback from employees, assessing changes in performance metrics, or conducting follow-up surveys or assessments.

- Flexibility
  The system should be flexible and adaptable to changing needs and circumstances. It should be reviewed and updated regularly to ensure that it remains relevant and effective in meeting the evolving needs of the organisation and its employees.

Copyrights 2023 Vocational Resources Australia. All Rights Reserved.

Training Needs Analysis

A training needs analysis (TNA) is a process of identifying the gaps between the current and desired knowledge, skills, and abilities (KSAs) of employees. It is a critical first step in developing effective training programs.

There are several reasons why organisations conduct TNAs. Some of the most common reasons include:

- To improve employee performance
- To comply with government regulations
- To prepare for new technologies or processes
- To attract and retain top talent
- To reduce costs

TNAs can be conducted in a variety of ways, including:

- Surveying employees
- Interviewing managers and supervisors
- Reviewing performance appraisals
- Observing employees at work
- Reviewing job descriptions
- Reviewing company data, such as turnover rates and customer complaints

Once the TNA is complete, the results can be used to develop training programs that are specifically tailored to the needs of the organisation and its employees.

Copyrights 2023 Vocational Resources Australia. All Rights Reserved.

Some of the benefits of conducting a TNA include:

- Improved employee performance
  TNAs can help identify areas where employees need additional training or development. This can lead to improved employee performance, which can boost productivity and profitability.

- Compliance with government regulations
  Many industries are subject to government regulations that require employees to have certain knowledge or skills. TNAs can help organisations identify these requirements and ensure that their employees are properly trained.

- Preparation for new technologies or processes
  As the world of work continues to change, it is important for organisations to ensure that their employees have the skills they need to use new technologies and processes. TNAs can help identify these skills and develop training programs to help employees acquire them.

- Attraction and retention of top talent
  In today's competitive job market, organisations need to do everything they can to attract and retain top talent. One way to do this is to offer training and development opportunities that help employees grow and develop their skills.

- Reduced costs
  TNAs can help organisations identify areas where they can reduce costs, such as by eliminating unnecessary training or by developing more efficient training programs.

Copyrights 2023 Vocational Resources Australia. All Rights Reserved.

While conducting a TNA, the following should be considered:

- Make sure the TNA is aligned with the organisation's goals and objectives.
- Tailor the TNA to the specific needs of the organisation and its employees.
- Use a variety of methods to collect data, such as surveys, interviews, and observations.
- Analyse the data carefully to identify the most pressing training needs.
- Develop a training plan that is based on the results of the TNA.
- Evaluate the effectiveness of the training program to ensure that it is meeting the needs of the organisation and its employees.

It is also important to:

- Get buy-in from top management
  TNAs are more likely to be successful if they have the support of top management.

- Communicate with employees
  Employees should be kept informed about the TNA process and its goals.

- Be realistic
  It is important to be realistic about the time and resources that are available for conducting a TNA.

- Be flexible
  The TNA process may need to be adjusted as new information becomes available.

Copyrights 2023 Vocational Resources Australia. All Rights Reserved.

- Be patient
  TNAs can take time to complete.

Types of Learning

Workplace trainings can be categorised in two broader types i.e. formal learning and informal learning. Both of them are discussed below:

Formal Learning

Formal learning is a structured, planned, and intentional learning experience that is designed to help learners acquire new knowledge, skills, or abilities. It is typically delivered in a classroom setting by a qualified instructor, but it can also be delivered online or through other means.

Formal learning is an important part of the workplace for a number of reasons. It can help employees:

- Stay up to date on the latest industry trends and best practices
- Develop the skills they need to do their jobs more effectively
- Advance their careers
- Improve their performance
- Increase their job satisfaction
- Reduce turnover

There are a number of different types of formal learning that can be offered in the workplace, including:

Copyrights 2023 Vocational Resources Australia. All Rights Reserved.

Onboarding Training

Onboarding training is the process of introducing new employees to a company's culture, policies, procedures, and products or services. It is an essential part of the employee lifecycle, and it can have a significant impact on employee retention, productivity, and satisfaction.

A well-designed onboarding program can help new employees get up to speed quickly and efficiently, and it can also help them feel welcomed and supported. This can lead to a number of benefits for the company, including:

- Increased productivity
  New employees who are quickly and effectively onboarded are more likely to be productive from day one.

- Reduced turnover
  Employees who are satisfied with their onboarding experience are less likely to leave the company within the first few months.

- Improved morale
  Employees who feel welcome and supported are more likely to be engaged and motivated in their work.

There are a number of different elements that can be included in an onboarding program, such as:

- Orientation
  This is the initial introduction to the company, and it typically includes information about the company's history, mission, vision, values, and culture.

Copyrights 2023 Vocational Resources Australia. All Rights Reserved.

- Policy and procedure training
  This training covers the company's policies and procedures, such as employee benefits, safety, and harassment prevention.

- Product or service training
  This training covers the company's products or services, and it helps new employees understand how they work and how to sell or service them.

- Shadowing
  This is where new employees shadow experienced employees to learn about their jobs and the company's culture.

- Feedback
  New employees should be given regular feedback on their progress, and they should be encouraged to ask questions.

The best way to design an onboarding program will vary depending on the size and complexity of the company, the nature of the work, and the budget.

There are a few general principles that can be applied to any onboarding program.

- Start early
  The onboarding process should start as soon as a new employee is hired. This will give the employee time to get familiar with the company and its culture before they start their job.

Copyrights 2023 Vocational Resources Australia. All Rights Reserved.

- Be comprehensive
  The onboarding program should cover all of the essential information that new employees need to know. This includes information about the company, its products or services, its policies and procedures, and its culture.

- Be personalised
  The onboarding program should be personalised to the individual employee. This means taking into account the employee's skills, experience, and learning style.

- Be ongoing
  The onboarding process should not end after the first few weeks or months. New employees should continue to receive training and support throughout their time with the company.

Copyrights 2023 Vocational Resources Australia. All Rights Reserved.

Instructor-Led Training

Instructor-led training (ILT) is a traditional form of training that involves a facilitator or instructor delivering content to a group of learners. ILT can be conducted in person or online, and it can be used to teach a wide variety of skills and knowledge.

There are many benefits to using ILT in the workplace, such as:

- ILT can be a very effective way to transfer knowledge. When an instructor is able to interact with learners in real time, they can answer questions, provide feedback, and correct misunderstandings. This helps to ensure that learners are able to master the material being taught.

- It can help to build relationships between learners and their colleagues. When learners are able to work together in a group setting, they can share ideas, learn from each other, and build camaraderie. This can lead to a more positive and productive work environment.

- ILT can help to improve employee engagement. When employees are given the opportunity to learn new skills and knowledge, they are more likely to be engaged in their work. This can lead to increased productivity, improved customer service, and a more competitive edge for the organisation.

Copyrights 2023 Vocational Resources Australia. All Rights Reserved.

Here are some best practices for creating an effective instructor-led training program:

- Start with a clear goal..
  What do you want learners to be able to do after completing the training?

- Choose the right instructor
  The instructor should be knowledgeable about the subject matter and have experience in delivering training.

- Design a learning experience that is engaging and interactive.
  Use a variety of teaching methods, such as lectures, discussions, activities, and assessments.

- Provide opportunities for learners to practice what they have learned.
  This can be done through hands-on exercises, simulations, or role-plays.

- Provide feedback to learners.
  This will help them to identify areas where they need to improve and to track their progress.

- Evaluate the effectiveness of the training program.
  This will help you to identify areas where the program can be improved.

Copyrights 2023 Vocational Resources Australia. All Rights Reserved.

eLearning

E-learning is a method of delivering educational content to learners through electronic devices such as computers, tablets, and smartphones. E-learning can be used to deliver a wide range of content, from basic training to advanced courses.

E-learning has become increasingly popular in the workplace in recent years. There are a number of reasons for this, including:

- Cost-effectiveness
  E-learning can be a cost-effective way to train employees. The cost of developing and delivering e-learning courses is typically lower than the cost of traditional training methods, such as instructor-led training (ILT).

- Flexibility
  E-learning can be delivered at any time and from any location, which gives employees the flexibility to learn at their own pace and on their own time. This can be especially beneficial for employees who have busy schedules or who work remotely.

- Scalability
  E-learning can be easily scaled to meet the needs of a large number of employees. This is in contrast to ILT, which can be difficult and expensive to scale up.

- Effectiveness
  E-learning can be just as effective as traditional training methods, if not more so. Studies have shown that e-

Copyrights 2023 Vocational Resources Australia. All Rights Reserved.

learning can lead to improved knowledge retention and skills acquisition.

There are a number of different types of e-learning courses available. Some of the most common types include:

- Self-paced courses
  Self-paced courses allow learners to progress through the material at their own pace. These courses are often used for basic training or for refresher courses.

- Live online courses
  Live online courses are delivered in real time, with an instructor leading the discussion. These courses are often used for more advanced training or for courses that require interaction with the instructor.

- Asynchronous online courses
  Asynchronous online courses are not delivered in real time. Learners can access the material at any time and can participate in discussions and activities at their own pace. These courses are often used for courses that require a lot of self-study.

When choosing an e-learning course, it is important to consider the needs of the learners and the goals of the training. For example, if the goal of the training is to improve knowledge retention, then a self-paced course may be the best option. If the goal of the training is to develop skills, then a live online course may be the best option.

E-learning can be a valuable tool for organisations that are looking to improve the skills and knowledge of their

Copyrights 2023 Vocational Resources Australia. All Rights Reserved.

employees. By choosing the right type of e-learning course and by providing learners with the support they need, organisations can ensure that their e-learning initiatives are successful.

Simulation Training

Simulation training is a type of training that uses simulated environments to provide learners with the opportunity to practice skills and knowledge in a safe and controlled setting. Simulation training can be used to train employees on a wide range of skills, including customer service, technical skills, and leadership skills.

There are many benefits to using simulation training in the workplace, such as:

- Simulation training can help to improve employee safety. By practicing skills in a simulated environment, employees can learn how to handle dangerous situations without putting themselves or others at risk.

- It can help to improve employee performance. By practicing skills in a simulated environment, employees can gain confidence and become more proficient in their work.

- Simulation training can help to reduce costs. By using simulation training, businesses can avoid the expense of sending employees to off-site training programs.

There are a number of different types of simulation training that can be used in the workplace. Some of the most common types of simulation training include:

Copyrights 2023 Vocational Resources Australia. All Rights Reserved.

- Computer-based training (CBT)
  CBT uses software to create interactive simulations that employees can complete on their own. CBT is a cost-effective and convenient way to train employees on a variety of topics.

- Virtual reality (VR)
  VR uses headsets and other technology to create realistic simulations that allow employees to experience different environments and situations. VR is a more immersive and engaging form of training than CBT, but it can also be more expensive.

- Role-playing
  Role-playing is a type of simulation training in which employees act out different scenarios. Role-playing can be used to train employees on a variety of skills, including customer service, conflict resolution, and leadership.

The type of simulation training that is most appropriate for a particular business will depend on the specific needs of the business and the resources that are available.

Copyrights 2023 Vocational Resources Australia. All Rights Reserved.

Coaching

Coaching is a process of helping employees improve their performance and achieve their goals. It is a collaborative relationship between a coach and a coachee, in which the coach provides support, guidance, and feedback. Coaching can be used to help employees develop new skills, improve their performance, or overcome challenges.

There are many different types of coaching that can be used in the workplace. Some common types of coaching include:

- Performance coaching
  This type of coaching focuses on helping employees improve their performance in their current role.

- Career coaching
  This type of coaching focuses on helping employees develop their career goals and strategies for achieving them.

- Executive coaching
  This type of coaching is designed for senior leaders, and focuses on helping them develop their leadership skills and abilities.

Coaching can be provided by a variety of people, including managers, HR professionals, external coaches, or even peers. The best type of coach for an individual will depend on their needs and goals.

If you are considering using coaching in your workplace, there are a few things you should keep in mind.

Copyrights 2023 Vocational Resources Australia. All Rights Reserved.

- First, it is important to have a clear understanding of the purpose of coaching. What do you hope to achieve by providing coaching to your employees? Once you know the purpose of coaching, you can develop a plan for how to implement it.

- It is also important to select the right coach for your employees. The coach should be someone who is qualified and experienced in providing coaching in the workplace. They should also be able to build rapport with your employees and create a safe and supportive environment for learning.

- Finally, it is important to provide ongoing support for your employees who are participating in coaching. This support can come from the coach, the manager, or HR. It is important to make sure that employees have the opportunity to discuss their progress and challenges, and to get feedback on their work.

Workplace coaching can be a valuable tool for helping employees improve their performance, develop new skills, and achieve their goals. If you are looking for a way to help your employees reach their full potential, consider using coaching in your workplace.

Copyrights 2023 Vocational Resources Australia. All Rights Reserved.

Mentoring

Mentoring is a powerful tool that can help employees develop their skills, knowledge, and career prospects. In the workplace, mentoring can be formal or informal, and it can be one-on-one or group based.

Mentoring is a relationship between a more experienced person (the mentor) and a less experienced person (the mentee). The mentor provides guidance, support, and advice to the mentee, helping them to develop their skills and knowledge. Mentoring can be a valuable asset to both the mentor and the mentee.

There are many benefits of mentoring in the workplace. For the mentee, mentoring can:

- Help them to develop their skills and knowledge
- Provide them with career guidance and support
- Help them to build their network
- Increase their confidence and self-esteem
- Improve their job satisfaction

For the mentor, mentoring can:

- Give them a sense of satisfaction and fulfillment
- Help them to stay up to date on industry trends
- Build their leadership skills
- Develop their own network
- Improve their communication and interpersonal skills

There are many different types of mentoring relationships. Some of the most common types include:

Copyrights 2023 Vocational Resources Australia. All Rights Reserved.

- Formal mentoring
  This is a structured relationship that is typically set up by the employer. Mentors and mentees are matched based on their interests and goals.

- Informal mentoring
  This is an unstructured relationship that develops naturally between two people. Mentors and mentees may be friends, colleagues, or even strangers.

- Group mentoring
  This is a type of mentoring in which a group of mentees are mentored by one or more mentors. Group mentoring can be a great way for mentees to learn from each other and to get different perspectives.

Copyrights 2023 Vocational Resources Australia. All Rights Reserved.

Informal Learning

Informal learning is a type of learning that occurs outside of a formal classroom setting. It can happen through everyday experiences, such as interacting with colleagues, taking on new challenges, or reading industry publications. Informal learning is often self-directed and driven by the learner's interests.

In the workplace, informal learning can be a valuable way for employees to develop their skills and knowledge. It can also help employees to build relationships with colleagues and to gain a better understanding of the company's culture and values.

There are many different ways that informal learning can take place in the workplace. Some common examples include:

On-the-Job Training

On-the-job training (OJT) is a type of training that occurs while an employee is performing their job duties. OJT can be provided by a supervisor, colleague, or other experienced employee. It can also be provided through self-study or online courses.

OJT is a common type of training in many workplaces. It can be a cost-effective way to train employees and it can help employees to learn the skills and knowledge they need to do their jobs effectively.

There are many different types of OJT. Some common types include:

Copyrights 2023 Vocational Resources Australia. All Rights Reserved.

- Coaching
  This type of OJT involves a supervisor or colleague providing one-on-one instruction to an employee.

- Job shadowing
  This type of OJT involves an employee observing another employee as they perform their job duties.

- Rotational training
  This type of OJT involves an employee rotating through different positions within a company. This can help employees to learn about different aspects of the company's business and to develop a broader range of skills.

- Experiential learning
  This type of OJT involves an employee learning by doing. This can involve completing projects, solving problems, or interacting with customers.

OJT can be a valuable way for employees to learn new skills and knowledge. It can also help employees to develop their confidence and to build relationships with colleagues.

If you are considering using OJT to train your employees, there are a few things you should keep in mind:

- Make sure that the trainer is qualified.
  The trainer should have the knowledge and experience necessary to teach the employee the skills and knowledge they need.

Copyrights 2023 Vocational Resources Australia. All Rights Reserved.

- Provide the employee with the resources they need.
  The employee should have access to the tools, equipment, and materials they need to complete their training.

- Provide the employee with feedback.
  The employee should receive regular feedback on their progress. This will help them to identify areas where they need to improve and to stay motivated.

- Measure the effectiveness of the training.
  It is important to measure the effectiveness of the training to make sure that it is meeting the needs of the employee and the job.

Peer-to-Peer Learning

Peer-to-peer learning is a type of learning in which learners share their knowledge and skills with each other. It can be done in a variety of settings, including the classroom, the workplace, and online.

There are many different ways to implement peer-to-peer learning. Some common methods include:

- Study groups: Learners form small groups to study together.

- Mentoring: More experienced learners mentor less experienced learners.

- Cooperative learning: Learners work together to solve problems or complete tasks.

Copyrights 2023 Vocational Resources Australia. All Rights Reserved.

- Jigsaw learning: Learners are divided into groups and each group is responsible for learning a different part of a topic.

- Webinars: Learners watch webinars presented by experts in their field.

- Online forums: Learners can ask questions and get answers from their peers.

Peer-to-peer learning is an effective way to develop skills and knowledge. It is also a cost-effective way to train employees. If you are looking for a way to improve employee performance and create a more collaborative work environment, peer-to-peer learning is a great option.

While implementing peer-to-peer learning it is important to:

- Make sure that the learners are interested in the topic.
  If the learners are not interested in the topic, they are less likely to be engaged in the learning process.

- Match learners with similar skill levels.
  This will help to ensure that everyone in the group is able to contribute to the learning process.

- Provide clear instructions and expectations.
  This will help to ensure that the learners know what is expected of them.

- Provide regular feedback.
  This will help to keep the learners on track and motivated.

Copyrights 2023 Vocational Resources Australia. All Rights Reserved.

- Celebrate successes.
  This will help to reinforce the learning and motivate the learners to continue learning.

Reading

Reading is a powerful tool for informal learning in the workplace. It can help employees stay up to date on industry trends, learn new skills, and develop their critical thinking skills. When done effectively, reading can be a valuable way for employees to improve their performance and contribute to the success of their organisation.

There are many different ways to incorporate reading into informal learning at work. Employees can read books, articles, blog posts, and other materials that are relevant to their jobs. They can also participate in book clubs or other reading groups, or attend conferences and workshops that feature speakers on topics of interest.

When choosing reading materials, it is important to consider the needs of the individual learner. What are their interests? What skills do they want to develop? What are the goals of the organisation? Once you have a good understanding of the learner's needs, you can start to identify appropriate reading materials.

It is also important to create a supportive environment for reading in the workplace. Encourage employees to take breaks during the workday to read, and provide them with access to a variety of reading materials. You can also create a reading nook or other designated space where employees can relax and read without distractions.

Copyrights 2023 Vocational Resources Australia. All Rights Reserved.

Here are some of the benefits of reading as informal learning in the workplace:

- Staying up to date on industry trends
  By reading industry publications, employees can stay up to date on the latest developments in their field. This can help them to identify new opportunities, solve problems more effectively, and make better decisions.

- Learning new skills
  Reading can help employees learn new skills that are relevant to their jobs. This can include technical skills, soft skills, and business skills. By developing new skills, employees can become more valuable to their organisations and increase their chances of career advancement.

- Developing critical thinking skills
  Reading can help employees develop their critical thinking skills. This includes the ability to analyse information, identify patterns, and solve problems. Critical thinking skills are essential for success in today's workplace, where employees are constantly bombarded with information and need to be able to make quick decisions.

If you are looking for ways to improve the learning and development opportunities for your employees, consider incorporating reading into informal learning.

Here are some additional tips for incorporating reading into informal learning at work:

Copyrights 2023 Vocational Resources Australia. All Rights Reserved.

- Make reading materials available
  Provide employees with access to a variety of reading materials, including books, articles, blog posts, and other materials that are relevant to their jobs. You can do this by creating a reading library in your office, subscribing to industry publications, or providing employees with access to online resources.

- Encourage employees to read
  Let employees know that you value reading and that you encourage them to take breaks during the workday to read. You can do this by setting a good example, by providing incentives for reading, or by creating a reading-friendly environment in your office.

- Provide opportunities for discussion
  Encourage employees to discuss what they have read with their colleagues. This can help them to solidify their understanding of the material, to get feedback from others, and to build relationships with their colleagues.

- Track employee progress
  Keep track of what employees are reading and how they are using the information. This will help you to identify areas where employees need additional support, and to make adjustments to your informal learning program as needed.

Copyrights 2023 Vocational Resources Australia. All Rights Reserved.

Conferences/ Workshops

Attending conferences and workshops can be a great way to learn new skills, stay up to date on industry trends, and network with other professionals. It can provide employees with opportunities to learn in a more flexible and self-directed way.

There are many different types of conferences and workshops available, so it is important to choose one that is relevant to your interests and needs. When choosing a conference or workshop, consider the following factors:

- Topic - The conference or workshop should cover topics that are relevant to your work or career goals.

- Speakers - The conference or workshop should feature speakers who are experts in their field.

- Format - The conference or workshop should be in a format that works for you. Some people prefer to attend live events, while others prefer to watch online presentations or read transcripts.

- Cost - The cost of the conference or workshop should be within your budget.

Once you have chosen a conference or workshop, it is important to prepare for it. This includes reading the conference or workshop agenda, researching the speakers, and coming up with questions to ask. It is also a good idea to bring a notebook and pen to take notes.

Copyrights 2023 Vocational Resources Australia. All Rights Reserved.

At the conference or workshop, be sure to participate in the activities and discussions. This is your chance to learn from the speakers, network with other professionals, and share your own ideas. After the conference or workshop, take some time to reflect on what you learned and how you can apply it to your work.

Attending conferences and workshops can be a valuable way to learn new skills, stay up to date on industry trends, and network with other professionals.

If you are looking for ways to improve your skills and knowledge, consider attending a conference or workshop.

If you are considering attending a conference or workshop, here are some tips to help you get the most out of it:

- Do your research
  Before you attend, be sure to research the conference or workshop to make sure it is a good fit for you. Read the agenda, learn about the speakers, and check out reviews from past attendees.

- Set goals
  Before you attend, take some time to think about what you hope to achieve. What do you want to learn? Who do you want to meet? What do you want to accomplish?

- Be prepared
  Be sure to bring everything you need, such as a notebook, pen, business cards, and any other materials that you may need.

Copyrights 2023 Vocational Resources Australia. All Rights Reserved.

- Be engaged
  Participate in the activities and discussions. Ask questions, network with other attendees, and share your own ideas.

- Follow up
  After the conference or workshop, be sure to follow up with the speakers and other attendees. This is a great way to stay connected and continue the learning process.

Online Courses

Online courses are a convenient and cost-effective way for employees to learn new skills and stay up to date on industry trends. They can be accessed from anywhere, at any time, and they offer a variety of learning formats, including video lectures, interactive exercises, and quizzes.

Online courses can be a valuable addition to any workplace training program. They can be used to provide employees with the skills they need to do their jobs effectively, to prepare them for new challenges, or to help them advance their careers.

There are many different types of online courses available, so it is important to choose one that is relevant to your needs. When choosing an online course, consider the following factors:

- Topic - The course should cover topics that are relevant to your work or career goals.

- Level - The course should be at the right level for your skills and knowledge.

Copyrights 2023 Vocational Resources Australia. All Rights Reserved.

- Format - The course should be in a format that works for you. Some people prefer video lectures, while others prefer interactive exercises or quizzes.

- Cost - The cost of the course should be within your budget.

Once you have chosen an online course, it is important to prepare for it. This includes reading the course syllabus, reviewing the course materials, and setting aside time to study.

During the course, be sure to participate in the activities and discussions. This is your chance to learn from the instructor and other students, and to share your own ideas. After the course, take some time to reflect on what you learned and how you can apply it to your work.

Online courses can be a valuable way to learn new skills, stay up to date on industry trends, and network with other professionals. If you are looking for ways to improve your skills and knowledge, consider taking an online course.

If you are considering taking an online course, the following should be considered:

- Choose a reputable course provider
  There are many different online course providers available, so it is important to choose one that is reputable and has a good reputation.

Copyrights 2023 Vocational Resources Australia. All Rights Reserved.

- Set realistic goals
  When you start an online course, it is important to set realistic goals for yourself. This will help you stay motivated and on track.

- Find a quiet place to study
  When you are taking an online course, it is important to find a quiet place where you can focus and avoid distractions.

- Take breaks
  It is important to take breaks throughout the day when you are taking an online course. This will help you stay focused and avoid burnout.

- Ask for help
  If you are struggling with a particular concept or assignment, do not be afraid to ask for help from the instructor or other students.

- Stay on track
  It is important to stay on track with your online course. This will help you avoid falling behind and feeling overwhelmed.

- Celebrate your successes
  As you complete modules and earn badges, be sure to celebrate your successes. This will help you stay motivated and on track.

Copyrights 2023 Vocational Resources Australia. All Rights Reserved.

Use of Technology

There are many different organisational technologies that can be used for workplace training and development. Here are a few examples:

- Learning Management Systems (LMS)
  An LMS is a platform that can be used to deliver and manage online training courses. It allows companies to create and deliver training content, track employee progress, and monitor performance.

- Virtual Reality (VR) and Augmented Reality (AR)
  VR and AR technologies are becoming increasingly popular in the workplace.

  They can be used to create immersive training experiences that simulate real-life scenarios. For example, VR can be used to simulate dangerous or expensive situations, while AR can be used to provide real-time guidance on complex tasks.

- Social learning platforms
  These platforms allow employees to collaborate and share knowledge with each other. They often include features like discussion forums, wikis, and social networks.

- Electronic Performance Support Systems (EPSS)
  EPSS are tools that provide employees with on-demand access to information and support while they are working. They can be used to provide just-in-time training, guidance, and resources.

Copyrights 2023 Vocational Resources Australia. All Rights Reserved.

- Gamification
  Gamification involves using game elements, such as points, badges, and leader boards, to make training more engaging and fun. It can be used to motivate employees and encourage them to learn and develop new skills.

Copyrights 2023 Vocational Resources Australia. All Rights Reserved.

Workforce Planning

Workforce planning is an essential aspect of any organisation's strategic planning process. It involves anticipating the future needs of the organisation and developing strategies to ensure that the workforce is capable of meeting those needs.

Workforce planning is important for several reasons. Some of the are outlined below:

- It enables an organisation to identify gaps in its current workforce and take proactive steps to fill those gaps. This can be especially important in industries that are experiencing rapid technological change or demographic shifts. For example, a healthcare organisation may need to hire more nurses to meet the needs of an aging population.

  Workforce planning can also help an organisation to identify and address skills shortages, which can be critical in industries where there is a shortage of skilled workers.

- Workforce planning can help an organisation to manage costs. By understanding its workforce needs, an organisation can plan for hiring, training, and development needs, and avoid the costs associated with reactive hiring or training.

- By identifying skills gaps, an organisation can focus its training and development efforts on those areas where it will have the greatest impact.

Copyrights 2023 Vocational Resources Australia. All Rights Reserved.

- Workforce planning can help an organisation to improve employee engagement and retention. By providing employees with opportunities for career development and growth, an organisation can increase employee satisfaction and loyalty. This can be especially important in industries where turnover rates are high.

- It can help an organisation to align its workforce with its strategic goals. By identifying the skills, knowledge, and experience needed to achieve those goals, an organisation can develop a workforce that is capable of meeting those needs.

- Workforce planning can help an organisation to manage risk. By understanding its workforce needs, an organisation can anticipate and mitigate risks associated with skills shortages, turnover, and succession planning.

- It can help an organisation to improve efficiency and productivity. By ensuring that the workforce has the right skills and is properly trained, an organisation can optimise its performance and improve its bottom line.

Copyrights 2023 Vocational Resources Australia. All Rights Reserved.

Workforce Planning Process

The workforce planning process involves the following steps:

1. Analysing the organisation's current workforce.
   This step involves analysing the current workforce in terms of skills, demographics, performance, and other relevant factors. This analysis helps identify gaps in the workforce and areas that need improvement.

2. Forecasting future workforce needs.
   Based on the analysis of the current workforce, the organisation can make predictions about the future workforce needs. This involves analysing factors such as industry trends, business goals, and changes in technology or regulations.

3. Identifying gaps and developing strategies to fill them.
   Once the future workforce needs are predicted, the organisation can identify the gaps between the current and future workforce. Strategies can then be developed to fill those gaps, such as hiring, training, and development programs.

4. Implementing workforce plans.
   After developing the workforce plan, the organisation can start implementing it. This includes recruiting and hiring new employees, upskilling existing employees, and other strategies to meet the future workforce needs.

Copyrights 2023 Vocational Resources Australia. All Rights Reserved.

5. Monitoring and evaluating the effectiveness of the workforce plan.
   After implementation, the workforce plan should be monitored and evaluated regularly to ensure that it is effective and meeting the organisation's needs. This includes tracking metrics such as employee turnover rates, productivity, and engagement.

Workforce Plan

A workforce plan refers to the strategy and actions a business or organisation takes to manage its human resources to achieve its goals. It includes analysing the current workforce, identifying future needs, and implementing actions to ensure that the right people with the right skills are in the right roles.

Key Components of a Workforce Plan

- Executive summary
  This section provides an overview of the workforce plan, including its purpose and objectives.

- Business Strategy
  This section outlines the organisation's overall business objectives and how they connect to the workforce plan.

- Priorities
  Defining priorities ensures that the goals and objectives of the organisation are aligned with the skills and talents of its employees.

  By identifying the most important roles and responsibilities, the company can focus its resources on

Copyrights 2023 Vocational Resources Australia. All Rights Reserved.

developing and training the employees who are best suited for those roles.

Prioritising also helps in allocating budgets and resources as per the company's goals. This leads to better productivity, higher employee engagement, and lower turnover rates.

Prioritization helps an organisation to be more proactive in addressing potential workforce trends, such as shortages or surpluses in certain job functions. By having a clear understanding of priorities, the organisation can better anticipate and respond to changes in the marketplace or industry.

- Workforce analysis
  This involves assessing the current workforce, including its skills, experience, and demographics. This analysis helps identify potential gaps in the workforce and areas where additional training or recruitment may be necessary.

- Workforce demand forecast
  Based on the organisation's goals and strategy, workforce planners must forecast the future demand for talent. This includes forecasting the number of employees needed, the skills required, and the timing of these needs.

- Workforce supply forecast
  This section estimates the future supply of employees based on current workforce trends and anticipated changes.

Copyrights 2023 Vocational Resources Australia. All Rights Reserved.

- Gap analysis
  This section compares the demand and supply forecasts to identify any gaps and potential risks.

- Workforce Strategies
  This section outlines the strategies the organisation will use to address the gaps and risks identified in the gap analysis.

  This section may include:

  - Recruitment and retention strategies
    Once workforce needs have been identified, organisations must develop strategies for recruiting and retaining the right talent. This may include developing new recruitment channels, offering competitive compensation and benefits packages, and creating a positive work culture.

  - Training and development
    Organisations must provide ongoing training and development opportunities to ensure that employees have the skills and knowledge needed to meet current and future demands. In this section appropriate T&D strategies are populated.

  - Succession planning
    With an aging workforce, succession planning is critical to ensure that the organisation has the right people in place to fill key roles as employees retire. Robust succession planning strategies and a plan should be part of the planning process.

Copyrights 2023 Vocational Resources Australia. All Rights Reserved.

  - Diversity and inclusion.
    Workforce planners must also consider the importance of diversity and inclusion in the workforce. This includes strategies to ensure that the organisation is attracting and retaining a diverse range of employees, and creating a culture that values and supports diversity.

- Action Plan
  This section provides a detailed plan for implementing the workforce strategies, including timelines and accountabilities.

- Budget.
  A budget is a crucial component of any workforce plan. It helps a company to allocate resources effectively, plan for future expenses, and ensure that operations run smoothly.

  In workforce planning, budgeting is especially important because labour costs are often the largest expense for a company. This means that careful consideration must be given to how much is allocated to hiring, salary, benefits, training, and other related costs. Without a clear budget in place, a company may overspend on labour costs or underinvest in critical areas like employee development and retention. This can lead to a variety of problems, including high turnover rates, low employee morale, and even financial instability.

  By having a budget in place, a company can make informed decisions about hiring, training, and

Copyrights 2023 Vocational Resources Australia. All Rights Reserved.

compensation, and can also prepare for unexpected expenses.

- Cost-benefit analysis.
  It is a process used to evaluate the potential benefits and costs of a particular decision, such as hiring new employees or investing in a new technology for the workforce.

  Cost-benefit analysis helps organisations make informed decisions by weighing the costs and benefits of different options. By doing so, they can identify the most effective and efficient ways to allocate their resources.

  In conducting cost-benefit analysis for workforce planning, it is important to consider all the costs and benefits associated with an action. For example, the cost of hiring and training new employees, the cost of implementing new technology, the opportunity cost of not investing in other areas, and the potential benefits such as increased productivity, reduced turnover, and improved quality. By considering all these factors, organisations can determine which decisions will have the greatest return on investment and are most aligned with their overall business goals.

  Cost-benefit analysis can also be useful in identifying potential risks and opportunities associated with different workforce planning strategies, helping organisations to make more informed decisions.

Copyrights 2023 Vocational Resources Australia. All Rights Reserved.

Determining Future Labour & Skills Need

Following are some of the strategies that businesses commonly use to determine future labour needs and their skill requirements:

- Analysing historical data.
  By looking at past trends in your business, you can get a good sense of how many employees you may need in the future. For example, if you noticed a spike in sales during a certain season, you may need to hire more employees to deal with the increased demand.

- Conducting regular workforce planning.
  Workforce planning involves analysing your current workforce and forecasting what your future needs will be based on your business goals. This can include identifying skills gaps and looking at potential changes in your industry.

- Employee surveys and feedback.
  Asking your employees how their roles could be improved or what new skills they would like to learn can help identify areas where you may need to hire new staff or provide training.

- Industry research.
  Keeping up with industry trends and changes can help you anticipate changes in labour needs and skills requirements. For example, if you work in a field that is becoming more automated, you may need to focus on hiring employees with strong technical skills.

Copyrights 2023 Vocational Resources Australia. All Rights Reserved.

- Collaboration with other businesses.
  Working with other businesses in your industry can help you stay informed about changes in labour needs and skill requirements. This can include participating in industry groups or attending conferences.

Determining Organisational Preferences

Determining an organisation's preferences regarding workforce can involve the following steps:

1. Research the organisation's mission and values.
   By understanding what the organisation stands for, you may get a sense of its priorities. For example, if the organisation values diversity and inclusion, they may have a preference for a diverse workforce.

2. Look at job postings.
   Job postings often include information about the qualifications the organisation is looking for in candidates. This can give you clues about what type of experience and skills the organisation values.

3. Observe the current workforce.
   Take a look at the employees who currently work for the organisation. This can give you an idea of what the organisation values and the type of people they like to hire.

4. Talk to current employees.
   If you have connections at the organisation, consider having a conversation about the workforce preferences. They may be able to share some

Copyrights 2023 Vocational Resources Australia. All Rights Reserved.

insights about what the organisation values in its workforce.

5. Check out the organisation's social media.
   Many organisations use social media to showcase their culture and values. By following the organisation on social media, you may get a sense of what they value in their workforce.

Strategic Direction, Objectives and Targets

Workforce strategic direction, objectives, and targets are critical components of effective workforce planning. By defining these elements, organisations can ensure that they have a clear understanding of their workforce needs and how they align with their overall business strategy.

Workforce strategic direction ensures that organisations have a clear plan for how they will meet their staffing needs over the long term. By identifying the skills and competencies that will be required in the future, they can develop targeted recruitment and retention strategies, and create development plans for their existing workforce.

Objectives and targets provide a roadmap for how organisations will achieve their strategic workforce goals. This can include everything from increasing diversity and inclusion, to improving employee engagement, to achieving specific productivity or cost-saving targets. By setting clear objectives and targets, organisations can focus their efforts and measure progress against their goals.

Copyrights 2023 Vocational Resources Australia. All Rights Reserved.

How Workforce Plan Relates to Strategic Plan

A workforce plan is a tool that organisations use to plan and manage their workforce. It involves analysing the current workforce's skills, knowledge, and abilities, and identifying future workforce needs to achieve organisational goals. A strategic plan, on the other hand, is a roadmap that outlines the long-term goals and objectives of the organisation, along with the strategies and actions needed to achieve them.

The workforce plan and strategic plan are interconnected because the workforce is essential to achieving an organisation's strategic goals. An organisation's workforce consists of its employees, contractors, freelancers, volunteers, and other staff members. These individuals have specific skills, knowledge, and abilities that contribute to the organisation's success.

The workforce plan defines the workforce required to execute the strategies outlined in the strategic plan. It forecasts the number of employees needed, their skillset, and the cost of acquiring and retaining them. This information feeds into the strategic plan, where it is evaluated and incorporated into the organisation's long-term objectives.

In other words, the workforce plan explains the organisational needs for achieving the strategic plan, and the strategic plan guides the creation of the workforce plan necessary to achieve it. As the organisation moves forward with its strategic plan, it uses the workforce plan to manage the workforce and ensure that it supports the strategic objectives by making the necessary adjustments to the workforce plan.

Copyrights 2023 Vocational Resources Australia. All Rights Reserved.

Importance of Consultation

Consultation is essential in workforce planning because it involves gathering input from all stakeholders, including employees, managers, and other relevant parties. By consulting with these stakeholders, workforce planning can be more informed, effective, and inclusive.

One of the main benefits of consultation in workforce planning is that it allows employees to have a say in shaping their own work environment. When employees are consulted, they feel valued and are more likely to be invested in the outcome of the workforce planning process. This can increase employee engagement and reduce staff turnover.

Consultation also provides a way for managers to identify and address potential issues before they become problems. When managers consult with their employees, they gain valuable insights into the skills, resources, and knowledge needed to achieve success. This can help reduce wasted resources and optimise productivity.

Labour Sourcing

Labour sourcing refers to the process of finding, selecting, and hiring workers to fill specific job positions within a company or organisation. This process typically involves reviewing resumes, conducting interviews, and checking references to find the best candidates for the job.

Labour sourcing can be done internally, by promoting existing employees, or externally, by recruiting from outside the organisation. It is an important part of human resource

Copyrights 2023 Vocational Resources Australia. All Rights Reserved.

management and helps companies build a skilled and effective workforce.

Some common labour sourcing options that businesses can consider:

- Internal sourcing
  This involves filling positions with existing employees within the company. This can be beneficial because it saves money on recruiting and training, and it can also boost employee morale by providing opportunities for career advancement.

- External sourcing
  This involves recruiting new employees from outside of the company. This can be done through job postings, recruitment agencies, or job fairs. This is a good option if the company is looking for new skills or experience that current employees don't have.

- Freelancers and contractors
  Hiring freelancers or contractors can be a cost-effective way to get work done without having to commit to a long-term employee. This is a good option for short-term projects or for work that can be done remotely.

- Apprenticeships
  This involves hiring entry-level workers and providing on-the-job training to develop the skills they need for the job. This is a good option for companies that need workers with specialised skills but have trouble finding them on the job market.

Copyrights 2023 Vocational Resources Australia. All Rights Reserved.

- Internships
  This involves hiring students or recent graduates for a short period of time to gain work experience and develop their skills. This is a good option for companies that want to test out potential employees without a long-term commitment.

- Employee referrals
  This involves asking current employees to refer potential candidates for open positions. This is a good option for companies that want to tap into the networks of their current staff to find qualified candidates.

These are some common labour sourcing options that businesses can consider. Each has its own advantages and disadvantages, so it's important to choose the option that best fits the company's needs.

Monitoring & Evaluation

Monitoring and evaluation (M&E) are critical components of a workforce plan. They help an organisation track the progress of its workforce plan implementation, measure the plan's success, and identify any necessary adjustments.

Below is a detailed discussion of workforce planning monitoring and evaluation strategies.

- Set clear goals and objectives
  The first step in M&E strategy involves setting clear goals and objectives. The goals and objectives should be specific, measurable, achievable, relevant, and time-bound (SMART). They should align with the

Copyrights 2023 Vocational Resources Australia. All Rights Reserved.

organisation's overall strategic plan and identify the critical workforce areas that require attention.

- Define performance indicators
  After establishing goals and objectives, the next step is to identify key performance indicators (KPIs) that will help track progress and measure success. KPIs may include employee turnover rates, employee engagement surveys, skill gaps analysis, and performance reviews.

- Collect data
  Workforce planning requires accurate data, and collecting data on a regular basis is essential for measuring progress. Data collection can be done through surveys, interviews, focus groups, and other methods. It is important to consider the sources of data, the frequency of data collection, and who is responsible for data collection.

- Analyse data
  Data analysis is crucial in identifying trends and patterns that inform decision-making. Workforce planners need to analyse data regularly to determine if the organisation is progressing towards its objectives or if changes in direction are required.

- Report findings
  Once data analysis is complete, the next step is to report the findings. Reports should be concise, easy to understand, and should inform key stakeholders, including senior management, HR, and other relevant departments.

Copyrights 2023 Vocational Resources Australia. All Rights Reserved.

- Take action
  Once workforce planning gaps are identified, action must be taken to address them. This may involve changes in recruitment strategies, employee training, restructuring, or any other action that aligns with the overall HR strategy.

- Review and adjust accordingly.
  Regular reviews of the workforce plan are vital to ensure that the plan remains relevant, effective, and aligned with the organisation's objectives. Workforce planners should make adjustments as necessary based on feedback from the stakeholders, new information, and changes in the business environment.

Recent Industrial/ Legal Changes

Recently, there have been a number of changes to Australian industrial and legal requirements that impact workforce management and planning.

Some of them are outlined below:

- One major change is the introduction of the Fair Work Amendment (Protecting Vulnerable Workers) Act 2017, which increases penalties for employers who breach workplace laws and expands the liability of franchisors for the actions of their franchisees.

- Another change is the introduction of the Modern Slavery Act 2018, which requires businesses with an annual turnover of $100 million or more to report on the risks of modern slavery in their supply chains.

Copyrights 2023 Vocational Resources Australia. All Rights Reserved.

- There have been ongoing discussions about potential changes to the Fair Work Act 2009, which could impact the way that workplace agreements are negotiated and the role of the Fair Work Commission in resolving disputes.

- The proposed introduction of the Industrial Relations Omnibus Bill 2020, which aims to streamline the industrial relations system and make it easier for employers to hire and manage their workforce.

- The introduction of the National Employment Standards (NES), which outlines the minimum entitlements for all employees in Australia. These standards cover things like hours of work, leave entitlements, and parental leave.

- The introduction of new anti-bullying laws, which provide employees with a way to make a complaint about workplace bullying and seek a resolution through the Fair Work Commission.

By staying informed about these changes and ensuring that their workforce management and planning strategies are aligned with the latest legal and regulatory requirements, employers can help to create a positive and productive workplace for their employees.

Copyrights 2023 Vocational Resources Australia. All Rights Reserved.

Relevant Technologies

There are several technologies that can be leveraged to support workforce planning. Some of these technologies include:

- Workforce management software
  This type of software can help automate many of the administrative tasks associated with workforce management, such as scheduling, time and attendance tracking, and employee performance monitoring.

- Predictive analytics
  Predictive analytics involves using data analytics and statistical models to forecast future workforce needs and identify potential talent gaps. This can help organisations make informed decisions about hiring and training.

- Artificial intelligence
  AI can help with workforce planning by automating routine tasks, such as resume screening and candidate matching. It can also help identify skills gaps and suggest training programs to address them.

- Collaboration tools
  Collaboration tools, such as project management software and video conferencing platforms, can help teams work together more effectively and efficiently, regardless of their location.

- Learning management systems
  These systems can be used to deliver training and development programs to employees, helping them to

Copyrights 2023 Vocational Resources Australia. All Rights Reserved.

build the skills needed to succeed in their current roles and prepare for future opportunities.

Risk Management

Risk management is essential in workforce planning because it helps organisations to identify and mitigate potential risks that may impact the workforce planning process.

Effective risk management enables organisations to proactively address potential risks and reduces the likelihood of negative outcomes.

In workforce planning, risk management involves analysing workforce data, identifying potential risks, and developing contingency plans to address those risks. For example, if an organisation is planning to hire new employees, the risk management process may involve identifying potential recruitment challenges, such as a shortage of qualified candidates or difficulty in attracting candidates with the necessary skills. The organisation may then develop contingency plans to address these challenges, such as expanding the recruitment pool or offering training programs to develop the necessary skills.

Effective risk management in workforce planning can help organisations to avoid costly mistakes, such as hiring the wrong employees or failing to address potential workforce issues.

It can also help organisations to capitalize on opportunities, such as identifying and hiring highly skilled candidates, or developing innovative workforce strategies.

Copyrights 2023 Vocational Resources Australia. All Rights Reserved.

Some of the common risks are discussed below:

- Inadequate forecasting
  Inaccurate forecasting can lead to a shortage or surplus of employees, causing problems such as inefficient resource allocation and increased labour costs.

- Insufficient data
  Lack of reliable data can hinder the accuracy of workforce planning, leading to ineffective decision-making.

- Changing business needs
  Business conditions can shift quickly, and if workforce planning is not agile enough to respond, the organisation may find itself with an ill-suited workforce.

- Misaligned objectives
  Workforce planning must align with the organisation's overall strategy, and if objectives are not aligned, it can lead to a lack of clarity and poor performance.

- Employee turnover
  High rates of employee turnover can negatively affect workforce planning, as it becomes difficult to accurately predict staffing needs.

- Legal and compliance risks
  Failure to comply with labour laws and regulations can lead to financial penalties and reputational damage.

Copyrights 2023 Vocational Resources Australia. All Rights Reserved.

- Lack of diversity and inclusion
  Failing to consider diversity and inclusion in workforce planning can lead to a lack of representation, decreased employee engagement, and difficulty in attracting and retaining top talent.

- Inefficient processes
  Poorly designed or executed workforce planning processes can lead to delays, confusion, and decreased productivity.

- Limited budget
  Inadequate budgeting can result in less-than-optimal staffing levels or inadequate investment in training and development programs.

- Inadequate technology
  Not having access to the right tools and technology for workforce planning can lead to inefficiencies, inaccurate data, and decreased agility.

- Employee burnout
  Overwork or high levels of stress can lead to decreased productivity, increased absenteeism, and increased turnover rates.

Copyrights 2023 Vocational Resources Australia. All Rights Reserved.

Trends and Emerging Practices

Following are some trends/ emerging practices impacting the workforce and/or workforce planning processes:

- Remote work becoming the norm
- Flexible work arrangements
- Increased use of automation and AI
- Augmented and virtual reality
- Gig economy and freelance work
- Emphasis on work-life balance
- Focus on mental health and well-being
- Diversity, equity, and inclusion
- Upskilling and reskilling programs
- Employee wellness programs
- Collaborative workspaces
- Cross-functional teams
- Flat organisational structures
- Performance-based pay
- Increased transparency
- Agile work methodologies
- Data-driven decision making
- Employee engagement and recognition programs
- Personalised learning and development
- Holacracy - self-management
- Mobile optimised work platforms
- Cloud-based work tools
- Crowd-sourced feedback
- Mobile workforces
- Blurred work and personal lives
- Focus on creativity and innovation
- A shift towards meaningful work
- Collaborative learning
- Increased use of chatbots and AI assistants

Copyrights 2023 Vocational Resources Australia. All Rights Reserved.

- Employee experience design
- Inclusive language and communication
- Increased focus on mental agility
- Virtual team building activities
- Increased use of wearables and IoT devices
- Intentional diversity initiatives
- Social responsibility
- Transparent communication
- Encouraging employee activism
- Increased focus on employee feedback
- Results-only work environments
- Focus on employee well-being and stress management
- Employee-driven cultures
- Increased use of predictive analytics
- Emphasis on employee retention
- Increased use of data to measure employee productivity
- Agile performance management
- Increased use of gamification
- Employee-driven corporate social responsibility initiatives
- Innovative approaches to employee engagement
- Increased use of employee perks and benefits
- Increased use of remote training and development.

Copyrights 2023 Vocational Resources Australia. All Rights Reserved.

THANK
YOU
for reading!!!
Please do not forget to
check our other volumes.

Empowering Leaders - Elevating Businesses

Uncover the Wisdom within our Five Incredible Volumes

Volume 1	Chapter 1	Workplace Communication
	Chapter 2	Critical and Creative Thinking
	Chapter 3	Emotional Intelligence
	Chapter 4	Personal Development
	Chapter 5	Leadership
	Chapter 6	Workplace Technology
Volume 2	Chapter 7	Continuous Improvement, Innovation, and Quality Management
	Chapter 8	Sustainability
	Chapter 9	Change Management
	Chapter 10	Health, Safety, and Risk management
	Chapter 11	Business Development and Marketing
Volume 3	Chapter 12	Business Operations
Volume 4	Chapter 13	Financial Management
	Chapter 14	Human Resources Management
Volume 5	Chapter 15	Project Management

RELEASE 1.0

© Vocational Resources Australia

www.ingramcontent.com/pod-product-compliance
Lightning Source LLC
LaVergne TN
LVHW062033101126
852251LV00025B/327
9798223180616